Institutional Engineering and Political Accountability in Indonesia, Thailand and the Philippines

Institutional Engineering and Political Accountability in Indonesia, Thailand and the Philippines

PATRICK ZIEGENHAIN

LSEAS

INSTITUTE OF SOUTHEAST ASIAN STUDIES

Singapore

First published in Singapore in 2015 by
ISEAS Publishing
Institute of Southeast Asian Studies
30 Heng Mui Keng Terrace, Pasir Panjang
Singapore 119614

E-mail: publish@iseas.edu.sg   • Website: bookshop.iseas.edu.sg

ISEAS Library Cataloguing-in-Publication Data

Ziegenhain, Patrick.
   Institutional engineering and political accountability in Indonesia, Thailand and the Philippines.
   1.   Government accountability—Indonesia.
   2.   Government accountability—Thailand.
   3.   Government accountability—Philippines.
   4.   Democratization—Indonesia.
   5.   Democratization—Thailand.
   6.   Democratization—Philippines.
   I.   Title.
JQ770 Z66   2015

ISBN 978-981-4515-00-9 (soft cover)
ISBN 978-981-4515-01-6 (E-book PDF)

Typeset by International Typesetters Pte Ltd
Printed in Singapore by Markono Print Media Pte Ltd

CONTENTS

LIST OF TABLES AND GRAPHS

Tables

Graphs

ABBREVIATIONS

Abbreviation	Full Name	Translation/Explanation
ABRI	Angkatan Bersenjata Republik Indonesia	Armed Forces of the Republic of Indonesia
AFP	Armed Forces of the Philippines	
AMIN	Anak Mindanao	Name of a Party List Group in the Philippines
ARMM	Autonomous Region of Muslim Mindanao	
Bappenas	Badan Perencanaan Pembangunan Nasional	National Planning Board (in Indonesia)
BPK	Badan Pemeriksa Keuangan	Supreme Audit Agency (in Indonesia)
CDC	Constitution Drafting Committee	In Thailand
CEO	Chief Executive Officer	
CNS	Council of National Security	In Thailand
COA	Commission on Audit	In the Philippines
CSC	Civil Service Commission	In the Philippines
DBM	Department of Budget and Management	In the Philippines

Abbreviation	Full Name	Translation/Explanation
DILG	Department of Interior and Local Government	In the Philippines
DP	Democrat Party (Phak Prachathipat)	In Thailand
DPD	Dewan Perwakilan Daerah	Regional Representative Council (in Indonesia)
DPID	Dana Penyesuaian Infrastruktur Daerah	Local Infrastructure Funds (in Indonesia)
DPR	Dewan Perwakilan Rakyat	National parliament in Indonesia
DPRD	Dewan Perwakilan Rakyat Daerah	Local parliament in Indonesia
e.g.	exempli gratia	for example
ECT	Election Commission of Thailand	
Ed.	Editor	
et al.	et alii	and others
etc.	et cetera	
f.	folio	and following (page)
FAO	Food and Agriculture Organization	United Nations
ff.	foliis	and following (pages)
GAM	Gerakan Aceh Merdeka	Movement Free Aceh
GDP	Gross Domestic Product	
Gerindra	Partai Gerakan Indonesia Raya	Great Indonesia Movement Party
GMA	Gloria Macapagal-Arroyo	President of the Philippines, 2001–10
GTZ	Deutsche Gesellschaft für Technische Zusammenarbeit	German Society for Technical Cooperation

Abbreviation	Full Name	Translation/Explanation
Hanura	Partai Hati Nurani Rakyat	People's Conscience Party
HCA	House Committee on Appropriations	In the Philippines
i.e.	id est	that is
Ibid.	Ibidem	at the same place
IDEA	International Institute for Democracy and Electoral Assistance	
INTOSAI	International Organisation of Supreme Audit Institutions	
IRA	Internal Revenue Allotment	In the Philippines
ISEAS	Institute of Southeast Asian Studies	In Singapore
JBC	Judicial and Bar Council	In the Philippines
Jr.	Junior	
KAMPI	Kabalikat ng Malayang Pilipino	Partner of the Free Filipino
KPK	Komisi Pemberantasan Korupsi	Corruption Eradication Commission (in Indonesia)
KPU	Komisi Pemilihan Umum	National Election Commission in Indonesia
LAMP	Lapian ng Masang Pilipino	Organization of the Filipino Masses
LAO	Local Administrative Organization	In Thailand
LDP	Laban ng Demokratikong Pilipino	Struggle of Democratic Filipinos

Abbreviation	Full Name	Translation/Explanation
LEDAC	Legislative Executive Development Advisory Council	In the Philippines
LGPMS	Local Governance Performance Management System	In the Philippines
LGU	Local Government Unit	In the Philippines
Menpan	Kementerian Pendayagunaan Aparatur Negara dan Reformasi Birokrasi	Ministry for Administrative Reforms (in Indonesia)
MILF	Moro Islamic Liberation Front	
MNLF	Moro National Liberation Front	
MoI	Ministry of Interior	In Thailand
MP	Member of Parliament	
MPR	Majelis Permusyawaratan Rakyat	People's Consultative Assembly (in Indonesia)
NCCC	National Counter Corruption Commission	In Thailand
NEDA	National Economic and Development Authority	In the Philippines
NGO	Non Governmental Organization	
OECD	Organisation for Economic Co-operation and Development	
PAD	People's Alliance for Democracy	In Thailand
PAGC	Presidential Anti-Graft Commission	In the Philippines

Abbreviation	Full Name	Translation/Explanation
PAN	Partai Amanat Nasional	National Mandate Party
PAO	Provincial Administrative Organizations	In Thailand
PDAF	Priority Development Assistance Fund	In the Philippines
PDI-P	Partai Demokrasi Indonesia - Perjuangan	Indonesian Democratic Party-Struggle
Pilkada	Pilihan Kepala Daerah	Election of local government head
PKS	Partai Keadilan Sejahtera,	Justice and Welfare Party in Indonesia
PLLO	Presidential Legislative Liasion Office	In the Philippines
PPP	Phak Palang Prachachon	People's Power Party (disbanded political party in Thailand)
SALN	Statement of assets, liabilities, and net worth	In the Philippines
SARA	Suku,agama, ras, antargolongan	Ethnicity, religion, reace, inter-group relations (in Indonesia)
SBY	Susilo Bambang Yudhoyono	President of Indonesia, 2004–14
TRT	Thai Rak Thai	Thais love Thais (disbanded political party in Thailand)
TV	Television	
UDD	United Front for Democracy Against Dictatorship	In Thailand
UK	United Kingdom	

Abbreviation	Full Name	Translation/Explanation
USA	United States of America	
UU	Undang-undang	Law (in Indonesia)
vs.	versus	
ZTE	Zhongxing Telecommunication Equipment	

1

INTRODUCTION

The establishment of democratic political systems of government is a difficult and protracted process. This particularly holds true for Southeast Asia. Despite various democratization attempts in the region, authoritarian setbacks seem to be a constant feature of Southeast Asian politics. The most serious and promising democratization efforts over the last decades were undertaken by Thailand, Indonesia, and the Philippines.

All these three countries became democratic in the so-called third wave of democratization (Huntington 1991). High hopes were set in the newly introduced democracies by democratic-minded people in the region. The re-start of Thailand's democracy with the 1997 Constitution was widely hailed as a political breakthrough to end decades of elite-controlled semi-authoritarianism. In the Philippines, the removal of dictator Ferdinand Marcos by the so-called People Power Revolution in 1986 offered a great chance to establish a full-fledged democratic order and to remove the authoritarian remnants. The same holds true for Indonesia after the downfall of long-time autocrat Soeharto in May 1998.

In the first years after the regime changes, there was rising optimism that a full-fledged democracy could be established in all three countries. However, disappointment over the implementation of the expected democratic consolidation soon became the dominant impression among analysts and ordinary people. Initial euphoria turned into frustration since the democratic promises did not always transfer into daily political practice and reality. Worse, particularly in Thailand and the Philippines, the political systems temporarily adopted authoritarian features and turned away from being liberal democracies. For some time, it was therefore justified to speak not of a weak democratic consolidation process but rather a veritable regression in democracy.

1

In Thailand, people witnessed a military coup in 2006, election boycotts, and about one decade of political violence and unrest, mostly not in the political institutions but rather on the streets. In the Philippines, the recent pork-barrel scandal made the dimensions of graft in public office visible to the general public. Previously, a president was impeached under legally dubious conditions, whereas his successor led the country into more or less open authoritarianism. Indonesia was spared from direct authoritarian backlashes, but the current political system is still marred by a multitude of corruption scandals and undemocratic power struggles at all levels of government. More than 350 Indonesian government officials have been jailed on corruption charges since 2002, including national ministers, provincial governors, dozens of members of the national parliament and high-ranking judges.

The struggles over democracy have been long and bitter in the region and many scholars have attempted to explain the various reasons. According to my understanding of the political dynamics in the region, one of the major weaknesses of young democracies — not only in Southeast Asia — is the mutual reinforcement between flawed elections, weak institutional oversight agencies, and an unclarified division of power between the national and the subnational governments. Arguing from an institutionalist perspective, my main working hypothesis of this study is that the democratization processes in Thailand, Indonesia, and the Philippines faced enormous resistance because of significant variations in the reforms to build and establish electoral, horizontal and vertical accountability. The democratization processes in these countries either moved forward but at a slow pace, stagnated, or in some cases even deteriorated since mechanisms of accountability often failed to work in political practice.

The main purpose of this book is thus to analyse the various mechanisms of political accountability in the three countries and to set them in connection with the democratization processes. Particular importance will be placed upon the institutional reforms by highlighting successes and shortcomings with regard to accountability.

I also take into account different levels of accountability, particularly the often overlooked subnational accountability. One specific value of this study is the inclusion of eventual interrelations between these different levels of accountability. By doing so, innovative strategies to build and establish different mechanisms of accountability can be discovered and novel strategies for systems of checks and balances can be explored. Insofar, this study aims to contribute to institutional problem solving in practice.

Institutional reforms and their consequences in democratizing countries are one of my main points of interest. Political systems are constantly shifting. However, their adaptability and flexibility vary to a great degree. Particularly democracies are in constant need to react to changing environments and have to respond to new challenges. Mainstream research on the state of democracy is usually conducted with status-quo analyses. Tracing the trajectories in a process-oriented analysis, however, gives more insight into the creation of institutional change and is thus more valuable than a simple result-oriented analysis. My focus thus lies not only on results, but rather on how and why developments happened.

Compared to other previous comparative studies on Southeast Asian politics, this book offers a comprehensive theoretical background on various dimensions of political accountability and a scientific analysis of political process based on a thorough literature review and first-hand interviews with political decision-makers in the three countries. The book covers political developments until early 2013 and thus deals with most recent political developments in Southeast Asia.

Concerning the time-frame of my study, I will put the focus on the years *after* the regime change and not the institutional transformation itself from authoritarianism to democracy. A reform of the central political institutions created in authoritarian times is inevitable in order to create a democratic political system. However, very often democratizing countries experience that the initial institutional configuration, which is the result of the new constitution or new laws passed shortly after the regime change, is not working in support of a further deepening of democracy. Thus, further institutional reform is necessary in order to promote and deepen the democratization process. In this study, I will not focus on the initial reforms after the regime change which led to the establishment of a democratic order. Instead, I will concentrate on the adjustments which took place afterwards in the so-called consolidation period. For example, I will not focus on the first democratic elections (the so-called founding elections) after the end of authoritarianism, but the reforms ahead of the second, third and following elections and their impact.

Since I will analyse institutional reforms after the introduction of democracy, the time-frame for this study depends on the specific conditions in the three countries under research. In the Philippines, I will start with the inauguration of the Constitution of 1987 and in Thailand with the People's Constitution in 1997. The Indonesian case is a bit more complicated. The end of the authoritarian rule occured in May 1998, but it took several years until the constitution was completely overhauled to meet democratic standards. The constitutional amendments only became effective after the presidential elections in 2004. The time between 1998 and 2004 can thus be regarded as a transitional period. Here, a series of reforms took place which have been covered extensively by various scholars (e.g. Bünte and Ufen 2009; Ziegenhain 2008; Crouch 2010). However, these reforms are not part of my assessment in this study since I will focus on reforms that deepen democracy rather than those aimed at producing democracy. Therefore, I will begin my assessment on institutional reforms in Indonesia in 2004 rather than 1998. So, the time-frame for my research begins for the Philippines in 1987, in Thailand in 1997 and in Indonesia in 2004, and ends for all three countries in early 2013.

This study takes an interdisciplinary approach crossing the disciplines of Political Science and Southeast Asian Studies. While political science often operates with a normative framework, Area Studies takes a rather empirical and fieldwork based approach. The latter includes what the anthropologist Clifford Geertz called "thick description" (Geertz 1973) — a first-hand method of data collection and interpretation. While my theoretical part will be rather normative (how accountability should be), my empirical analysis will be rather factual (how accountability is in reality). Insofar, my study combines the two approaches from the two different disciplines.

Since my study focuses on institutional reforms concerning accountability, it is necessary to lay down what kind of accountability concept I am using. This will be done in chapter 2.2. Currently, the "empirical research into accountability is fragmented, episodal, and scarce" (Brandsma and Schillemans 2012, p. 1). Most of the current political science discourse on accountability is either conceptual or theoretical, discussing the various meanings of the term itself. There is a dearth of empirical studies on accountability, despite its importance in recent governance debates, most likely due to ambiguity in meaning of the term and difficulties in finding measurable parameters (Biela and Papadopoulos 2010, p. 2). When the focus is empirical, the studies generally concentrate on singular cases and do not include a comparative dimension. In this study, however, I will develop a concept of accountability and then assess it empirically in several countries and in a comparative perspective.

I will thus analyse in what ways institutional reforms on different dimensions of accountability (the independent variable) determined the quality of democracy (the dependent variable). These institutional reforms can be seen as a kind of a deliberate institutional engineering (Sartori 1994) of relevant actors in order to effect the quality of democracy. My research questions are therefore:

(1) What kind of institutional reforms have been deliberately undertaken by, or forced onto, policy-makers with the goal of transforming political accountability?

(2) What was their impact on the respective democratization processes?

(3) What lessons can be drawn from a comparative perspective?

After the introduction, in which I present the research framework of this study at a glance, I will go into more theoretical details in the second chapter. This includes — besides the presentation of the research methodology and the case selection — the conceptualization of institutional changes and accountability as well as the theoretical discussion of possible outcomes of democratization processes, namely consolidation, stagnation, and regression.

In the chapters 2.4 to 2.6, I will discuss the three dimensions of political accountability in which institutional reforms can take place: electoral, vertical, and horizontal accountability. In the empirical part of this study, I will put these theoretical dimensions to test. Specifically, I will analyse the effects of political reforms on accountability in Indonesia, Thailand, and the Philippines. Finally, I will draw some general conclusions from a comparative perspective on the impact of institutional reforms concerning accountability for the democratization processes of Thailand, Indonesia, and the Philippines.

2

RESEARCH FRAMEWORK

2.1 METHODOLOGY AND SELECTION OF CASE STUDIES

This study will use a mix of qualitative and quantitative research methods, but with a clear preference towards qualitative research findings. Since the impact of institutional reforms can hardly be expressed in figures and numbers, an in-depth analysis provides more insight and leads to more realistic results. Therefore, the primary research method will be the analysis of significant scholarly literature on democratization as well as relevant literature on Philippine, Thai, and Indonesian politics. If available, statistical material and organization data from the countries under research were also included as well as (legal) official documents such as constitutions, laws, and regulations.

In order to raise the quality of the evaluation, I conducted qualitative interviews with local experts during various field trips to Manila, Bangkok, and Jakarta and other cities in the Philippines, Thailand, and Indonesia.

Interviews with Southeast Asian government officials, parliamentarians, and politicians provided additional first-hand experiences and gave a local voice to the assessments in this study. To avoid a partisan bias, the selection of the interviewed politicians and government officials included the different political camps in the respective countries and members of the government as well as opposition forces.

To obtain further background information, I also conducted a variety of interviews with local journalists, NGO activists, political analysts and scholars. The purpose of these interviews was to cross-check assumptions and to get additional information. Often a personal interview with an expert gives you more country-specific insights than just the study of his or her publications.

The interviews in Indonesia were supported by the German development cooperation agency GTZ (*Deutsche Gesellschaft für technische Zusammenarbeit*), for which I produced an evaluation study of their portfolio in good governance and decentralization in 2008. Most interviews were conducted in Indonesian language (*Bahasa Indonesia*) with a few in English. Most interviews in the Philippines were facilitated by the local branches of the Friedrich-Naumann-Foundation and Friedrich-Ebert-Foundation, while in Thailand the local branches of the same organizations helped to organize the interviews.[1] The interviews did not follow a strict questionnaire, since the questions were adapted to the function of the interviewee. The statements which are quoted in this study have not been tape-recorded, but written afterwards from notes during the interviews. Therefore, they should not be taken as official statements, but rather as informal information given to the author.

Additionally, I used written sources and documents in the local languages of Indonesia and the Philippines. Summing up, I used a triangulation method which combines literature review, document analysis, quantitative data, and in-depth interviews with relevant actors for the verification and cross-examination of results.

Selection of Case Studies

The target of this study is to analyse and compare the development of democracy in three different Southeast Asian countries: Thailand, Indonesia, and the Philippines. The Southeast Asian region had been dominated by authoritarian rule for a long time. Only a few countries have so far started democratization processes in order to transform authoritarian rule into pluralistic, liberal and competitive democracies. Among these, Thailand, Indonesia, and the Philippines are the most important.[2] These three countries embarked on democratization processes within the last twenty years which have had, and continue to have, difficulties to further consolidate democracy. And yet, there were remarkable institutional reforms in all three countries in recent years, which influenced the course of the respective democratization processes.

Thailand, Indonesia, and the Philippines have significant differences concerning their political systems including presidential and parliamentarian democracies, proportional and plurality election systems, and different forms of state organization. Besides some geographical and cultural similarities, they are all major players in the Southeast Asian region, each having large populations and considerable political and economic influence. Consequently, these countries serve as suitable research objects for this case study, which takes a most similar case study approach.

Indices of democratic development, such as the US based Freedom House Index,[3] illustrate the development of political freedom and civil liberty in the three countries on a basic level. The Philippines, which have been rated "free" between 1996 and 2004, are rated as "partly free" since 2005. Thailand, which was assessed as "free" between 1998 and 2004, was downgraded to "partly free" in 2005 as well. In 2006 and 2007 the military *coup d'état* in September 2006 resulted in a rating of "not free". The return to democracy following the December 2007 elections raised the rating to "partly free" in 2008. Indonesia was assessed for the first time as "partly free" in 1998 after the regime change. In the following years the values for political liberties continued to grow until the country was rated as "free" in 2005.

The data from the Freedom House Index give a clear distinction of the democratic development in the three countries. In Indonesia, the quality of democracy could be maintained and even improved slightly in recent years. In Thailand and the Philippines, however, the trend temporarily showed not only stagnation, but rather a decline of democracy in the mid-2000s before improving in recent years. Graph 2.1 depicts the development of democracy in the three countries with the data of the Freedom House Index. Despite similar initial conditions, the graph indicates significantly different trajectories in the three countries.

The very different developments in the three countries underline my skepticism against structural democratization approaches. If political analysts would have been asked to predict the democratic prospects in Thailand, Indonesia, and the Philippines in the late 1990s, they would have never guessed the status of democracy as it is today. None could have foreseen that Indonesia — a huge, populous, highly fragmented country riddled with separatist conflict, a large Muslim majority, and very little democratic experience — would have become the most democratic country in Southeast Asia. On the other hand, Thailand's chances for democratic consolidation and political stability were forecasted generally much brighter.

Graph 2.1
Development of Democracy According to the Data of Freedom House

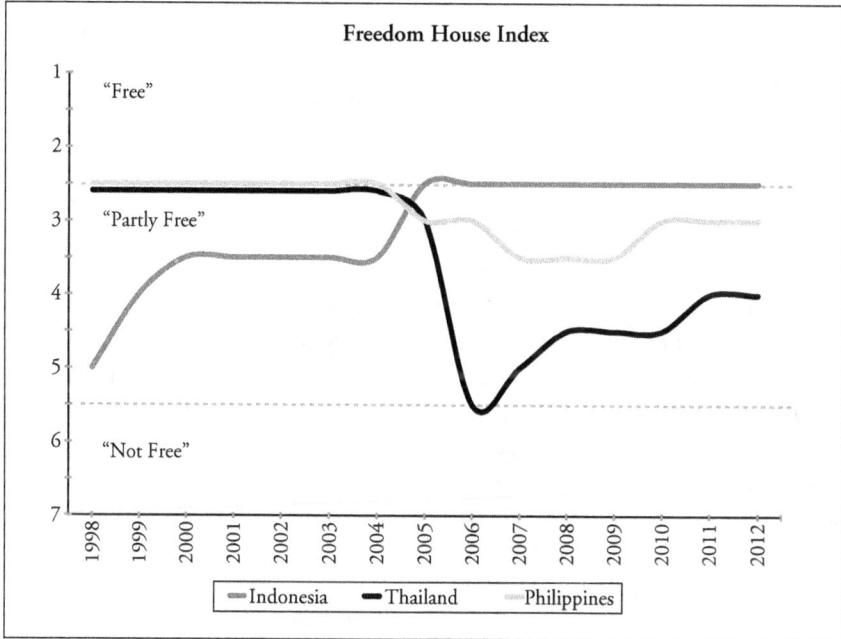

Freedom House Index

Indonesia   Thailand   Philippines

2.2 INSTITUTIONAL ENGINEERING

Within the literature of democratization processes there is a wide-ranging debate on the various factors which impact the stability, consolidation or regression of democracy. While some authors (e.g. Huntington 1991) focus on the "big" structures such as macroeconomic, social, historical, cultural, or religious preconditions for democracy, others (e.g. O'Donnell and Schmitter 1986) would rather concentrate on the concrete actions of certain political elites and their behaviour in crucial situations (i.e. actor-oriented approach). Neither approach, however, adequately considers the impact of political institutions on the development of democratization processes. Larry Diamond rightly argues:

> If the shallow, troubled, and recently established democracies of the world do not move forward, to strengthen their political institutions, improve their democratic functioning [...], they are likely to move backward, into deepening pathologies that will eventually plunge their political system below the threshold of electoral democracy or overturn them altogether (Diamond 1999, p. 64).

An institution in this sense can be defined as "a system of rules including not only formal legal rules that might be prosecuted by a court system but also norms that actors will generally respect and whose violation might be sanctioned by social disapproval, loss of reputation or withdrawal of cooperation" (Scharpf 1997, p. 38). According to institutionalist approaches, institutions limit and condition the behaviour of political actors. The preferences and the behaviour of the actors are thus determined by an institutional set-up. Institutions are thus understood as "coordination devices that resolve collective action problems" (Schedler 1999a, p. 333).

The main target of this study is to analyse the reform of political institutions and their outcome for the democratization processes in three case studies. Therefore, I will pursue an actor-centred institutionalist approach. This approach tries to combine actor-centred and institution-centred approaches in an integrated framework. The advantage of this approach is that it bridges theoretical perspectives and the observed reality of political interaction within institutional settings that, at the same time, enable and constrain the scope of this interaction (Scharpf 1997, p. 36).

While traditional institutionalism emphasizes the importance of institutions as independent players, neo-institutionalism also takes into consideration the influence of individual actors and juxtaposes them to the institutions in which they operate. Nevertheless, neo-institutionalists regard political behaviour as the product of institutional structures, such as rules, norms, expectations and traditions, which strongly limit the individual scope of action (March and Olsen 1984, p. 736).

This analysis of individual actor behaviour within a changing institutional environment is suitable for gaining a better understanding of political developments. Political systems are composed of structures/institutions and norms/rules/procedures, which bring together political and social actors (both individuals and groups) into rule-based interaction. Therefore, I will adopt neo-institutionalism as a methodology in this study. This approach is particularly adequate to analyse the three dimensions of accountability (electoral, vertical and horizontal), which shape by its specific institutional settings the scope of action for the actors herein.

Process Tracing

In order to single out the importance of institutional reforms, I will adopt the process-tracing research method to provide acceptable explanations. Process tracing is a methodology "well-suited to testing theories in a world marked by multiple interaction effects, where it is difficult to explain outcomes in terms of two or three independent variables" (Hall, quoted in George and Bennett 2005, p. 206). Tracing the process that has led to a certain outcome is inevitable if one tries to identify potential causes. Particularly in theoretically-oriented case studies historical actions are at the core of the process-tracing method, since they address the questions of processes and their outcomes. The analysis of institutional reform within a specific context, meaning the actual measures and their causal effects in a certain frame of time in a particular political system (chapters 3 to 5) can be seen as theoretically-oriented historical cases.

Process tracing is generally used for intensive case studies with the aim to analyse data on the causal mechanisms that link processes and events with the observed effects. The process-tracing method tries to identify the intervening causal process between independent variables and the outcome of the dependent variable. By closely following (tracing) the causal process from the independent variable of interest (institutional reforms concerning accountability) to the dependent variable (development of the democratization process) one can better identify the relationship between the two variables. It attempts as well to show the causal chain and causal mechanism between the two mentioned variables. By testing hypotheses with this method, the number of cases cannot be high. The testing is therefore based on "relevant, verifiable causal stories resting in differing chains of cause-effect relation, whose efficacy can be demonstrated independently of those stories" (Tilly 1997, p. 48).

Process tracing permits causal inference on the basis of a few cases. It can "greatly reduce the risks of the many potential inferential errors that could arise from the isolated use of Mill's methods of comparison, congruence testing, or other methods that rely on studying covariation" (George and Bennett 2005, p. 223). However, there are still some explanatory limits of the process-tracing approach, since a complete elimination of potential rival explanations is still very difficult. In order to avoid a confirmation bias, yet, it is necessary to study alternative explanations for the outcome.

Persistance and Change of Institutions

In most political systems there are many relatively enduring features of political life, particularly institutions which often cannot be changed *ad hoc*. Therefore, the relatively inflexible nature of institutions hinders institutional change. As Bingham Powell rightfully remarked: "Things that are institutionalized tend to be relatively inert, that is, they resist efforts at change" (Powell 1991, p. 197). New governments often promise to revise major reforms of the previous government. However, in many or even most cases, they do not touch the issues again, even when they were fierce opponents of the reform measures while in opposition.

In established democracies, institutions are often taken "for granted", so that they are beyond periodic conscious scrutiny. Since the standard political science research is conducted in long-standing democracies, most analyses focus on "explaining continuity rather than change" (Mahoney and Thelen 2010, p. 4). The persistence of institutions is in these cases, however, "not a matter of unreflective adherence, but the outcome of exercises of power and interpretation" (Hall 2010, p. 217). In young democracies, on the contrary, institutions are usually objects of active reinterpretation by relevant actors after a very short time. Here, institutions are in most cases not based on settled agreements that can be taken for granted at all times, but rather as "objects of continuous contention" (Hall 2010, p. 219). Institutional change is more typical of young and fragile democracies. The stability of institutions is accordingly always contested in young democracies (Sandschneider 1995, p. 120). More democratically open political systems provide more opportunities to a wider range of actors to pursue institutional changes than do authoritarian regimes dominated by a closed circle of elites.

Institutional change does not happen accidentally, except in times of an external shock, when urgent and immediate measures have to be taken. Otherwise, institutional change is incrementally prepared, structured, and organized by political actors. Therefore, these kinds of changes can be described rather as reform, since they are based on a reform agenda of important political actors. The term "to reform" is commonly understood to mean "to improve by alteration, correction of error, or removal of defects, or to put into a better form or condition". Reforms thus have a rather positive connotation. However, institutional change and political reforms do not automatically result in a positive outcome. In the context of this study, the term "reform" is used to describe *measures aimed at achieving change for the better*, which of course depends on the perspective and the intentions of those who initiated institutional changes/reforms. This does not automatically mean that the outcome of the reforms did lead to the intended improvement.

In this study, I will differentiate between gradual institutional change over time (evolutionary change) and replacements, which at one specific point of time, lead to a complete overhaul of various rules and institutions. The former refers, for example, to an incremental change of a constitution by amendments. The US Constitution passed in 1787 was amended twenty-seven times. The first ten, known as the Bill of Rights, were ratified simultaneously in 1791. The following seventeen were ratified separately over the next two centuries. So, the constitution maintained its main features, while several amendments were necessary in order to keep it in accordance with democratic principles and the changing *zeitgeist*. The 15th amendment in 1870 allowed previously excluded people from all races to participate in elections, while the 19th amendment in 1920 allowed the suffrage for women.

An example of a more abrupt constitutional change was the new Basic Law (*Grundgesetz*) of the Federal Republic of Germany in 1949, which replaced the Weimar Constitution from 1919. The complete institutional set-up was drastically overhauled, while only some minor features (such as the colours of the flag) remained. The Basic Law is a good example for the argument that only "exogenous shocks ... bring about radical institutional reconfigurations" (Mahoney and Thelen 2010, p. 2).

However, these kinds of drastic institutional changes are rather an exception to the rule. Institutional arrangements usually do not emerge and/or break down in a very short time, but are rather subject to gradual change. Institutions are usually based on endogenous developments that often unfold by degree and over time. Particularly in democracies, political change "unfolds incrementally, without dramatic disruptions like ... wars and revolutions" (Streeck and Thelen 2005, p. 4).

In most cases, institutional continuity with punctual adaptation is the rule. In this regard, path dependency plays a major role. The institutional legacies from the past limit the freedom for institutional innovation. It is a widely spread and erroneous notion that massive, abrupt shifts in institutional forms are more important and consequential than slow and incrementally occuring changes (Mahoney and Thelen 2010, p. 2). In fact, the vast majority of institutional changes are gradual and often they have more impact than sudden changes. Unfortunately, the general public and the majority of scholars prefer to concentrate on abrupt and dramatic changes rather than for gradual transformations (Heilmann and Ziegenhain 2008). For example, the Arab spring generated a surge of media coverage and scholarly articles whereas the ongoing and relatively unspectacular reform process in Myanmar receives comparatively much less attention. It is no wonder then that Mahoney and Thelen complain that slow but nevertheless important reforms related to institutions are "too often left out of institutionalist work" (Mahoney and Thelen 2010, p. 2). This particularly refers to scholarly transition and democratization research. After the initial major institutional reforms, which were necessary in order to democratize the political system, further "periods of rapid institutional change occur rarely. In general, institutions, like species, change only incrementally" (Geddes 1996, p. 35).

Institutions have a strong influence on actor behaviour, but at the same time they are also objects of strategic action by those actors themselves (Hall 2010, p. 204). In other words, there is a mutual correlation between actors and institutions. The latter also reflect the outcome of conflicts among different actors. There are some cases in which "the power of one group (or coalition) relative to another may be so great that dominant actors are able to design institutions that closely correspond to their well-defined institutional preferences" (Mahoney and Thelen 2010, p. 8). On the other hand, if there are equally strong contenders, the institutions themselves may even be the unintended outcomes of conflicts or ambiguous compromises among actors. In other words, institutional changes are often a by-product of distributional struggles between political actors, which can compromise on a reform that none of these actors explicitly sought.

Therefore, institutions that are based on agreements and compromises between various political actors often have a dynamic component. They are vulnerable to changes and shifts, if one would put it in a negative sense, or, expressed in a more positive way, flexible to adaption in a changing environment. The necessity of institutional stability and the need for change over time are an ever occurring feature of politics. Those who support the existing structures argue for stability and continuity, while the reformers underline the need for transformations due to social, economic, and other forms of change within a society.

Institutions, and particularly rules, are not just designed, but must be applied to the daily life of a society. Institutional changes must be interpreted and enforced by other state and private actors. While the designers may have good intentions about the outcomes of an institutional reform, the reality could be quite different. Public officials, policemen, and the judiciary are thus very important for the effectiveness and outcome of institutional change, since they have to interpret, implement, and enforce every political agreement or rule.

Often, reformers are weak and ineffectual if important state and non-state actors with vested interests are wary of change. As early as in the sixteenth century, political philosopher Niccolò Machiavelli concluded that there is nothing more difficult to carry out nor more doubtful of success nor more dangerous to handle than to initiate a new order of things; for the reformer has enemies in all those who profit by the old order, and only lukewarm defenders in all those who would profit by the new order (Machiavelli 1514, p. 173).

Institutional reforms are thus usually not easily agreed upon. When the reforms are enacted, they are frequently won against the express will of defenders of the present circumstances (Schedler 1999a, p. 337). Very often, reforms are delayed since the institutional winners benefit from the current status and expect to lose in alternative futures. Powerful interest groups that face significant material and immaterial losses from reforms will inevitably oppose them, and often use their resources and influence to contest any changes to the status quo (Grindle and Thomas 1991, p. 100f.). Reformers thus often depend on the goodwill of broad and unstable coalitions supporting reform measures. An important factor in the success or failure of any reform is the kind of relationships between the various interest groups in favour of or opposed to the intended measures.

Political self-interest is often the reason for supporting certain institutional arrangements and refusing others, particularly for opportunists. By doing so, the decision-makers prioritize their individual short-term interests over possible long-term outcomes. Procedural consensus is more probable, if the participants do not expect to lose all the time and that no dire consequences for themselves will follow when they lose (Valenzuela 1992, p. 83).

However, if one assumes only narrowly defined self-interest as the basis of all political action, then the assessment of political reforms becomes overly pessimistic. If policy-makers are only conceptualized as "rent-seekers", then little can be expected from the outcome of these reforms. Reality shows that policy elites in developing countries are often much more aware of societal problems and try to undertake serious efforts to address political problems (Grindle and Thomas 1991, p. 4f.). Therefore, it makes sense to include selfish interests for political change but not to treat it as the primary motive of political action.

Institutional Change and Democratization

Institutional changes can have significant impact on the quality of democratic procedures. However, they are not panacea for all political and social problems. Even deeply grounded institutions, such as constitutions, "amount to little if elites and constituents refuse to observe them. But it is precisely these shortfalls that assessments of democracy's quality seek to spotlight" (Case 2007, p. 7). Institutional change may force elites to change their tactics but not necessarily their motivations.

Thus, assessments of democracy's quality must take into account that in trying to rectify shortcomings, institutional reforms must be combined with deeper attitudinal changes. As Diamond and Morlino argue, "the diffusion of liberal and democratic values at both popular and elite levels" (Diamond and Morlino 2004, p. 23) is of utmost importance for democratic deepening, while institutional reforms are only a tool towards this end. Therefore, my analysis necessarily includes actor behaviour that is directed at adjusting institutional frameworks.

Major institutional reforms are typical features of the democratization period (O'Donnell and Schmitter 1986) in which the constitution is revised, new institutions are created or former authoritarian institutions are transformed in order to fit for a democracy. These institutional changes have a significant impact on the behaviour of the political actors and the policy outcome of the political system. The reform of political institutions also always has an impact on the manner of political decision-making processes. For instance, the Polish Sejm or the Hungarian Parliament played for decades a completely subordinate role under communist rule. Their members had to be supporters of the government and their main function was to serve as a tool of acclamation. In changing the personal composition by transforming the access rules (from previously appointment or uncontested elections to competitive elections in a pluralist party system) and by substantially enlarging the competencies, the political role and the functions of these institutions were transformed completely. Institutional change thus became a catalyst for democratic reform and offers opportunities for the improvement of democratic quality.

Democracy is not immutable, but is rather an ever changing process concerning the polity (institutional setting), the political in- and outputs, and the ways and means of binding decision-making. Once a country reaches a certain democratic level, it "cannot just lean back, relax, and enjoy" (Diamond, Plattner, and Schedler 1999, p. 1). Often, new democracies experience many difficulties in practising essential democratic standards in everyday politics. Corruption, clientelism, arbitrary exercise of power or ongoing human rights violations are among the most typical problems that young democracies face. These deficiencies reveal the underlying problems of public accountability and rule of law.

Obviously, the improvement of democratic conditions inevitably requires reforms. But it is not so obvious what kind of reforms are most suitable. It is often assumed that systemic institutional reforms, in particular, have the potential to significantly impact the quality of democracy in a given political system. Institutional engineering seeks to systematically improve problematic parts of a democracy, just as a mechanic would replace some broken parts of a malfunctioning car. The study of institutional engineering represents an underexplored field of the "new institutionalism" in political science. Neo-institutionalist scholars have discussed intensively the effects of different institutional settings, but neglected the analysis of institutional reforms (Schedler 1999*b*, p. 336). Therefore, my approach will also include a process-tracing perspective, which is part of a historical institutionalist approach. Such an approach is adequate to the specific problems of institutional change (Hall 2010, p. 205).

2.3 ACCOUNTABILITY AND DEMOCRATIC QUALITY

Democratization processes are not one-way streets. Some may lead to a further deepening and finally consolidation of democracy, others may stagnate, while others may break down. It must be taken into account that not every transition away from authoritarian rule can be considered as a transition towards democracy. As O'Donnell pointed out, many democratization processes may lead to authoritarian regressions or to hybrid regimes (O'Donnell 1996). Some democracies that have appeared in recent decades have in fact regressed back into authoritarianism (Diamond 2003, pp. 18–20). At the same time, Welzel (1996, p. 54) documented that there is a threshold of fifteen years for the consolidation of new democracies. If they survive the first fifteen years after their creation, it is extremely unlikely that they will collapse.

If the quality of democracy improves to a sufficient level over a long period of time, then it is justified to speak of a democratic consolidation. Democratic consolidation can be defined as a process which transforms the unorganized and inconsistent processes of political decision-making, which are typical for the transition period after the end of authoritarianism, into more stable structures and procedures. It also implies the effective functioning of state institutions in a political system which enjoys a broad public legitimacy. The decision-making mechanisms must be independent of the ruling figures and parties.

Another possible outcome of a democratization process is the stagnation of democratic quality at a medium level. Here, some features of democracy are implemented while others remain inchoate or deficient. In place of continuity, sporadic oscillation characterizes the quality of democracy. Such political systems move neither towards democratic consolidation nor to straightforward authoritarianism, but are rather trapped in a hybrid zone between the two.

The third possible outcome of democratization processes is regression. This scenario has been neglected for a long time in scholarly research on democracy. However, it makes more sense today to study these cases further since the research on reasons and patterns of the decline of democracies will stimulate the debate on democratic transition processes as a whole. For the most part, the breakdown of fragile democracies does not occur all at once or in a short span of time, but is rather "the culmination of a longer process, an incremental political change that has evolved over a more or less prolonged period" (Linz 1978, p. 3). The main problem of these broken democracies is a slow erosion and gradual weakening of the democratic process caused, not by a sudden *coup d'état*, but from within, by those who were elected to lead the democracy (Huntington 1996, p. 9). The regression of democratic regimes is thus, in general, a dynamic process of crisis and loss of democratic quality over several years for which the democratic elite itself is responsible to a great extent.

If the quality of democracy in a given country declines continuously, it is a matter of opinion whether this development is a failure of democratic consolidation or a regression of democracy. Young democracies have more difficulties to avoid a regression than established democracies. Their central political institutions often lack the acquired trust of their counterparts in older democracies. Political stability is generally also a problem. The legacy of the authoritarian past can be difficult to overcome, possible veto actors can still be powerful, and furthermore, the turmoil surrounding the regime change does not contribute to political stability.

Since the 2000s, the study of democratization has moved away from questions over transitional pathways and institutional design to conceptual issues of democratic quality. The debate centres on concepts of democracy, wherein various indicators and criteria are used to assess the quality of democracy. It is important to mention some important features that determine the research agenda.

Many theories on democratization are based on the ten criteria[4] for democracy presented by Robert Dahl in his polyarchy model (Dahl 1971, p. 3). Since then, it is a scholarly consensus that the term democracy

contains at least two basic parts: free/fair elections and pluralism/
competition. This minimalist definition declares electoral contestation and
open participation as the core elements of democracy.

Nonetheless, while a liberal democracy necessarily includes civil
liberties and elections, it is necessary to take into account potential executive
abuses, human rights violations, unconstitutional veto actors and corrupt
practices that negatively influence the quality of democracy. Elections and
civil liberties alone do not prevent these undemocratic practices. Dahl's
definition of democracy thus delineates only the minimum criteria for
democracy.

Among the most contestable points of Dahl's criteria is his neglect
of the importance of the rule of law. Leonardo Morlino contends that
indicators by which to assess democracy's quality are hierarchically
linked. For him, in direct contrast to Dahl, the rule of law serves as "a
prerequisite for all other dimensions" (Morlino 2004, p. 15). The rules of
democracy can be perfect, but as long as nobody diligently guards these
rules and sanctions perpetrators, the political order cannot work properly
in a democratic sense. Political accountability must be institutionalized
in order to be effective. Institutions such as constitutions and laws, but
also courts and supreme courts are thus important factors for sustaining
democratic substance. However, other political institutions such as
national and local parliaments are also significant in this regard. Hence,
"the study of political institutions is integral to the study of
democratization because institutions constitute and sustain democracies"
(King 2003, p. 7).

If important state institutions, such as national parliaments, the
bureaucracy, or the judiciary, fulfill their functions properly, the overall
quality of democracy is improved. From that point of view, the restructuring
of political institutions have significant impact on the development of
democratization processes in general. American scholar Larry Diamond
includes well-functioning institutions in his criteria for democracy and
emphasizes the constraint of executive power by other government
institutions such as parliaments, an independent judiciary and other
mechanisms of horizontal accountability (Diamond 1999, p. 11). Other
crucial points for democracy are the protection of minority interests and
the safeguarding of human and civil rights by all state and executive
actors. Additionally, potential veto players, which endanger the existence
of a democratic order, such as the military, should be subordinated to
civilian authority.

This study defines democracy under Dahl's criteria with the addition of Diamond's more detailed list. Besides the electoral accountability of free and fair elections, which Dahl underlines, the dimension of horizontal accountability, emphasized by Diamond, will play a significant role in this study. Analysing the quality of democracy involves "various indicators [that] can be analysed on a case-by-case basis" (Morlino 2004). The quality of democracy depends on various factors. Specifically, according to Diamond and Morlino (2004, p. 22):

- a regime must satisfy citizens' expectations regarding governance (quality of results)
- a regime must allow citizens, associations and communities to enjoy extensive liberty and political equality (quality of content)
- a regime must provide a context in which the whole citizenry can judge the government's performance through mechanisms, such as elections, while governmental institutions and officials hold one another legally and constitutionally accountable (procedural quality)

This study focuses on the third factor, the criteria of procedural quality, which includes "popular control over public policies and policy makers through the legitimate and lawful functioning of institutions" (Diamond and Morlino 2005, p. xi). I will adopt the following three criteria for assessment of the procedural quality of democracy:

- Electoral Accountability
- Vertical Accountability
- Horizontal Accountability

A functioning legal framework and stable institutional setting are preconditions for working accountability mechanisms (Pridham 2000, p. 93). Accountability, however, does not only depend on institutional factors but also on actors' behaviour and configurations. Informal practices, which are not necessarily covered by the institutional setting, will also be included in my assessment.

Political accountability can be analysed in the horizontal as well as in the vertical dimensions, with "each form thereby reinforcing the other" (Morlino 2004, p. 20f.). Limits on quality result in rich opportunities for executive abuses and corrupt practices. Damage along one dimension may weigh heavily upon others, leading to a creeping autocratization (Merkel 2004, p. 43). Merkel further argues that this trend may not automatically lead to authoritarianism. Rather, these mixed results may become manifest in various forms of so-called "defective democracies" (Merkel 2004).

Diamond and Morlino identify that improvement along one dimension (such as participation) can have positive or negative effects on others (such as equality and accountability). However, a dilemma can emerge wherein "there can be trade-offs [making] it impossible to maximize all of them at once" (Diamond and Morlino 2004, p. 21). Institutional reforms often lead to such trade-offs; they may gain ground in one area and lose ground in another. For example, an institutional reform may lead to more accountability at the cost of less decisiveness.

Under the gaze of scrutiny, governments may be more reluctant to undertake new and overdue initiatives. They "cannot deliver what citizens need if they are hampered by mechanisms of oversight and sanctioning agencies" (Mainwaring 2003, p. 4). Constitutional crises and a power vacuum can emerge if oversight bodies block political decision-making. Such situations, particularly when occur between the executive and legislative branches, can put the country in a gridlock. Excessive accountability can be problematic since it can lead to risk-avoiding behaviour. Furthermore, "governments that are immobilized by oversight mechanisms are sometimes perceived by voters or power groups as being indecisive, ineffective, or inept" (Mainwaring 2003, p. 4). It is thus a crucial question of institutional design as to how to create accountability mechanisms that enhance policy-making accountability without undermining the effectiveness of governments.

In this regard, it is important to refer to differentiation between majoritarian and consensus democracy by Arend Lijphart (Lijphart 1999). The former refers to a so-called Westminster democracy, where fast decision-making of democratically elected one-party governments is intended. Majoritarian democracies focus on the concentration of powers in representative, central-level political institutions. The political system of the UK was for a long time a perfect example of majoritarian democracy (thus the name *Westminster Democracy*).

In a classical Westminster system of government, a single party

> wins a majority of seats and takes government office. The party then is well positioned to transform its programme into government policy and can be held accountable by the voters in the next general election. This clearness of political representation and accountability makes the beauty of the Westminster model (Müller and Meyer 2010, p. 1066).

But even at the home of the Westminster democracy, in the United Kingdom, some consensus tendencies have been implemented in recent years, such as the regional representation for Scotland and Wales. In contrast to the UK, most other European political systems belong to the other type of democracy.

Consensus democracy delineates a democracy in which the inclusion of as many actors as possible in decision-making processes is intended to aid in creating compromises. This more consensus-oriented form of democracy includes a wide variety of actors in a given polity, often through decentralization and the need for supermajorities. Consensus democracy is characterized by broad executive power-sharing in multi-party cabinets, a balance of power between the executive and legislative branches of government, multi-party-system instead of a two-party system as typical for majoritarian democracy, a proportional election system, strong bicameralism consisting of two chambers with symmetric powers, federalism or decentralized state configuration and an independent judicial review on political issues such as laws.

Accountability

Accountability is a pivotal term for this study and requires a thorough discussion and nuanced definition. Like the concept of democracy, the meaning of accountability is contested. Moreover, its "admission into the pantheon of democratic values" happened only in recent decades. Although the term has existed in the English language for a much longer time, its widespread use beyond the more restricted contexts of financial accounting started only in the mid-1980s as part of new public management (Mulgan 2003, p. 9). It is specifically an Anglo-American phenomenon originating with the Thatcher Government in the UK and the Clinton-Gore Administration in the US who brought the term from financial to political use. Nowadays it finds daily use in politics and academia. There is no exact equivalent of the political meaning of "accountability" in other languages. For example, French, Spanish, German, and Japanese do usually translate accountability as responsibility and do not distinguish semantically between "responsibility" and the Anglo-American sense of "accountability" (Bovens 2007, p. 449).

Accountability cannot be divorced from its context. One must always know who is accountable to whom and specify what type of accountability is meant (Mulgan 2003, p. 10). Stapenhurst and O'Brien identify accountability as "a relationship where an individual or body, and the performance of tasks or functions by that individual or body, are subject to another's oversight, direction or request that they provide information or justification for their actions" (Stapenhurst and O'Brien 2008, p. 1).

Accountability serves as a blanket term for various concepts, such as transparency, responsiveness, and integrity. In American scholarly and political discourse, it is synonymous for political *desiderata* such as "good governance" or "good virtuous behavior", particularly of persons in public positions (Behn 2001, pp. 3–6; Bovens 2010, p. 2; Bovens 2007, p. 449). Likewise, the concept is often implemented to prevent or punish perceived inappropriate, unethical, or illegal actions by public officials (Weisband and Ebrahim 2007, p. 1). Accountability implies that groups or persons held accountable have some degree of autonomy and that their decisions are scrutinized afterwards by one or several other autonomous actors. To use the famous words of such radically different historical figures, Vladimir Ilyich Lenin and Ronald Reagan, accountability is to "trust but verify".

Accountability is an inherent feature of a full-fledged democracy. Since abuse of power, arbitrary decision-making, clientelism, cronyism, corruption, rent-seeking, impunity of state actors despite human rights violations, and waste of state funds are not uncommon features in new democracies, the necessity of accountability mechanisms is self-evident. This is in accordance with Scott Mainwaring's statement that "one of the important emerging challenges for improving the quality of democracy revolves around how to build more effective mechanisms of accountability" (Mainwaring 2003, p. 4). Or in other words,

> together with delegation and representation, accountability is one of the cornerstones of democracy. Delegation involves endowing another party with the discretion to act, representation is about the interests that are at stake, and accountability is meant to ensure that the exercise of discretion is checked (Brandsma and Schillemans 2012, p. 1).

Mechanisms of accountability can improve the democratic quality of a political system if they deter public officials from exploiting public office for private gains and protect civil liberties from their personal interests. In other words, they keep officials responsive to citizens' preferences rather than their own. Mechanisms of accountability are also designed to accomplish the proper use of public funds and the fair treatment of citizens. As Behn stated, "accountability for the use (or abuse) of power is nothing more than accountability for finances and fairness" (Behn 2001, p. 9). Therefore, accountability processes are intended to make public officials observe norms of fairness and efficiency in the appropriation and expense of public money.

Democratization processes change relationships between individuals and the state, as "clients become citizens and bureaucrats become public servants" (Fox 2007, p. 1f.). Citizens are more capable of holding public officials accountable than are clients towards an anonymous bureaucracy. Improvements concerning accountability increase democratic legitimacy and contribute to a better assessment of government and institutional decisions and thus more confidence in institutions and political leaders (Biela and Papadopoulos 2010, p. 3). If the general public does not trust those in power, it often assumes that nobody controls abuses of power. Under such conditions, the hope for a new and young democracy turns to despair.

The distinction between accountability as a mechanism and as a virtue that Dutch scholar Mark Bovens introduced (Bovens 2010) will prove useful in this study. As a virtue, accountability is seen as a character trait of individuals or institutions, which lines up with a normative framework. Studies dealing with accountability in this sense, try to evaluate the behaviour of public officials. They "formulate a set of substantive standards for good governance and assess whether officials or organizations comply with these standards. These are basically studies about good public or corporate governance" (Bovens 2010, p. 18).

In this study, however, I will treat accountability as a mechanism. Here, accountability is used in a more narrow sense. It is an institutional relation or arrangement in which a person or institution can be held accountable by another institution through specific mechanisms which make the actions and intentions of the observed institution clearly identifiable and scrutinizable. The focus lies not on the behaviour of individual actors, but rather on the systemic interrelations between various actors, which must justify its actions before another autonomous institution and answer to inquiries by other bodies in public. Therefore, the concern of my study is not so much good governance but rather mechanisms of political control.

Going Beyond the Limits of Principal-Agent Models

The concept of accountability is connected with the principal-agent model. In a democracy with people's sovereignty, citizens act as principals that "elect candidates to office as their agents; and, between those elected politicians who oversee the work of public administrators and other bureaucrats who act as their agents and, by extension, as agents of the public" (Weisband and Ebrahim 2007, p. 4). However, the principal-agent model is not suitable for every accountability relationship in practice, since the people as the principal have fewer possibilities to guide the agents as explained in the model. Additionally, most public bodies are both objects and agents of accountability. A legislator is accountable to the electorate, but is at the same time legally empowered to hold the executive branch to account. Michael Philp recently criticized that the relationship between accountability and democracy "has often become overloaded and distorted partly by being put to the service of theoretical models (such as principal-agent theory) and partly by being seen as responsible for satisfying a wide range of normative demands" (Philp 2009, p. 28). Since I agree with Philp, I will not frame this study from a principal-agent perspective.

Accountability in a political context has two basic aspects — answerability and enforcement. The former refers to the duty of public officials to inform and explain to the general public of their actions. Answerability includes the obligation of public institutions, such as government, to be transparent about their actions and the reasons for these actions (Lauth 2007, p. 56). Furthermore, they ought to give an explanation not only to the general public but also to institutions of accountability which are designed for this task (accounting agencies). Nowadays, in a society dominated by mass media, answerability belongs less to the information on certain policies but rather the justification of them.

Enforcement is the other fundamental aspect of accountability, which distinguishes it from other relationships between political actors. Enforcement entails the ability of the general public or the institution of accountability to sanction the offender or correct the contravening behaviour (Stapenhurst and O'Brien 2008, p. 1). Sanctions may include "disciplinary measures (such as dismissals), civil remedies, penal sanctions (such as fines), budget cuts, or 'softer' sanctions such as negative publicity" (Biela and Papadopoulos 2010, p. 5). In a political sense, formal sanctions may also include impeachment, removal from office, or legal punishment by a court. Additionally, sanctions may also have informal consequences, such as loss of reputation within the party or publicly, alienation from political allies and coalition partners as well as negative publicity resulting in decreasing re-election chances (Lauth 2007, p. 60).

Accountability thus means the "capacity of accounting agencies to impose sanctions on powerholders who have violated their public duties" (Schedler 1999a, p. 14). The necessity of sanctions must be underlined as an integral part of the concept of accountability. If agencies of accountability expose wrongdoings of other branches, but do not impose sanctions, they will commonly be regarded as toothless and weak. In a democracy, this frustrates the general public. Particularly, when the enormity of the scandal is great, sanctions are absolutely necessary. Or as Mulgan put it, "heads should roll. If heads stay stubbornly in place, as often happens, we think that accountability has been denied. In other words, accountability implies an element of retributive justice in making the guilty pay for their wrongdoing" (Mulgan 2003, p. 9).

In this study, I am following a compliance-based model, which "regards public office as a potential source of temptation to be guarded against by the careful shaping of behaviour through scrutiny and incentives and penalties" (Philp 2009, p. 37, see also Elster 1988, p. 127), since the political systems in Southeast Asia cannot be regarded as consolidated democracies and the temptation to abuse power is quite high.

Answerability and enforcement are usually dependent on the individual rights of the agency of accountability. For example, legal courts have explicit sanctioning rights, while the power of auditing institutions seems to be limited to the acquisition of information. However, this information can become a powerful tool when forwarded to institutions that have sanctioning power (Biela and Papadopoulos 2010, p. 8).

Graph 2.2 depicts the mechanism of political accountability. An actor is accountable to a forum, which he should inform about his conduct. In turn, the forum (accountability agency) debates and then judges the actor's behaviour, from which either formal or informal consequences follow.

Graph 2.2
Schematic Diagram of Accountability

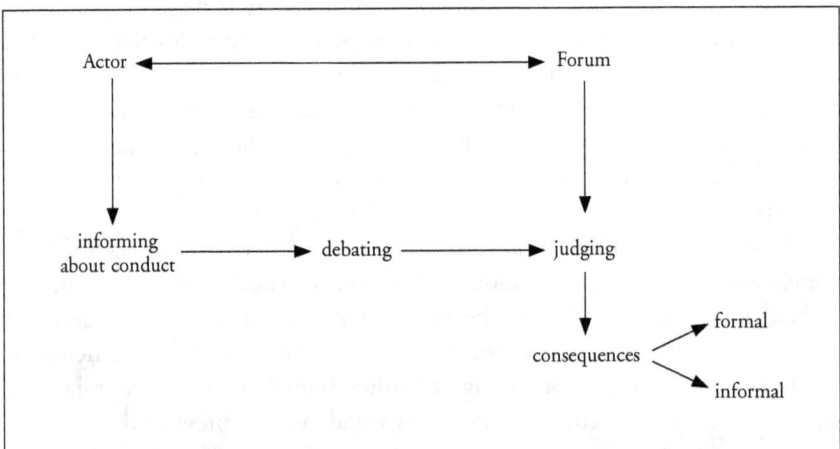

Source: Bovens (2007), p. 454 with modifications by the author.

Accountability can be used in different contexts and with a wide variety of different understandings. The definition and understanding of accountability varies to a great extent among the scholarly community. Over time, more and more elements have been classified as part of accountability, turning it into an "ever-expanding concept" (Mulgan 2000). A great number of debates concentrate on the most appropriate definition and on typologies that include the assumed multiplicity of accountabilities (Brandsma and Schillemans 2012, p. 1). Many approaches generally complain about the complexity of accountability relationships, since they are conceptualized in many different ways (Biela and Papadopoulos 2010, pp. 2–4).

One of the most extensive typologies for different subtypes of accountability is provided by Mark Bovens, who identified not less than fifteen types of accountability. He distinguishes between the nature of the forum, the organizational form of the actor, the aspect of conduct under investigation (financial, procedural, product) and the nature of the obligation (Bovens 2007, p. 461). Despite its value for identifying all kinds of assumed accountability, it remains unclear if this approach has a practical value to capture the accountability processes in practice. Scott Mainwaring differentiates between political and legal accountability (Mainwaring 2003, p. 11). In my study I explicitly include political accountability since in politics, sanctioning is not limited to legal transgressions and encroachments, but also to political decisions.

It is clear that an accountability regime consists of at least six elements: "Who, to whom, about what, through what process, by what standards and with what effect" (Mashaw 2006, p. 118). In democratic political systems, many interconnected accountability relationships exist in which actors are held accountable for their actions. Since these mechanisms of accountability "differ in their criteria and consequences it is important … to distinguish them into *qualitatively different kinds of accountability* [my emphasis]" (Lord and Pollak 2010, p. 973).

In order to reduce complexity, I will differentiate between three kinds of accountability, which I regard as essential for a further deepening of existing democracies: electoral, vertical, and horizontal accountability. These three forms of accountability address the problems of mutual reinforcement between flawed elections, weak institutional oversight agencies, and unclarified distributions of power between the national and the subnational governments as mentioned earlier.

First, electoral accountability refers to the mechanism in which citizens hold those in power accountable for their actions via elections. Electoral accountability is the most quoted and probably most important feature of the concept of accountability. The importance of fair, free, and competitive elections and the inherent accountability of the elected are at the core of the concept of a liberal democracy. In this study, I will use the term electoral accountability for what is otherwise often described as vertical accountability.

However, elections are not the only mechanism through which citizens can hold those in power accountable. As I will explain in more detail in chapter 2.5, citizens and institutions at the local level play an important role, on the one hand in exercising accountability towards local governments, and on the other hand in impacting national politics. I reserve the term "vertical accountability" in my study to correspond to the German term *"vertikale Gewaltenteilung"* (literally, *vertical division of power*) that refers to the division of political power and interaction between national and subnational levels of government. I will not deal extensively with federalism and federal systems of government, since in all the three countries under research such systems do not exist. Instead, I will focus on the prevailing decentralization processes which shifted power from the national to subnational state levels.

The third dimension of accountability is the horizontal dimension, which I define as the configuration and the relations between the executive, legislative, and judicial branches of government within a system of "checks and balances". The difference between accountability and checks and balances is a fine one. Checks and balances are mostly mechanisms of accountability. The main distinction is "whether an actor has the constitutional/legal capacity to request an accounting of a public official's (or agency's) dicharge of dutores or to impose sanctions on that official" (Mainwaring 2003, p. 17). A typical example is a legislature's investigation committee, which is acting as a mechanism of accountability. Additionally, (independent) government agencies such as anti-corruption commissions, auditing courts, etc., also play a role in the horizontal dimension of accountability. A more specific outline of these three dimensions of accountability will be presented in the following sub-chapters.

Since I am assessing the impact of institutional reforms concerning these three dimension of accountability on democratization processes, this study will analyse the following:

• Electoral accountability refers to the party and election system. The electoral system can be defined as the tool for selecting and ending political leadership as well as the method to translate votes into seats for legislatures. As political parties are usually a central part of the electoral process, they must be analysed as well in this dimension.

- Vertical accountability, as described in this study, refers to the enhancement or hindrance of the national government's accountability to subnational institutions. This includes also reforms referring to local autonomy and the quality of democracy at the local level. Thus, I will focus on measures related to the degree of local autonomy and the functioning of democracy at the local level.
- Horizontal accountability refers to the reconfiguring of the systems of "checks and balances" in order to increase or decrease the accountability of the elected government *vis-à-vis* the other branches of government.

Graph 2.3 illustrates my research approach:

Graph 2.3
Research Approach

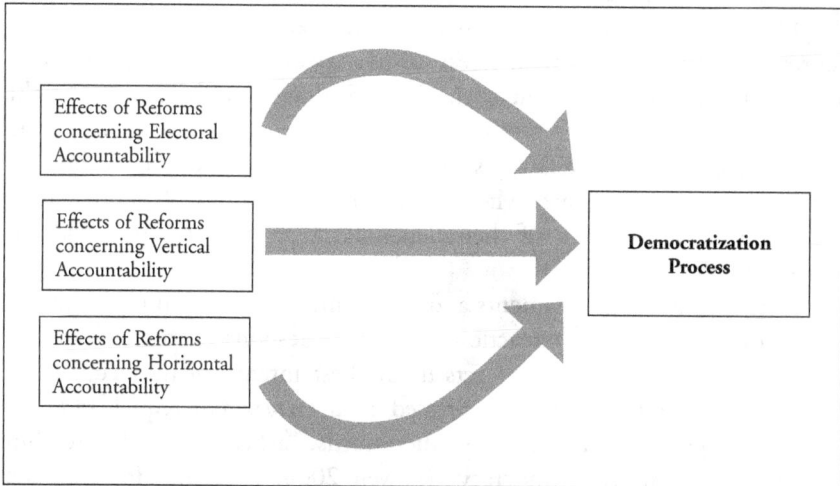

2.4 ELECTORAL ACCOUNTABILITY

Electoral accountability is the most quoted form of accountability, not least since elections are the most important instruments of democracies. Elections are an essential institution for democracies since they have two major functions. First, they legitimize leadership as the choice of the majority of the people. Second, they make leaders accountable for their actions. Elections "are by themselves too weak to guarantee 'decent' government. They are a necessary but by no means a sufficient condition" (Diamond, Plattner, and Schedler 1999, p. 2) for working electoral accountability in a democratic sense. In liberal democracies there is a common understanding that representatives should be selected, authorized and held to account by free, fair, and general elections. A democracy is in this sense seen as public control with equality (Lord and Pollak 2010, p. 971).

The democratic quality of elections depends on the degree of political freedoms before polling day, even before the electoral process itself has started. It must be asked whether opposition parties are allowed, and if they can act free from suppression. Political liberties also include sufficient opportunities for all parties and candidates to present themselves in campaigns and the media and to voice their political statements without any restrictions. Elections are thus always connected to a great extent with civil and political rights. According to Dahl, free and fair elections cannot take place unless and until these basic rights and liberties are firmly protected (Dahl 1992, p. 246).

Electoral accountability is strongly connected with the idea that representatives act in the interest of the people since they are held accountable by voters in regular elections. Suffrage is a fundamental right in a democracy since it is meant to link the preferences of citizens to the behaviour of policy-makers. It is in this sense that one of the authors of the Federalist Papers, James Madison, described elections of politicians as the "habitual recollection of their dependence on the people" (Madison 1788a, p. 352).

In democracies, governments and representatives ought to represent the wishes of the people. Their actions should be responsive to these wishes. It is not only that government acts in the best interest of the people, but that those interest have been expressed in a transparent, equal and free way by the people themselves. In other words, "a benevolent dictatorship is not a representative democracy" (Powell 2004, p. 273). However, the representatives should not only listen to what the citizens want. To ensure that this relationship ensues, institutionalized arrangements must be in place and reliably functioning. Elections are the most common arrangement to guarantee this responsivess. Citizens can force governments to follow their wishes if they "can induce the incumbents to anticipate that they will have to render accounts for their past" (Manin, Przeworski, and Stokes 1999b, p. 40). To be re-elected, representatives must therefore anticipate the wishes of the electorate and adjust their actions accordingly (Maravall 2009, p. 910). Ideally, only those representatives who act in the best interests of a majority of citizens are re-elected and those who do not are thrown out of office.

Since in liberal democracies incumbents always anticipate the retrospective reaction of voters in the forthcoming elections, governments need to act in the interests of as many citizens as possible. If governments are accountable in this way, repeated elections will lead also to representation (Maravall 2009, p. 935). The retrospective control of incumbents and judgement of representatives by citizens after a certain time-frame (usually three to five years) on election day is essential for the concept of electoral accountability. Elections offer citizens the opportunity to act as a "rational god of vengeance and reward" (Key 1966, p. 568). Elections thus give voters the chance to hold governments to account for their past actions. The concept of elections as a sanctioning mechanism is at the core of what electoral accountability means. In other words, elections are a "contingent renewal accountability mechanism, where the sanctions are to extend or not to extend the government's tenure" (Manin, Przeworski, Stokes 1999*a*, p. 10).

Accountability is not only a retrospective measure ("throw the rascals out"), but also a prospective measure (selecting the right candidate). The mechanisms and processes of "selection and sanctioning inevitably interact" (Fearon 1999, p. 83). A rational voter might sanction an official by not voting for him/her anymore, but also has the choice whom to elect. However, one must be aware that citizens' control over elected politicians is "at best highly imperfect in most democracies". Furthermore, regular elections are "not a sufficient mechanism to insure that governments will do everything they can to maximize citizens' welfare" (Manin, Przeworski, and Stokes 1999*b*, p. 50).

Horizontal and electoral accountability are connected. Rulers bind themselves through institutional mechanisms of accountability since they fear that voters would punish them in the next elections if they fail to do so. This electoral connection, however, is in reality not that plausible. Voters tend to give other issues such as policies a higher priority than institutional matters. Therefore, governments are unlikely to expect "electoral benefits from subjecting themselves to regular accountability; or the other way round, they are unlikely to fear the electoral costs of unaccountable decision-making" (Schedler 1999*b*, p. 335). Additionally, multifaceted governmental structures, such as coalition and divided government, "blur lines of responsibility and make it more difficult for voters to assign responsibility and sanction governments on the basis of their performance" (Hobolt, Tilley, and Banducci 2010, p. 3). Under such circumstances, voters cannot clearly assign responsibility for government performance. Accountability is hardly possible if it is not clear who is responsible for government actions and policies (Aarts and Thomassen 2008, p. 7).

Electoral accountability assumes that citizens are to some degree rational and informed. In practice, however, many citizens tend to lack basic information and instead make decisions on ideological grounds rather than performance. Elections are in a sense "inherently a blunt instrument of control" (Manin, Przeworski, and Stokes 1999*b*, p. 49). While government must decide on a multitude of issues, voters judge only on a few. They often cast their votes on short-sighted issues that are only relevant around election day. Elections occur only periodically and their effectiveness at securing electoral accountability is disputed, particularly if there are "inchoate party systems, high voter and party volatility, poorly defined issues, and sudden policy reversals that prevail in most polyarchies" (O'Donnell 1998, p. 113). This multitude of factors impacts the efficacy of electoral accountability.

If there are constitutional limitations on re-eligibility like in many presidential systems, electoral accountability is limited. In the United States, for example, a president is allowed to serve only two terms. In his or her second term, voters no longer wield the weapon of refusal to re-elect him or her. If there are no re-election possibilities, elections cannot work effectively as an accountability mechanism. Instead, in such cases an election functions more as a selection (i.e. prospective measure) than as a retrospective measure to hold the incumbent accountable.

Though legislators are directly elected in presidential and parliamentary systems of government, they differ in electoral accountability. In parliamentary systems, the government is only indirectly accountable to the voters through their elected representatives. The prime minister is not elected directly by the people but by a majority vote in parliament. In contrast, in presidential systems, the head of the executive branch (i.e. the president) is directly elected by the electorate and therefore directly accountable to them. In both systems, the legislatures are elected directly. Accountability is also limited when the presidency and the legislature are controlled by different parties in a presidential system of government (Manin, Przeworski, and Stokes 1999*b*, p. 47). Here, divided government blurs accountability when compromises have to be made between the executive and the legislative branches of government. In these cases, responsibility for policies is shared and the voters cannot discern clearly who is responsible for what. The same problem can occur in parliamentary systems of government if a second chamber forces a gridlock with the prime minister and the majority of the first chamber.

Electoral Systems

In a broader sense, electoral systems also include all formal and informal rules and practices that encompass the electoral process before and after polling day. Electoral systems determine the rules by which the representation of the people — the sovereign in democratic political orders — takes place. In a more precise way, elections can be defined as the mode in which votes are transferred into parliamentary seats or how a president is elected.

Elections are of the utmost importance for the consolidation of young democracies. The design of the electoral system is a crucial part of institutional engineering (Sartori 1994), since it is, among others, a decisive variable for access to power, the configuration of the party system, and possibilities for civil participation. The selection of a certain kind of electoral system also determines the inclusiveness of the main state institutions. Inclusiveness is understood here as the degree to which all segments of society are represented in the political institutions.

In general, there are two types of electoral systems for legislatures — plurality and proportional election systems. The plurality election system turns votes into representation by dividing the polity into several constituencies and then electing the candidate who receives the majority of votes in each district. The working of this system requires that the electorate has a clear choice between two (or sometimes more) competing parties or party coalitions.

In contrast, in proportional systems representation is directly proportionate to the overall number of votes received by competing parties at the level of the polity itself. The major function of elections in these electoral systems is to create a parliament that mirrors the electorate as a whole. In parliamentary systems this election mode has effects on government formation. Since the outcome of proportional elections is often a multi-party system in which no single party holds the majority, the formation of the government in a parliamentary system is the result of coalition talks between two or more parties. In such systems, the government is in most cases accountable to a coalition (Müller and Meyer 2010, p. 1066). Coalition governments blur responsibility and make elections, as an instrument of accountability, a rather dull tool. Even if a government party is punished by the voter with a high loss of mandates, it can still be part of the new government if it manages to form a coalition with other parties.

With a proportional system for parliamentary elections, the composition of the legislature will possibly be more representative and, at the same time, more fragmented than with a plurality election system. The relative advantage of being better in accordance with a multitude of political, social, ethnic, and minority stances is counterweighed by its difficult decision-making process. Plurality systems usually give more priority to efficiency and effectiveness of the government. In other words, if the aim is to establish an electoral system that facilitates voters to, as it were, "throw the scoundrels out" in order to sanction poor performance, plurality systems have two clear advantages. First, parties that lose votes in the elections tend to lose a far higher proportion of the parliamentary seats. Second, a change of majority and thus a new government as a direct consequence of popular election is far more common in countries with a plurality election system (Lord and Pollak 2010, p. 979). The chances for voters to effectively vote a government out of office in a parliamentary system are thus higher with a plurality election system.

However, proportional election systems are not *per se* worse in terms of accountability because plurality systems also have major weaknesses. There is usually a huge discrepancy between the percentage of votes and the percentage of parliamentary seats for political parties. For example, if the incumbent legislator wins his constituency with a relative majority of 40 per cent, 60 per cent of the votes which may be divided between two or three candidates are not considered for the composition of the legislature. Though that 60 per cent makes up the majority, they are still unable to remove the incumbent legislator despite his poor performance. Electoral accountability is limited in such cases. Additionally, plurality election systems lead to an over-representation of some parties to the detriment of others. It may also happen in a plurality election system that the party that receives the most votes does not receive the highest number of representatives.

Proportional election systems often lead to a division of power between various parties. Here, accountability is strengthened since the control of the government is not exercised by the voters only but also by coalition partners. Proportional systems underline the value of political equality, since they count each vote equally in the apportionment of representation (Lord and Pollak 2010, p. 980). No vote is lost and even smaller parties have their fair chance to be represented. Proportional representation is therefore important for political parties that lack the means to win a constituency seat, but nevertheless represent important segments of society. If electoral losers are inadequately represented, the democratic legitimacy might decline. Additionally, the degree of inclusiveness has an impact on the stability of the democracy, since inclusive political institutions prevent the dominance of a political oligarchy.

However, if the preference of the electoral law is less concerned with a formal division of power and primarily influenced by the extent to which voters can identify a single government that they can reward or punish (Hobolt, Tilley, and Banducci 2010, p. 4), plurality election systems have clear advantages. They are better at institutionalizing electoral accountability, since they give priority to public control instead of other actors. They are based on the value of autonomy that the people have in choosing and penalizing their own rulers.

The existence of a certain voting system has a direct relation to the tendency towards a more majoritarian or consensus-oriented type of political system. Plurality systems are a central part of Lijphart's model of majoritarian systems, while proportional voting systems belong to his consensus model of democracy (Lijphart 1999). Certain elements of a proportional election system are necessary if one wants to reduce distortions between the number of votes and parliamentary seats and, at the same time, give minorities adequate representation. If the target is to create more system stability and reduce party fragmentation and polarization, plurality voting elements are a usual means. Due to their impact on the party system, plurality voting systems tend to hinder anti-system parties and can increase system stability. Often, first-past-the-post systems have a stabilizing tendency towards the centre since moderate candidates have better chances to win.

Electoral rules for a parliamentary election may either foster a personal or a party vote. In a party vote with a closed-list system, a party has the right to nominate and rank candidates. If that selection process is not decentralized and democratic, there is no real accountability between legislators and voters (Moreno, Crisp, and Shugart 2003, p. 113) since the party leadership can determine who gets a good position on the list. To avoid this, several countries started experiments with open lists, where voters could reorder the list. By doing so, the legislators should be more responsive to voters instead of the party leadership.

For all these reasons, there is often a "very delicate balance in the design of electoral rules" (Moreno, Crisp, and Shugart 2003, p. 113). If too much emphasis is laid on personal votes, political parties will be weakened and legislators will tend to demand patronage from the executive. In contrast, if too much weight is put on party votes, legislators depend on the party leadership and not on the voters.

As mentioned above, the decision for a certain electoral system is also connected with a tendency towards majoritarian or consensus democracy. As Lijphart stated, the electoral system is likely to be the most suitable and effective instrument for changing the nature of a particular political system on the continuum between majoritarian and proportional democracy (Lijphart 1994). As we will see in the following chapters, the reform of electoral systems was an attempt to strengthen certain aspects of the political system referring to the dimensions of majoritarianism versus power-sharing democracy in all three countries under research.

Parties and Party Systems

The development of electoral accountability in democratization processes is not only influenced by the institutional setting concerning the electoral system, but also by the party system. Particularly in parliamentary systems of government with a proportional election system, voters transfer their votes to political parties and thus play a major role in exercising electoral accountability.

Not only do political parties structure elections in plurality election system, but even more so in proportional election systems. Even if voters are not familiar with individual candidates, they can gain some orientation by looking at their party affiliation. Voters can expect that members elected under their respective party labels have common goals on a given policy issue. This link between individual candidates and parties allows voters to understand their own choices and actions, giving "political parties as enduring organizations an incentive to live up to their claims in representing the voters" (Müller and Meyer 2010, p. 1066). Reforms concerning the political parties and the party system have thus a direct impact on the dimension of electoral accountability.

The question whether parties play an important role in politics is to some extent dependent on institutional features such as the electoral system. The importance of the type of electoral system for the shaping of political parties and party systems is beyond controversy in political science. In general, it is assumed that proportional election systems favour the strength of political parties, since they decide on the positions of candidates on the party list. Accordingly, parties determine who gets a real chance to be elected and who does not. The way the executive function of government is institutionalized is also important for the relative power of political parties. Parliamentarian systems of government require stricter party discipline from individual legislators in order to safeguard the government majority in parliament. In presidential systems, legislators have generally more autonomy from their respective parties, since the government does not necessariliy need to be supported by a legislative majority to stay in power.

Presidentialism as well as a plurality voting system for parliament strengthen the role of individual persons and decrease the role of political parties, particularly through their recruitment function. As a result, the intermediary function of political parties as instruments of regulation and coherence is undermined in such systems. Nevertheless parties can gain some importance in presidential systems if they have the power to nominate the presidential candidate. In the United States, for instance, all presidents since 1869 were either candidates of the Republican or the Democratic parties. Being nominated by one of these two parties was and is half the battle towards gaining the presidency. This explains the relative power of political parties even in presidential systems with a plurality voting system.

Democratic political parties can be important instruments of accountability. According to mainstream democratic theory, parties provide a crucial connection between ordinary citizens and governmental processes. If citizens vote for a certain party platform, they presume that the elected party will exert some pressure on its representatives after election day to stick to the party line. It is also assumed that parties should follow voters' preferences and "control the government, both if they are in power or in opposition" (Maravall 1999, p. 166).

Many prime ministers in parliamentary systems lost the support of their own parties and were thus forced to step down. For example, the British Prime Ministers Margaret Thatcher (Conservative Party) and Tony Blair (Labour Party) had to step down during their terms due to intra-party revolt against them. Since parties want to increase their popularity, they can choose a scapegoat strategy to get rid of a party leader or head of government in order to improve their chances in the next election. It was in this sense that the parties and not the voters who ended their terms of government. In fact, between 1950 and 1990 about 50 per cent of the prime ministers in parliamentary systems were not removed by elections but by their parties (Maravall 2009, p. 923). In terms of electoral accountability, these examples can be seen as prospective measures in order to be in better accordance with the people's wishes. The parties (and only indirectly the voters) hold their leaders accountable in this way.

For electoral accountability to work, legislators should be aware that they need to serve a particular district/constituency, but also not to neglect their party affiliation. Moreno, Crisp and Shugart found out that in Latin America, candidate selection processes are generally overly centralized, leading to legislators who are more responsible to the party leadership than to their voters (Moreno, Crisp, and Shugart 2003, p. 111). Every legislator faces the problem of finding the right balance between accountability to his or her party and, at the same time, individual accountability to his or her constituents. If national political parties are excessively powerful, legislators tend to neglect their constituencies, to exaggerate party networking, and to prioritize good relations with the party's leadership. If, in addition, political parties are "excessively top-heavy, dominated by national leaders, then legislators will have little incentive to articulate the interests of the voters whom they supposedly represent" (Moreno, Crisp, and Shugart 2003, p. 110).

In contrast, if political parties are excessively weak or extremely decentralized, legislators are often less concerned about national, and even less so international, policies. They extensively care about their constituency and the electorate therein. At the national level, political parties cannot exert pressure on their representatives, and the legislature as a whole cannot engage in collective actions to check the government, effectively resulting in weak horizontal accountability.

A weak institutionalization of the party system can also undermine the ability of the electorate to hold politicians individually and political parties collectively accountable. If political parties "are short-lived electoral alliances, when 'personalism' trumps party label, when party switching is rampant, it is more difficult to identify whom to blame or credit for particular outcomes" (Hicken 2006a, p. 44). In such a system, voters cannot easily reward or punish the performance of their representatives, resulting in a flawed electoral accountability.

The importance of political parties and party systems, particularly in the consolidation period of democratization processes, has been stressed by various scholars. Robert Dix, for instance, wrote that "although it seems that strong parties are not necessary for inaugurating democratic regimes (also they might be helpful in doing so), they are almost certainly necessary for the long-term consolidation of broad-based representative government" (Dix 1992, p. 489). Solid party institutionalization "helps to order, stabilise and legitimise a more democratic contest for power" (Randall and Svasand 2001, p. 95). Parties and party systems are thus important indicators for the progress of the quality of democracy towards an achievement of democratic consolidation (Pridham 1990, p. 2). The existence of functioning political parties who fulfill their roles as mediators between citizens and the state is essential for a further deepening of democracy.

Electoral Reforms and Democratization

After the end of authoritarian rule and the start of democratization, a crucial choice for a specific electoral system has to be made. Path dependency is central here, since once a country decided for a certain type, it will often stay with that type, only to modify it later. The prevailing electoral system is usually influenced by national traditions such as historical models (e.g. that of the former colonial power) or pre-authoritarian democracy. In pacted transitions,[5] the former regime party, which allowed competitive founding elections, nearly always opted for a strong president and majoritarian electoral system since they expected the best possible outcome for their interests. They often count on their existing power at the local level (Geddes 1996, p. 21f.), where local leaders are often still incorporated in the previous regime party. Smaller and younger parties, which are not sure about their voters' base, usually support a proportional election system, which guarantees their representation in the state institutions even with relatively low voter support.

Another factor, which decision-makers include in their considerations for opting for a certain type of the electoral system, is whether their own party has a great number of charismatic and popular personalities or a certain degree of local bosses who always win a majority in their region. In such cases, they clearly support majoritarian electoral elements. Parties whose structures are dominated by the national leadership and who lack influence at the regional level would prefer a closed-list proportional election system. In such a system, the leaders can significantly influence the order of the list and hence the chances of the candidates.

Since the focus of this study is the period after democracy has been established, I will not concentrate on the electoral system which was used in the first elections after authoritarianism, but rather on the electoral reforms afterwards. This study takes for granted that "the celebration of relatively free and fair elections does not represent the end of the struggle for democracy, but the first step in the broader search for truly accountable government" (Ackerman 2009, p. 4). The attention of the international (donor/media) community is often focused on the so-called founding elections, the first elections after the regime change. Following elections are generally "less glamorous than the landmark contests that gave birth to democracy" (Bratton 1998, p. 51). And yet they are even more crucial for the further development of the democratization process than the first elections, since they often clearly indicate the development and possible consolidation of democracy. In his study, Michael Bratton has noted a remarkable decline in quality in the second elections in sub-Saharan Africa (Bratton 1998). Such a regression of democracy can have many reasons, but one could have been a flawed electoral process.

In young democracies, the electoral systems are not only part of the initial constitutional engineering, but also frequently discussed as a variable in order to support the consolidation of democracy. Electoral reforms have "played and will continue to play a preeminent role in the discussion of political-institutional reform" (Nohlen 1996, p. 44). The reforms are an important means of counter-attacking the reduction of democratic quality and thus the regression of democracy. The deepening of democratic consolidation requires an electoral process, which is accepted by all major political actors and the ordinary voters. Improvements on the electoral component have a decisive impact on the development of the quality of democratic regimes as a whole. Electoral reforms can deepen democracy insofar as the elections have the potential to enhance "legitimacy by procedure" for the whole democratic political system.

Institutional reforms are needed if the electoral accountability mechanism is flawed. The legitimacy of democracy declines if elections are generally seen as divergent with democratic standards. Inadequate attention to the preparations and processes of elections, but also unclear regulations concerning the determination of electoral results, often lead to stagnation or regression of democratization processes (Elklit 2001, p. 64). Institutional change could be a solution if the electoral system does not contribute to the deepening of democracy. Electoral reforms are therefore an attempt to identify where electoral processes and results failed to meet the basic principles of democracy and then to modify the electoral rules. The modes of electing political leaders as well as the conversion of votes into seats for parties in parliaments are the typical ingredients of electoral reform. These issues are usually defined in election laws if not in the constitution itself. Therefore, the process of institutional reform concerning electoral rules is, in most cases, a complex and disputed topic.

Reforms of the electoral system are often influenced by the perceived necessity of the political actors, often those in power. These elites "often only legislate institutional changes they consider instrumental to advance their own immediate interests" (Elklit 2001, p. 70). Therefore, electoral reforms are often made in the political interest of those who have majorities or other powers to amend them. In this sense, the reforms are rather an attempt to strengthen the political power of these individuals and groups. This prevalent feature, however, might be negative for the legitimacy of future elections. Therefore, Nohlen recommends that the most important political actors, including those in opposition, must agree to electoral reforms (Nohlen 1996, p. 54), since the electoral system is a fundamental part of the democratic system as a whole.

Nevertheless, democratic electoral rules are only one of many institutional preconditions for a sustainable development towards democratic consolidation. The

> simplest way to get politicians to act in the public interest is to create incentives for them to do so. And the incentives, to which politicians respond most readily, because they are the most important to their survival and continuation in office, are electoral ones. Change the rules governing how politicians are elected to office, and you can change their behavior (Harvard Kennedy School Indonesia Program 2010, p. 86).

Electoral reforms resulting in qualitatively better elections will not automatically solve all problems within a democratization process, but they are a crucial component. Thus it is not far-fetched to rate the reform of the electoral system as a key — or perhaps the key — to reform the whole political system (Nohlen 1996, p. 44).

The chapters on electoral accountability in Thailand, Indonesia, and the Philippines will be structured in the following way: first, I will analyse problems of post-founding elections in the three mentioned new democracies. I will then assess institutional changes concerning the national parliament and a possible second chamber. In a final step, I will discuss reforms concerning political parties and their contribution to electoral accountability.

2.5 VERTICAL ACCOUNTABILITY

As already mentioned, I understand vertical accountability as an important part of the relationship between central and local levels of a political system. Citizens and institutions at the local level play a crucial role, on the one hand, in exercising accountability towards local governments, and on the other, in impacting national politics. This analysis is quite challenging since detailed studies on "how accountability expands vertically from local to the national level or vice versa ... are still lacking" (Fox 2007, p. 10).

Most analysts differentiate between two major forms of decentralization approaches — deconcentration and devolution. Deconcentration means "to extend the scope or reach of central government and to strengthen its authority by moving executive agencies controlled by the center down to lower levels in the political system" (Crook and Manor 1998, p. 6). In this approach, authority and political space are not given to the local level, which follows the orders of the national government. Rather, power remains centred at the national level. Devolution is a form of power-sharing between the central government and subnational authorities. The latter receive legally defined areas of competence and autonomy for tax-raising and public expenditures. In addition, they have discretion or decision-making power for local regulations. In deconcentrated states, local leaders are appointed by the state bureaucreacy or the national government. In contrast, in devolved states local leaders are elected by the constituents.

Institutional reforms concerning vertical accountability usually address processes of centralization and decentralization. While centralization means the reallocation of competences from local government units to the central government; decentralization is the opposite process, meaning "a transfer of power away from central authority to lower levels in a territorial hierarchy" (Crook and Manor 1998, p. 6). Currently, decentralization processes, often in connection with democratization processes, are a phenomenon which can be observed in all parts of the world. The third wave of democratization (Huntington 1991) in the 1980s and 1990s was accompanied by a similar wave of decentralization measures. Of the seventy-five countries with a population of over five million people, sixty-three started or continued with decentralization measures in the 1980s and 1990s (Selee 2004). In Southeast Asia, decentralization can be seen as a "post-authoritarian response" (Alicias and Velasco 2007, p. 4), since real and effective reform measures concerning decentralization only took place after the end of authoritarian rule.

Decentralization alone, however, is not necessarily in accordance with democratic principles. After all, authoritarian regimes also try to broaden their legitimacy by deconcentrating state powers in order to control more efficiently the state territory. Thus, decentralization must include the principles of devolution in order to successfully contribute to democratization processes. Devolution is *a priori* anti-authoritarian, since it is by definition the dispersion of central government powers. It helps to counter the possible excessive domination of an authoritarian national executive branch.

French political thinker Alexis de Tocqueville argued in the same direction. By comparing the American and French political systems in the early nineteenth century, he stressed the importance of a vertical division of power. For him, decentralization and local self-government were major institutional safeguards for individual liberty and protection against democratic despotism (Malixi 2008, p. 4).

Decentralization can contribute to democratization for many reasons. Devolution enhances political competition, since the opposition at the national level can win executive positions in subnational units. By doing this, the opposition can still prove its abilities and gain governing experience at the local level and is thus not completely excluded from decision-making after a loss in the national elections. Shared responsibilities between central and local government lead to power-sharing in political decision-making. Not only is the national government responsible for policies but also governments at the local level. If one of these levels governs poorly, the repercussions can be addressed by its counterpart in a system of shared responsibilities. At the same time, the good policies of one level can be blemished by the other. Particularly, what is enacted on paper at the national level might be implemented quite differently at the local level.

If decentralization takes place in the form of devolution, a diffusion of executive power follows. Decentralization thus includes lessening the prerogatives of the previously dominating national executive and strengthening the consultation mechanisms between the two government levels. Decentralization prevents power concentration at the national level. The propensity of central governments or elites "to become all-powerful can also be controlled or counteracted by stronger local or regional governments" (Van de Sand 1999, p. 14). The best way to promote democracy via decentralization is to reform central powers and to strengthen the ties that bind the central to the local. In this perspective, the effects of a decentralization programme would not only be restricted to the local level but at the same time affect the central government.

Due to the territorial differentiation of political power which devolution initiates, a new vertical dimension of power-sharing emerges. The divergence of the political system into different levels dissolves the concentration of power in the hands of a central government. This separation and limitation of power can strengthen consultation mechanisms among the state institutions. Decentralization thus can lead "toward vertical power-sharing among multiple layers of government" (Norris 2008, p. 157).

Additionally, federal and devolved local governments can force the political actors to enter negotiations and find compromises among themselves. These interactions can lead to a more cooperative style of government (Rüland 1993, p. 182). These typical negotiation procedures make decentralization a power-sharing tool and a consensus element, which leads to a more consensus-style oriented democracy (Lijphart 1999).

By analysing local democracy, it is important not only to focus on the presence and character of local government structures, but to also consider the national political environment in which such structures exist (Hutchcroft 2001, p. 33). Therefore, it is necessary to analyse the interactions between central and local levels of government. In order to assess the correlation between the quality of democracy at the local level and the overall quality of democracy at the national level, I created a policy cycle as an analytical tool to single out these various factors.

Graph 2.4 depicts the flow of influence, starting first with national influences on the local level, usually national laws and regulations which set important parameters for local governance. This impacts the quality of democracy at the local level, which in turn influences the quality of democracy at the national level. Graph 2.4 illustrates my approach:

Graph 2.4
The Vertical Accountability Cycle

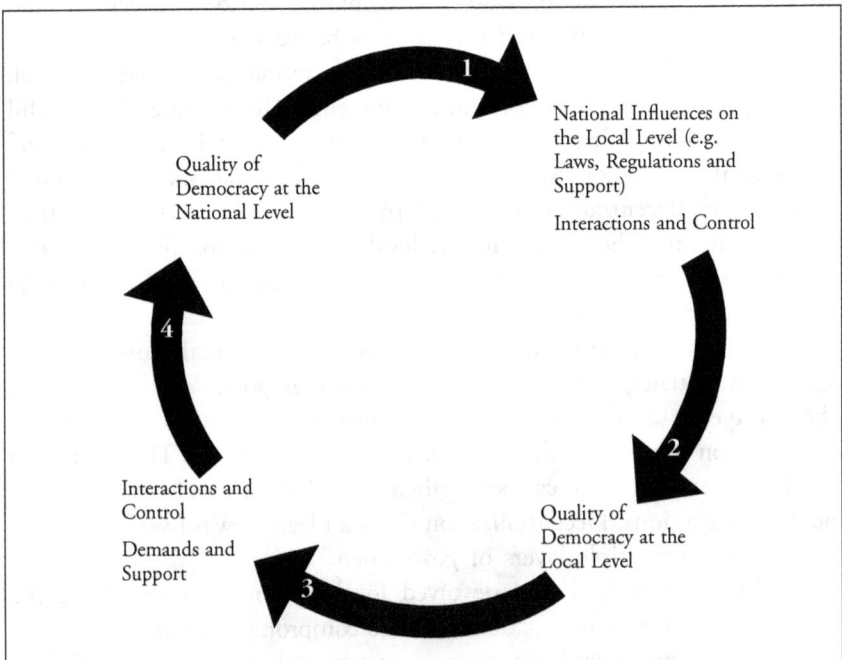

Source: By the Author.

National Influences on the Local Level

If decentralization was started after years of authoritarian rule, one of the main reasons would be the fostering of a new democracy in general, and specifically an increase in legitimacy for the current democratic national government. Some national government might also intend to deepen democracy by increasing accountability and participation. However, of equal importance are often more practical reasons, such as better public service delivery and more efficient implementation of government programmes. Another intention may be the diminishment of tensions in some areas where ethnic or religious minorities live. National governments often consider giving these regional groups more autonomy in order to reduce local resentments against the nation state and its government. In any case, the national government initially determines the rules under which local governments operate at the beginning of a decentralization process.

The relationship between the central government and subnational branches concerning the balance of autonomy and accountability is a disputed topic. Decentralization reforms are intended to change principal-agent relationships between citizen and state. This can be done in two ways. One is the enhancement of citizens' powers to select their agents by electing local officials directly. The other is the transfer of autonomous policy-making rights from central to local officials (Hiskey 2006, p. 2).

Devolution necessarily requires that the power of appointment for local government officials is removed from the central and transferred to the local. Such a step is additionally a strong indicator of non-clientelistic government policies, since the surrender of the appointment of local government positions takes away important tools of patronage from the national government.

Local governments benefit if their legitimacy derives from local elections and if they have autonomy in selecting their staff. If the central government interferes in these matters, the decentralization process has not yet turned into devolution. The revenues from the local budget are another indicator of autonomy. If local governments do not have the power to raise their own taxes and to allocate other sources of income, they are still subject to central control over the power of the purse (Hiskey 2006, p. 4).

Though local governments are equipped with significant autonomy, they are in practice still subject to the scrutiny of national governments. This occurs by means of a variety of accountability instruments which tend to have a top-down direction. National governments tend to have the upper hand in what ought to be a mutually accountable relationship.

They are in a better position to supervise local governments and to take punitive measures in the case of local power abuse, whereas there are fewer possibilities for the local governments to hold the national government accountable. In such cases, "local governments are accountable to higher-level hierarchies for their conduct. This often creates a relationship of upward accountability or dependence on central authorities, which may contradict the arguments about local discretion and accountability" (Yilmaz, Beris, and Serrano-Berthet 2010, p. 262).

Accordingly, decentralization warrants caution. The decentralization of roles and responsibilities must be meaningful if it were to be a constructive mechanism for increased legitimacy of democracy. To ensure that it is meaningful, there are various measures which influence the quality of democracy at the local level. Among the most decisive factors is the extent of autonomy that is granted to local government units. More powers for local governments/parliaments often result in a better quality of democracy at the national level. If the local institutions are able to build up their own personal resources and improve the local capacities to govern, the dependence on state supervision will decrease.

Another significant aspect of national-local relations is fiscal regulations, whether taxes are divided between national and local levels, and to what degree each level pays for public services delivery. Particularly poor regions depend on financial support from the national government, since they do not have the personal and financial capacities to adequately provide public services. In such cases, the country as a whole benefits from well-developed fiscal equalization mechanisms, which support lagging regions and result in spatially balanced growth (Hill 2007, p. 73). Furthermore, a national government could offer programmes to reward good governance with financial and other incentives.

Beside financial support, the national government is also expected to improve the capacities of local governments to manage their responsibilities. These local capacities are necessary in order to shift from reliance on government allocations to local fund-raising mechanisms. Fiscal support without capacity-building measures is often not sufficient. Hal Hill cautions that "transferring major expenditure and revenue responsibilities to local governments without first strengthening their institutional capabilities is likely to result in waste and inefficiency" (Hill 2007, p. 86). Building local capacities refers to cooperation with local experts, think-tanks, and NGOs, which could lead to a self-acquired knowledge base. If local institutions have sufficient capacities, they can develop accurately fitting solutions for local problems instead of following orders from above.

The influence from the national to the local level is thus twofold: democratic decentralization must not only empower local governments by giving them autonomy and responsibilities, but also by providing financial support for institution and capacity building. Additionally, the national level should ensure that democratic principles are respected at the local level. Since local governments often have little experience in democratic decision-making, it is very difficult to build responsive governance systems that ensure that local governments are held accountable by their own citizens and institutions (Eckardt 2007, p. 2). Thus, it is also the task of the national government to prevent power abuse and corruption within local government, at least in the early stages of a decentralization process.

It is seemingly paradoxical that a strong central government is required for effective decentralization. The central government must make the initial decision to disperse its power through decentralization mechanisms. In a well-organized inclusive process, it ought to re-define its own role and that of local governments in a comprehensive way. If the central government fails to do so,

> the less likely are the rules of the game to be defined transparently and coherently, the less orderly will be the process of decentralization, the less likely is it that local governments will be prepared to assume increased revenue raising responsibility, and the more likely it is that local governments will lobby to the central government for special favours and exemptions (Hill 2007, p. 89f.).

Therefore, what initially seems to be a paradox is in fact an essential condition for a successful devolution. A decentralized system of government can only work effectively if the central government supports the decentralized units by delivering good national governance (Hill, Balisacan, and Piza 2007, p. 42).

Democratic Quality at the Local Level

The evaluation of local politics, or patterns of local political activity, offer realistic insights for evaluating the qualitative features of a country's political systems, both locally and at the national level (Choi 2011, p. 3). However, it is difficult to gain a general assessment of the quality of democracy at the local level since there are usually dozens or even hundreds of local government units. Some may be more democratic, while others might be rather authoritarian. Therefore, this study moves towards a broad and representative picture of the state of local democracy, including both worse and best cases.

An analysis of democracy at the local level necessarily involves the two crucial dimensions of accountability — answerability and enforcement. If these two dimensions prevail, political awareness among ordinary citizens rises. It can rightly be argued that accountability is "higher at the local level, since citizens who are better informed about government performance can vote these governments out of office" (Eckardt 2007, p. 5).

It is obvious that the decisions made at the national level have an impact on every citizen. Democracy in everyday life depends on national political decisions, but citizens may feel the consequences of local decisions more directly than those from the faraway capital. Citizens' experiences with local government are a critical determinant of their views towards the larger political system. There is less distance between citizens and their representatives at the local than those at the national level. Thus, policies adopted at the local level are more tangible for average people and might be closer to citizens' real needs and wishes. Additionally, the chances for political participation increase in a devolved political system and the likelihood for becoming involved in politics (e.g. becoming a candidate) is higher.

Devolution offers greater political opportunities for civil society and otherwise marginalized groups to mobilize. This can create a new political dynamism towards greater empowerment and participation (Alicias and Velasco 2007, p. 6). This power gives citizens a greater stake in politics, and as a consequence, produces a more vibrant and dynamic democracy. In this sense, devolution can be an effective instrument to support the deepening of democracy. It has a "great potential to stimulate the growth of civil society organizations ...; prevent widespread disillusionment with new policies from turning into a rejection of the entire democratic process ...; [and] boost legitimacy by making government more responsive to citizen needs" (Diamond 1999, p. 124f.). In agreement, Antlöv demands that "politics need to be built from below, because this is ... where people can translate national policies into local programs, and where local issues [can] become national ideology" (Antlöv 2003, p. 74).

Vertical accountability is the means through which citizens, mass media and civil society seek to enforce standards of good performance on officials. This does not only apply to the national level, but also to the local level, on which citizens have a far more realistic influence. Local officials can be better scrutinized by the local people who know them and can access them. Ordinary citizens are often more aware of their political possibilities if they witness the mismanagement of local public officials. The actions of local governments are in this sense strongly influenced "by the effectiveness of political accountability systems ensuring public control of [local] government actions" (Eckardt 2007, p. 3). Hence, the conditions for the two crucial components of accountability — answerability and enforcement — must operate effectively at the local level in order to improve the quality of democracy. However, the outcome of decentralization hinges "heavily on how local actors (with varying interests and capacities) shape and respond to new opportunities" (Choi 2011, p. 21). In the end, their behaviour determines whether decentralization contributes to a deepening of democracy or not.

Local Influences on the National Level

Decentralization reshapes power relations between local citizens, local governments and the national government. By transferring powers and autonomy to the local level, the national government will have to accept a growing number of demands from local governments, local interest associations and citizens. The channels through which the demands are made vary. In some political systems, formal and institutional channels — for example, an assembly of local governments or common commissions of state and local level officials — are the decisive negotiation fora. In other polities, informal channels between influential local elites and central government members, often along party or patronage lines, are more influential.

The institutionalization of local level participation can lead to a higher potential of deepening democracy in the whole country. It seems plausible that "without grassroots democracy, it is impossible to sustain democracy at the national level" (Antlöv 2003, p. 74). Since local governments are generally closer to ordinary people, they often know more about public needs and interests. Local experiences can lead to demands which the national government has to take seriously. Often, these demands from the local are more pragmatic and solution-oriented than projects from technocrats in the national ministries. Decentralized government structures thus support the accountability of the national government to the wishes of particular regional governments.

The institutional structure of decentralization has implications not only for the subnational level, but also for national governance. An example for the importance of local influences on national politics is Argentina. Here,

> the subnational political sphere, especially at the provincial level, is a
> key arena for Argentine politics and policy-making. Almost every single
> important policy issue at the national level in the last two decades
> has been negotiated somehow by the President and his/her ministers

(or operators) with provincial governors, who subsequently instruct national legislators from their provinces to go along (Ardanaz, Leiras, and Tommasi 2010, p. 5).

Hence, regional demands can be decisive for national politics.

Local politicians, who care for national politics, try to influence national policies in order to safeguard the local interests of their constituency. However, well representing local interests is one issue, political and economic power is another. From the viewpoint of local politicians, the possibility of acquiring national positions presents a good opportunity to gain access to otherwise unavailable financial resources (de Dios 2007, p. 190). This could be obtained after being elected for national parliament or appointed as high-ranking national government official.

The interactions between local and central levels of government can be manifold. However, in states with devolved local governments the national government is held more accountable than in centralized states. In decentralized systems of government, local and national governments have to exercise checks and balances on one another. The balance of power between these two institutions is determined by their constitutional or legal competencies. Particularly, subnational capacities to monitor, supervise and limit central government discretion is of utmost importance for vertical accountability (Fox 2007, p. 39). Devolution, with its inherent relevant possibilities for local government units, offers significant opportunities to improve national government accountability by exerting high pressure from below (Yilmaz, Beris, and Serrano-Berthet 2010, p. 259). Additionally, vertical accountability might be higher if members of the opposition are elected to rule in several provinces or districts.

Decentralization and Ethnic/Religious Minorities

Decentralization can be advantageous for the resolution of ethnic and religious conflicts. Giving local autonomy to these groups can not only be useful for the reduction of violence, but also for the improvement of the quality of democracy. According to Linz, "few multinational states have been stable democracies" (Linz 1978, p. 65). Ethnic and religious minorities themselves often feel disadvantaged by the national government and demand more autonomy, and as a last resort, a secession. In such cases, the national army under the control of the national government tries to violently suppress regional conflicts. These separatist tendencies and the human rights violations of the military further weaken the legitimacy of the democratic order and contribute to the regression of democracy.

The significant impact of decentralization on ethnicity and religious conflicts is that local autonomy opens avenues for negotiations between the central government and the insurgents. More powers for local governments offer more possibilities for the protection of the interests of minorities, which in turn can improve the chances for peace. Additionally, decentralized government structures allow the adjustment of national policies according to local customs and culture. This might help to reduce ethnic and religious tensions in multi-ethnic and multi-religious states. Decentralization can thus be seen as a tool to ameliorate local disaffection with the capital in the country's centre. If violent conflicts diminish, the overall quality of democracy rises.

At the same time, decentralization can also contribute negatively to the development of democracy in multi-ethnic and multi-religious societies. Sometimes, local autonomy might be used to favour members of the ethnicity or religion of local rulers to the detriment of minorities. And so, decentralization may encourage intolerance towards these minorities, exacerbate inequalities and foster ethnic and religious conflict. In such situations, minorities are excluded from exercising accountability on local politics. Consequently, if "subnational political elites manage to exclude part of the electorate from democratic competition, then national political leaders will have little incentive or capacity to be accountable to those citizens" (Fox 2007, p. 40).

The Transformation of National-Local Relations and Their Impact on Democracy

There is no direct causal link between democratization and decentralization. The latter "only presents a political opportunity to deepen democracy" (Alicias and Velasco 2007, p. 5). The cycle model I presented above can be read in terms of a negative influence on democracy between central and local governments. In this "vicious cycle", poor governance from the national level may result in authoritarian features at the local level. Local bosses may become, as it were, "little kings" who adopt authoritarian features in their local governance. Corruption, which in centralist states is quite a problem of the national capital and its political elites, may spread actually to small towns and villages. Bad governance and power abuse at the local level then quasi-automatically loop around back to national politics.

It is therefore wrong to assume that there is *per se* a direct positive correlation between decentralization and democratization. In their comparative study of South Asian and West African countries, Crook and Manor (1998) come to the conclusion that decentralization is not always positive for improving local governance and accountability. Decentralization can only be successful in promoting democracy if it is combined with institutional reforms at the national level (Crook and Manor 1998, p. 304). If the democratization process at the national level stagnates or deteriorates due to a lack of democratizing reforms, local level governance is also often not in accordance with democratic standards.

In terms of accountability, decentralization often contributes to more channels for citizens to hold those in power accountable. It is necessary, however, that citizens clearly know who is to blame for what. Otherwise, decentralization may reduce accountability if the lines of authority are opaque, so that citizens have difficulties knowing who is responsible (Rose-Ackerman 2005, p. 19). In such situations, local leaders can blame the national government for policy failures and vice versa.

Additionally, some authors argue that decentralization may in fact create or deepen local enclaves of authoritarianism. If local elites that rule in a certain area for generations by authoritarian means receive more autonomy from the central government without promoting accountability mechanisms, decentralization may in fact lead to a less democratic rule (Diamond 1999, p. 132f.; Hutchcroft 2001, p. 43). Since the degree of illiteracy, poverty and inequality correlates to the degree of political awareness, rural citizens might also have more difficulties in controlling their local rulers. As a result, some authors argue that the lower the level of government, the greater is the opportunity for vested interests to capture political process (Bardhan and Mookherjee 2000, p. 135ff.). Decentralization thus "risks a descent into parochialism that leaves national interests behind" (Rose-Ackerman 2005, p. 217). If political accountability is incomplete at the local level, decentralization can in fact create powerful incentives for local bosses to dominate local politics and to divert public resources in favour of their own ambitions rather than those of the broader community (Eckardt 2007, p. 5).

However, it must be considered that even if these local bosses cannot be held accountable by the national government, they are still, at least in theory, dependent on the electoral support of their local constituency. In other words, "local political strongmen who rule with impunity will be more likely to use their positions of power for personal gain than those who must answer to the electorate" (Hiskey 2006, p. 12). In such cases, decentralization might not be the panacea for overcoming traditional and feudal[6] social orders, but at least offers opportunites for a solution, insofar as elections might contribute to changing local power relations.

Re-Centralization

National governments can not only give further autonomy to the subnational level, but also revert these processes. Re-centralization processes take away the powers of local governments and concentrate power back at the national centre. Such re-centralization measures were historically often paralleled with a regression of democracy and served as prelude to authoritarianism. In 2004, the President of the Russian Federation, Vladimir Putin, transformed the formerly powerful Federation Council and the elected state governors into weak, dependent and powerless appointees. This centralization of the national political system went hand in hand with a concentration of power in the president and a turn towards authoritarianism.[7]

Re-centralization reduces the vertical accountability of the national government to the wishes of any particular region or locality (Seabright 1996, p. 65). There are no more channels of mutual exchange, which contribute positively to the quality of democracy, but rather top-down directives. It is obvious that the consequences of centralization as a means for maximizing power by one or a few omnipotent men have a largely negative impact on democratization. But it does not necessarily follow that the opposite value, decentralization, is *per se* positive in any regard (Fesler 1965, p. 538 f.).

In chapter 4, I will analyse the kind of institutional reforms concerning local democracy and centre-local relations that were undertaken in the three countries under research. I will start with an assessment of the legal framework in order to determine the level of autonomy and powers of the local governments. I will then examine how democracy functions at the local level. In the next step I will take a closer look at the degree to which ethnic conflicts and separatism in troubled regions were effectively reduced by minority representation and decentralization. Finally, I will analyse the interactions between central and local governments and determine in which ways accountability relations are structured.

2.6 HORIZONTAL ACCOUNTABILITY

Vertical and electoral accountability are necessary tools to control the behaviour and actions of those in power. However, practice has shown that vertical and electoral accountability alone are not enough to prevent abuses of power. The authors of the Federalist Papers already stated that "a dependence on the people is, no doubt, the primary control on the government: but experience has taught mankind the necessity of auxiliary precautions" (Madison 1788*b*, p. 322). Thus, the introduction of elements of horizontal accountability and of a system of checks and balances between different political institutions at the national level became instruments to restrain abuse of power by the executive.

Particularly in young democracies, which had excessive power abuse by the executive in their authoritarian past, the scope of action for presidents and other chiefs of government must be institutionally restricted in order to stabilize democracy. The authors of the Federalis Papers caution that "power is of an encroaching nature and that it ought to be effectually restrained from passing the limits assigned to it" (Madison 1788*c*, p. 308). In this sense, horizontal accountability is a "necessity for democracy to protect itself from its own potential for self-destruction" (Schmitter 1999, p. 59).

Liberal democracy requires governments to not only be accountable to their citizens (and the local governments) but also subject to restraint and oversight by other public agencies. This refers to official state institutions such as the legislature or the supreme court. Horizontal accountability refers thus to the capacity of governmental institutions to check abuses by other public agencies and branches of government. In addition, other independent state agencies, which control and scrutinize government actions, are also often necessary to safeguard horizontal accountability. These institutions, which work as agencies of restraint, such as independent electoral commissions, auditing agencies, anti-corruption bodies, and ombudsmen also contribute to horizontal accountability.

Networks of relatively autonomous institutions of accountability are necessary to provide horizontal accountability. Consequently, horizontal accountability refers to actions "with the explicit purpose of preventing, cancelling, redressing and/or punishing actions (or eventually non-actions) by another state agency that are deemed unlawful, whether on grounds of encroachment or of corruption" (O'Donnell 2003, p. 35). In political practice, state agencies and individual political actors are in constant exchange with each other. During decision-making processes they *de facto* or *de jure* consider the decisions and actions of other institutions. This interaction can lead to relations of mutual control.

If one takes the two dimensions of accountability, answerability and enforceability seriously (Schedler 1999*a*, p. 14ff.), legislatures should have the right to require from the executive information about government actions without delay and also that they have the right to impose sanctions on unconstitutional behaviour. The effectiveness of horizontal accountability depends also ultimately on decisions by courts, especially in major cases. Thus effective horizontal accountability is dependent on the cooperations and coordinated efforts of various state agencies, particularly the legislature and the courts.

Actions of horizontal accountability are often very dramatic. If president and parliament are in a deep confrontation, the stability of the whole political system might suffer. Actions of accountability between the supreme state institutions may create highly visible and costly conflicts (O'Donnell 2003, p. 45) and thus damage the legitimacy of any democratic system. This holds particularly true if the actors in these conflicts are perceived by the general public as being motivated mainly by partisan reasons. Political competition is a necessary feature of democratic processes. However, if horizontal accountability is not about democratic principles but rather a power struggle among the political elite, the general public will perceive these actions quite negatively.

A dynamic equilibrium between major actors is important for horizontal accountability. If one actor can dominate the others, the democratic regime is in danger of becoming unconsolidated and prone to authoritarian rule. The "absence or weakness of institutional restraints on the state also greatly diminishes the quality of democracy" (Diamond, Plattner, and Schedler 1999, p. 2). Without effective institutions that can provide credible restraints, particularly on powerful executives, the quality of democracy tends to stagnate or regress.

If the duly authorized state agencies of oversight and investigation fail to discover responsibility for power abuse and cannot react with sanctions, the horizontal accountability of governments is put in danger. O'Donnell defined these state agencies as legally empowered and willing and able to take actions from routine oversight to criminal sanctions or impeachment in relation to possibly unlawful actions or omissions by other agents or agencies of the state (O'Donnell 1998, pp. 117, 119). In order to work effectively they must have sufficient autonomy in regard to the other state institutions they are intended to control. To guarantee the independence and autonomy of state institutions is not easy in practice, since all of them try to maximize their power. In other words, it is an extremely difficult task "to provide some practical security for each, against the invasion of the others" (Madison 1788c, p. 308).

According to American scholar Thomas Carothers (2002, pp. 10–14), problems of democratic consolidation in developing countries can be characterized in two ways. Either there is a so-called "feckless pluralism", where deficits in horizontal checks and balances result in stalemates where accountability is blurred, or in so-called "dominant-power politics", where the neo-authoritarian tendencies of the executive leadership is not effectively controlled by other state institutions. Both types of "defective democracies" (Merkel and Croissant 2003) are the product of deficiencies in the relationship between the executive and the legislative branches of government. Either the unchallenged dominance of the chief executive leads to a "delegative democracy", or the parliamentary preponderance results in gridlock situations and political stagnation. Presidential systems of government are particularly prone to such deficiencies since both the executive and the legislative branches are directly legitimated by elections and can both rightfully claim to represent the people.

Horizontal accountability is extremely weak or non-existent in what O'Donnell termed "delegative democracies" (O'Donnell 1994). This type of democracy has features that are in accordance with democratic principles, but is characterized by a strongly majoritarian bias. Referring to numerous examples of Latin American presidents, O'Donnell highlights the overstretching of powers by directly elected presidents. After election day, they often feel being entitled to govern as he or she deems fit. Such delegative presidents make continuous efforts to further weaken the development of institutions that limit the scope of his or her decision-making. In the eyes of rulers in delegative democracies, accountability to other institutions, particularly to those with no direct electoral legitimacy, "appears as a mere impediment to the full authority that the president has been delegated to exercise" (O'Donnell 1994, p. 60). Particularly in not yet old-established democracies, the executive is often very active in reducing or altogether eliminating all sorts of agencies of horizontal accountability. The elected government feels entitled to implement its policies and does not want to be restricted by other state agencies. This could mean, for instance, reducing the legislative function of legislatures by the extensive use of decrees instead of laws, or by trying to influence court decisions by exerting public or personal pressure on the judges.

Another frequent occasion for governments to reduce horizontal accountability is during a political and/or economic crisis. Here, governments often feel the need to show their will of survival and the ambition to regain force and authority. Thus, it will often take measures that broaden the powers of the executive government and reduce that of other government institutions. The reduction of horizontal accountability limits the quality of democracy. The government claims that these efforts are necessary in order to protect the democratic state in a temporary situation.

Other developing countries, which were more involved in internal struggles about the persistence of democracy, however, tend to use even more drastic measures. Typical solutions proposed in democracy-endangering circumstances are the strengthening of the powers of the executive by decrees or constitutional amendments, the granting of emergency powers to the head of government, the suspension of the legislature and the ignoring of supreme court decisions. If the political instability has separatistic causes, then it could interfere with regional or local governments by undermining their local autonomy. Another measure could be the engagement of the army, police, or other security forces to suppress opposition forces.

However, the impact of such steps, which are undertaken to save democracy, is ambiguous. To gain authority, the government uses measures which have rather authoritarian features. The quality of democracy is thus further deteriorated by the described measures of governments under pressure. Very often, a breakdown of democracy is not caused by the actions of militant anti-system opponents, but often by democratically elected rulers who do not keep to democratic and constitutional principles and instead exercise their power excessively. If the opposition is suppressed and not allowed to make use of the constitutional mechanisms for control of the government, the more the democracy moves to an authoritarian regime. By disesteeming essential democratic liberal freedoms, the continuity of democratic rule is at stake. The violation of constitutional norms, abuse of power, disregard of civil liberties, and excessive violence by democratic governments is one of the main causes for the breakdown of democracies (Linz 1978, p. 92). If the principle of horizontal accountability is also kept in crisis situations, this danger could be reduced.

Another feature of feeble horizontal accountability can occur if the control of government is not taking place in formalized institutional relationships within a system of checks and balances, but rather in informal power networks. In delegative democracies, the place of well-functioning institutions "is taken by other nonformalized but strongly operative practices – clientelism, patrimonialism, and corruption" (O'Donnell 1994, p. 59). If political decision-making does not take place in a constitutionally regulated way, but by backroom dealings, bribes and other forms of money politics, the dimension of horizontal accountability is severely damaged.

Executive-Legislative Relations

Legislatures are usually referred to as "the single most important check on executive power" (Fox 2007, p. 35). Therefore, their constitutional and legal competencies for the supervision of government are of utmost importance for the working of horizontal accountability. However, practice matters more than paragraphs. A legislature must therefore take its task to watch, control, and prevent power abuses of the executive, or more specifically the government seriously in their daily work. Elections and the resulting electoral accountability are the most important instrument to keep rulers answerable to citizens. In the long period between elections however, the people's representatives in the legislature have to ensure that the government acts in accordance with the preferences of the people. An inherent feature of legislative work is thus "to gain policy concessions by using their capacity to criticize, embarrass, delay, and obstruct the government" (Ziegenhain 2008, p. 40).

The interventions of legislators with government initiatives are compatible with democratic principle since the legislators are elected as representatives of the people. Since legislatures represent a more diverse institution than the executive, legislatures are often estimated as more responsive and permeable to civil society and organized citizens (Fox 2007, p. 36). The latter can turn towards the people's representatives with their grievances and demand intervention in cases of inadequate government decisions. Legislatures can thus work as a vehicle for public voice and a means through which citizens can request parliamentary sanctioning for inappropriate government actions (Stapenhurst and O'Brien 2008, p. 2). The main task of legislatures is therefore to safeguard the people's interests against irresponsible actions of government such as waste of public funds. In addition, they should expose corruption, power abuse and lack of efficiency among the national government (Mezey 1979, p. 16).

In order to fulfill the answerability dimension of accountability, the executive branch must be willing to supply accountability agencies, particularly the legislative with sufficient information and enough time to react. If a government obstructs the delivery of material or is responsible for delays, then the legislature cannot work effectively. However, every government, even in established democracies is interested in not being scrutinized too thoroughly. Therefore, the provision of information is often a tug-of-war between the executive and legislative branches.

Answerability also refers to the notion that legislatures should be arenas contributing to transparency in the political process. In public debates, which are reported in the media, the general public can witness which political questions are on the agenda of the political parties and the government. The different arguments on a certain policy issue gives the interested public an idea why this policy is intended and what are the possible advantages and disadvantages.

The other feature of accountability, the sanctioning mechanism, is exerted by legislatures in various ways. A group of legislators can address the members of the executive branch directly and initiate different processes to punish governmental misconduct. Typical instruments for legislatures are investigative committees and question periods, in which the plenum or specific committees call upon government officials to account for their actions and investigate certain questionable government policies. High public attention is ensured (and intended) when legislators summon high-ranking government officials or even the head of government members and "grill" them publicly. Here, the legislators want to focus public attention on the actions of the executive branch via media coverage. Legislative supervisory mechanisms such as interpellations, investigative committees and public hearings have the intention to clear up executive irregularities. However, in most cases the more or less hidden agenda of such actions is to arouse public interest in the alleged mismanagement or wrongdoings of the government (Ziegenhain 2008, p. 40).

One of the main accountability mechanisms is the legislative process. If the majority of a legislature does not agree with government initiatives, they will negotiate with government officials on the amendments of bills. If the legislature must be convinced in supporting the bill, the executive branch must give reasons and explanations for the new bill. Legislatures are therefore places for deliberative consultations, in which supporters of the prime minister/president and members of the opposition can exchange arguments. In most democracies, legislatures must agree to government bills before they can become effective. This results in veto possibilities for legislatures. Depending on individual constitutional provisions, there might also be mutual or suspensive veto rights of both the executive and legislative sides. Another traditional prerogative of legislative power is the control of the budget. Governments need the financial means in order to pursue their policies. The power of the purse gives the legislatures an important instrument to hold the government accountable and to limit executive scope of action. Many legislatures must also agree to personal appointments of important government officials. In this sense, they also can effectively exert control towards the executive branch.

Another possibility for legislatures to sanction executive offenses is to call the third state power, the supreme or constitutional court for action. Depending on the constitutional provisions, this step can be either very dramatic or daily business. In such cases, a group of legislators must provide sufficient evidence for governmental power abuses so that the court can initiate an investigation with a final judgement.

The sharpest "weapon" of legislatures is the removal of government. In parliamentary systems of government, a certain number of legislators can push for a vote of no confidence. In these systems, the reasons for such a move must not be of criminal nature. Political reasons, for instance the breakaway of a coalition party within the government coalition, or widespread dissatisfaction with government performance can lead to a vote of no confidence. If a majority of the legislature supports the motion, the prime minister has to resign and the government is overthrown.

In presidential systems of government, the removal of the president is more difficult. Here, the legislature can start an impeachment only for legal and not for political reasons. The president or other high-ranking government officials must have committed a serious crime in order to be removed from office. Usually, impeachment processes are rare and very dramatic in presidential systems of government.

In general, the functions of legislatures are dependent on the system of government under which they operate. In a parliamentary system, the tight control and supervision of government actions is usually undertaken by the opposition, which constitutes the parliamentary minority. The majority of the legislators supports the government and usually has no intention to question government actions. This so-called fusion of powers in parliamentary systems of government has several implications for executive-legislative relations. Generally, the possibilities for parliaments to control governmental actions are reduced in practice. The scrutinizing is undertaken by the opposition which is always the minority in the legislature. Decisions cannot be stopped by these minority parties, but often they have possibilities for delaying decision-making and also make government bills to the subject of a public debate. Adherence to the party line is very important for the government's party or the government's coalition in parliamentary systems. If there are too many dissenters, the survival of government is in serious danger giving the opposition the chance for a successful vote of no confidence.

In presidential systems of government, executive and legislative are elected separately resulting in a separation of powers. The essence of exchange is that the two branches are independent since they have separate bases of authority but they need to cooperate in order to fulfill their tasks. Therefore, their functions overlap (Moreno, Crisp, and Shugart 2003, p. 95). In other words, legislature and executive are separate institutions sharing powers. The legislature as a whole (and not only the minority of the legislature as in parliamentary systems of government) is tasked to control government actions. Due to the "proaccountability potential of the separation on powers" (Fox 2007, p. 35), legislatures are generally more important as an agency of horizontal accountability in presidential systems of government. The legislature can block legislation initiated by the president, whereas the president can veto legislation and has also some discretion over the enforcement. Thus, each of the two needs the support of the other branch.

Irrespective of the system of government, legislatures can only work effectively as agencies of horizontal accountability if the political system, in which they operate, offers them a high degree of participation in decision-making. According to Mezey and Olson (1991, p. 19), the following factors result in a high intensity of legislative involvement in political decision-making processes. Democratic and non-authoritarian government structures obviously support the relative strength of legislatures. Additionally, Mezey und Olson state that decentralized administrative structures (in contrast to centralist government) also favour a more powerful legislature. Additionally, a non-fragmented party system, which nevertheless consists of more than two parties is beneficial for effective legislatures. Under such conditions, a more efficient working structure than in two-party systems prevails. The intensity of participation of legislatures is also higher if political parties are less hierarchical structured and the parliamentary party discipline is not too high.

A more professionalized legislature, which is financially and in organizational matters independent, and is composed of politically experienced members has better chances to counterbalance governmental powers. Additionally, an institutionalized system of committees within the legislature with a parallel structure of the executive departments works more efficient and effective than a legislature with unstructured temporary committees.

Controlling by Jurisdiction: Constitutional and other High Courts

The judiciary is as a third state power also tasked to ensure horizontal accountability. Particularly its most important national institutions, be it a constitutional court or a supreme court, bear the responsibility of watchdogs concerning the actions of other state institutions. An independent judicial power should (together with the voter, parliament, and independent government organizations) check, prevent, and punish power abuses by those in power. These judicial institutions also "have been given the power to request that account be rendered over public expenditures, the exercise of coercive powers, and the fair and equal treatment of citizens" (Bovens 2010, p. 16).

The accentuated location of supreme and constitutional courts in the system of checks and balances often results in a high legitimacy among the general public so that other branches of government can be expected to respect and follow their decisions. The high respect that supreme and constitutional courts usually enjoy stems from their assumed independence and impartiality, which is in direct contrast to the group interest oriented positions and partiality of governments, politicians, and political parties. The judiciary should thus be independent and free from executive or legislative interference. This is also the logical consequence of the application of the principle of separation of powers. This principle in regard to the judiciary is also applied in parliamentary systems of government where a fusion of power between the executive and the legislative branches takes place. Here, as in presidential systems, constitutional courts serve as checks on the parliamentary majority (Moreno, Crisp, and Shugart 2003, p. 89).

In order to work effectively in a system of checks and balances, the most important national judicial institutions should be free from pressure by the government. Additionally, the judges should not fear the possibility of being replaced after critical decisions. To diminish the chances of bribery, judges should receive attractive salaries, which cannot be reduced after critical decisions. The problem of judicial independence is in practice in most democracies that the nomination and/or appointment of supreme court judges takes place either by the president, the parliament, or by a mixed commission of both institutions. Thereby, the legislators and the government can influence the promotion of judges which they deem suitable. If a president, for example, appoints an ordinary judge to a much better paid and respected supreme court position, he or she often expects that the chosen candidate later express his gratitude by deciding in his or her favour, or in a similar political direction. However, in order to be independent, judges should not be politically accountable to anybody. If their judgements are under constant pressure of political actors, their impartiality and objectivity "becomes questionable, and where that happens the constitutionality and consolidation of the system is threatened" (Philp 2009, p. 39). In order to avoid such negative development, Dodson and Jackson propose the following five measures to guarantee judicial independence:

- Merit selection on non-partisan assessment of objective qualifications
- Relatively long or lifetime terms of office/No possibilities for removal for unpopular decisions
- Removal for official misconduct (corruption, incompetence, etc.) should be grounded in clearly articulated standards
- Adequate resources in terms of staff and finances
- Legal and political culture that accepts the supremacy of the law (Dodson and Jackson 2003, p. 232)

Judicial independence, however, can be ambiguous, since "most judicial accountability mechanisms depend primarily on self-monitoring and regulation, rather than on external oversight" (Fox 2007, p. 37). If effective control mechanisms *vis-à-vis* the judiciary are limited in order to save its independence, the power of the judiciary can become very extensive. In severe cases, an unpopularly elected institution can dominate the people's representation and the elected government.

The competencies of supreme and constitutional courts vary from country to country. Particularly supreme courts are the highest court of appeal after lower judicial entities. Consequently, the main task of supreme courts is the supervision of decision from lower courts. The most important task in terms of accountability, however, is the right of judicial review and the right to decide if laws are in accordance with the constitution. Supreme and constitutional courts may even overturn laws passed by the legislature on constitutional grounds and that their decisions are final and binding. Since laws are political constructs, they may reflect the interests of political forces, which may not necessarily be in accordance with the constitution. Thus, it is necessary that supreme and constitutional courts are empowered to anticipate or overcome such constitutional violations of the executive branch through judicial review (Mahfud 2009, p. 2).

Critics argue that this judicial activism turns supreme courts into a sort of supreme law-making body that lacks electoral accountability and is not democratically elected. Yet, courts can prevent power abuse of ambitious governments by declaring their legal actions null and void. In terms of horizontal accountability, the supreme or constitutional court thus presents an important veto player (Tsebelis 1995) and constitutional check for power-hungry governments.

Another main task of supreme and constitutional courts is the mediation between state institutions over competences and procedures. If there is a conflict between the executive and the legislative branch, the judiciary might decide who correctly interpreted the constitution and who did not. Critics say that this results in a judicial interference in political disputes. Often, court decisions have been criticized for injecting the court into the political arena.

Additionally, in presidential systems, involvement in impeachment procedures against high-ranking government officials, most importantly the elected president, also belong to the typical tasks of supreme and constitutional courts. In general, the legislative (as a popularly elected entity) determines whether a case against an executive official is initiated and decides whether the process is moving forward. However, the supreme court (as an unpopularly elected entity) must often give assent or finally decision.

The prohibition of political parties represented in executive or legislative can also be a constitutional right of supreme and constitutional courts in terms of horizontal accountability. However, this instrument is not often used in democracies and if applied, then only as a highly controversial measure of last resort. In some countries (such as Germany) parties can be dissolved forcefully if their platform and actions proved to be unconstitutional. In other countries, criminal actions such as money politics and vote-buying are also sufficient reasons for party prohibition.

Independent State Agencies

Traditionally, horizontal accountability is exercised by the three state powers (executive, legislative, and judiciary). In recent years, however, independent accountability agencies have been created throughout the world to improve systems of checks and balances. The creation of these agencies particularly took place in the fragile democracies of developing countries in the Southern hemisphere. This process has occurred "with particular strength in new democracies under pressure from civil society and international actors to find innovative ways to bring accountability beyond electoral politics" (Ackerman 2010, p. 266).

This led to a growing phenomenon of reassignment of political power from democratic institutions (particularly parliaments and governments) to various non-elected bodies (Maggetti 2010, p. 1), which are responsible for various monitoring tasks. If they perform effectively and without external pressure, they can serve as a positive force for accountable governance. The specific value of independent agencies is that they can offer "a fresh perspective on governance and ... [have] the potential to be brave enough to take on central issues that have been swept under the rug for years" (Ackerman 2010, p. 271).

There is a huge variety of independent accountability organizations who deal with specific aspects of checking executive actions. Independent audit institutions have the function to hold the executive accountable when using public funds and resources, whereas an ombudsman is usually tasked with answering to and caring for the concerns of average citizens, an electoral commission may organize and check electoral procedures.

The powers and independence of these agencies varies to a great extent. Generally they are legally assigned to oversee, prevent, and discourage unlawful actions or omissions of other state agencies, on the national as well as the subnational levels. Some of them are tasked with sanctioning or promoting the sanctioning of other state institutions (O'Donnell 2003, p. 45).

The power of independent organizations depends not only on their ability to sanction directly. Some provide accountability rather in the sense of answerability. For example, an audit commission checks the financial expenditures of the government and then demands explanation for discovered irregularities. Usually, such audit commissions have no instruments to ensure that their decisions and resolutions are fulfilled. Since they do not possess a direct punitive function, they still have the opportunity to forward their findings to the parliament or supreme court, who might have sanctioning powers. In this case, the audit commission promotes the sanctioning, but does not itself sanction directly. Another means for exercising accountability might be to inform the general public via the media and thereby create public awareness for executive misconduct. In this sense, independent state agencies act more like pressure groups than as state institutions. With broad popular support and sufficient media coverage, they can nevertheless gain substantial influence. Without these two factors, the power of many independent state agencies might be quite limited in practice.

In the face of the three powerful branches of government, independent agencies operate with some disadvantages. In some cases, they are marginalized or ignored altogether. This is often the case "since the work of accountability agencies is by nature 'uncomfortable' for other areas of government" (Ackerman 2010, p. 269).

Autonomous institutions of accountability are usually kept apart from government officials and from the people. Separation from government officials is logical as the independent institutions are tasked to monitor and eventually sanction government wrongdoings. Members of independent institutions of accountability should be free from government interference and the fear of being replaced, not re-elected, or punished, in order to function effectively. Their actions should generally be in accordance with criteria "that are professional rather than partisan or 'political'" (O'Donnell 2003, p. 45). But even when they are highly professionalize, endowed with sufficient resources, independent of the whim of the executive, and insulated as much as possible from the latter, they still can be vulnerable to corruption or government co-optation (O'Donnell 1999, p. 44).

Furthermore, as in the above mentioned case of the supreme and constitutional court judges, the autonomy and independence of these agencies "puts them in a delicate situation since it is not always clear to whom they themselves are accountable. This is the classic problem of second-order accountability" (Ackerman 2010, p. 270), or of "*Quid custodiet ipsos custodes*" (who guards the guardians)? The generally low legitimacy of independent agencies of accountability is therefore problematical because "considerable public authority is delegated to these unelected non-majoritarian bodies, producing a 'net loss' of legitimacy for political institutions" (Maggetti 2010, p. 5). The autonomy of independent state agencies therefore clashes with the principles of electoral accountability (Diamond, Plattner, and Schedler 1999, p. 3). Since members of independent accountability organizations are themselves unaccountable, they are exposed to charges of being undemocratic and partial.

If the independence of the agencies is not guaranteed they can end as an authoritarian cover-up. They can also be accused of acting against the will of the majority, or of overstepping their legal and constitutional boundaries. For these reasons, independent accountability agencies are perceived ambiguously by the public. From one perspective, they are seen as having the potential to improve the quality of democracy and creating public legitimacy for government's action. They can be regarded as a pioneer of state reform. From the other perspective, since they are appointed by those in power, they are seen as a continuation of the corrupt practices of the previous regime. Under such conditions, faith is low that the newly created accountability agency will be an authentic break with the undemocratic past (Ackerman 2010, p. 267). Even worse, some authors claim that, particularly in Latin America, such agencies are created by less democratic government in order to boost their legitimacy and apparent accountability without actually changing their undemocratic and corrupt behaviour. The "proliferation of entities of superintendence in Latin America, then, must be seen as largely a product of discontent with the functioning of accountability and it represents an effort to find a way around the problem without tackling the roots of the accountability deficit" (Moreno, Crisp, and Shugart 2003, p. 82). In such situations, they are accountability agencies only in name.

In chapter 5, I will analyse what kind of institutional reforms concerning horizontal democracy were undertaken in the three countries under research. I will first focus on executive-legislative relations, then on executive-judiciary relations. Finally, I will examine independent watchdog organizations, such as counter-corruption commissions, audit agencies, and election commissions.

Notes

[1] I would like to particularly thank Siegfried Herzog and Rainer Adam from Friedrich Naumann Foundation and Mirko Herberg, Vesna Rodic, and Marc Saxer from Friedrich Ebert Foundation.

[2] Recent democratization efforts in the Republic of the Union of Myanmar, the Democratic Republic of Timor-Leste, Malaysia, and other Southeast Asian countries could not be included in this comparative study.

[3] The Freedom House Index is an annual assessment of the perceived degree of democratic freedoms worldwide. It rates these two freedoms on a scale from 1 (most free) to 7 (least free). If a country receives a value between 1.0 and 2.5 is regarded as "free", whereas a value between 3.0 and 5.0 means "partly free" and a value between 5.5 and 7.0 results in a rating as "not free". More information on the methodology can be found at <http://www.freedomhouse.org>. The Freedom House Index rates the developments of the previous year. For example, the assessments from 2008 are presented in the Freedom House Index of 2009. In the tables of this chapter, I refer to the years under assessment and not to the year of publication.

[4] The ten criteria from Robert Dahl are freedom to form and join organizations, freedom of expression, right to vote, eligibility for public office, right of political leaders to compete for support/votes, alternative sources of information, free and fair elections, and institutions for making government policies depend on votes and other expressions of preference.

[5] In pacted transitions, moderate authoritarian regime elites and the opposition jointly negotiate a transition to democracy (O'Donnell and Schmitter 1986).

6   The word "feudal" refers to the dominant social system in medieval Europe, in which the nobility held lands and the large majority of the ordinary people were subjects working as peasants for the land owners with little rights and limited freedom.

7   In 2012, Russia returned to the direct elections of governors, in fact decentralizing presidential powers in the wake of nationwide protests following the parliamentary elections in December 2011.

3

THE ELECTORAL
ACCOUNTABILITY DIMENSION

As has been described in chapter 2.4 institutional reforms concerning electoral accountability are very important in order to analyse the progress of democratic deepening in a political system. In the following, I will apply the criteria from chapter 2.4 to draw conclusions on the democratization processes in Thailand, Indonesia, and the Philippines and will proceed in this order. Starting with Thailand, I will illustrate and analyse major features of the post-founding elections. In a next step, I will then take a closer look at processes of institutional engineering and assess institutional changes concerning the electoral accountability of the national parliament and the second chamber. Finally, I will present and discuss reforms concerning political parties and their contribution to electoral accountability. The same structure and proceeding will be applied in chapters 3.2 to Indonesia and 3.3 to the Philippines.

3.1 THAILAND

The 1997 Constitution

Thai electoral regulations are usually very closely defined in their respective constitutions. Since the transition from an absolute monarchy to a constitutional one in 1932, Thailand has been able to maintain a constitution for more than ten years only between 1932 and 1946. Frequent changes were made due to the numerous coups the country witnessed. As every new regime wanted to create a system of government that suited its own vision, a plethora of constitutions was decided upon. The constitution became a tool of those in power only to be replaced when power switched hands. In other words, Thai constitutions "have functioned as mere political documents serving the interests of the executive branch" (Klein 1998, p. 17), or rather that of the coup plotters.

Some constitutional principles remained untouched, however. The King's role as head of state in the constitutional monarchy was never questioned, as well as the corresponding parliamentary system with a prime minister as head of government. The 1997 Constitution differed from the previous fifteen in that it was drafted as a part of the democratization process by a representatively composed Constitutional Drafting Assembly[1] instead of being drafted by the ruling powers. Hence, it was commonly called the "People's Constitution" and generally regarded as the most democratic constitution Thailand had ever seen. Some Western observers were even convinced that "the 1997 Constitution represents a revolution in Thai politics. It was a bold attempt at conferring greater power to the Thai people than had ever been granted before. It was a demonstration of the political capital possessed by the progressive forces of pluralism since they succeeded in getting the document passed" (Chambers 2002, p. 20). The newly established democracy seemed to have a very solid foundation by virtue of the constitution, which was understood to be "unlike all previous Thai constitutions … fail-safe, foolproof, cast-iron, lasting and eternal" (McCargo 1998, p. 7). The 1997 Constitution was meant to transform the undemocratic past and facilitate democratic consolidation.

The major political actors themselves had only indirect influence on the 1997 reforms concerning the electoral system. Since the 1997 Constitution was mostly drafted by academics and other expert groups, the influence of these partisan politicians was limited so that the constitutional changes can be seen as rather exogenous (Hicken 2009, p. 127f.).

Thus, the drafting of the constitution threatened some of their vested interests. However, the political momentum to let the constitution pass was strong. The Asian Economic Crisis of 1997/98 revealed serious mistakes within the political and economic sphere. The new constitution was regarded as a suitable tool to effectively combat the consequences of the crisis. Additionally, the legislators who had the final say on the constitution were not allowed to modify the draft document. Although there was some initial resistance, the members of the National Assembly eventually passed the Constitution almost unanimously. Thus, the "constitutional draft became a symbol of the government's commitment to difficult but needed political and economic reforms" (Hicken 2009, p. 129). It was also a signal to both traditional elite and military elements that political times might have changed and power might have to be pursued differently. Finally, as the constitution took effect amidst Thailand's economic fragility, it was a clear message to the business and political elite that transparency, good governance, accountability, and political stability were matters which must be immediately and adequately addressed (Chambers 2002, p. 20).

In this sense the 1997 Constitution "was drafted to prevent further coups".[2] The economic crisis of 1997/98 and the new constitution paved the way for the rise of Thaksin Shinawatra (McCargo 2005, p. 512).

Electoral System of the 2001 Elections

As mentioned above, Thailand has always had a parliamentary system of government in times of democracy after 1932. Thai voters elect the government by voting individuals and parties into the national parliament. These elected representatives then go on to elect the prime minister as head of government. In contrast to the presidential systems of the Philippines and Indonesia, the resulting elections in the House of Representatives are always decisive for the election of the prime minister. Since the House majority elects and supports the prime minister, the people can only vote indirectly for the head of government.

The electoral rules of the 2001 elections, which took place on 6 January, were in accordance with Sections 98–100 of the 1997 Constitution. Of the total 500 seats, 400 were elected with a first past-the-post election system in single member districts. The remaining 100 were distributed among political parties through a proportional election system in a single nationwide constituency. Voters had two ballots papers, in each of which they had to tick one box, one for a preferred constituency candidate and one for a preferred party on the national level. Since the two parts of the election system are functionally separated and operate under different electoral formulae, the Thai election system can be described as a segmented or parallel system, similar to those in Japan, South Korea and Taiwan (Nelson 2007, p. 2).

The election system of the 1997 Constitution brought various institutional reforms concerning electoral accountability that contrast with previous election systems. The former plurality election system that consisted of various multi-seat districts was replaced by a strict majority system of 400 single-seat districts, giving the electoral system a more majoritarian tendency. The newly introduced proportional elements did not counterbalance this trend since they made up only one fifth of the seats. Additionally, smaller parties were further disadvantaged by the 5 per cent threshold for the party-list seats.

The 2001 election brought a clear electoral victory for the Thai Rak Thai (TRT) party led by Thaksin Shinawatra, which was short of an absolute majority by only two seats. Table 3.1 depicts the exact election results:

Table 3.1
Result of the 2001 Elections in Thailand

	Constituency Mandates	Party-List Mandates	Total Number of Mandates
Thais love Thais Party/			
Thai Rak Thai	200	48	248
Democrat Party/Prachathipat	97	31	128
Thai Nation Party/			
Chart Thai	35	6	41
New Aspiration	28	8	36
Chat Phattana	22	7	29
Seridham	14	0	14
Ratsadon	2	0	2
Social Action	1	0	1
Thin Thai	1	0	1
Total Number	**400**	**100**	**500**

Source: Election Commission of Thailand, quoted in Phongpaichit and Baker (2009, p. 89).

The reforms of the 1997 Constitution "drastically revamped Thailand's electoral and political landscape" (Hicken 2009, p. 130). TRT's landslide victory in 2001 was the first time in Thai history that one party won nearly half of parliament's seats. As can be seen in Table 3.1, TRT candidates won 200 of the 400 constituencies with a relative majority.

Thai political scientist Siripan Nogsuan argued that the majoritarian electoral system in the 1997 Constitution was intended to "encourage the emergence of a strong one-party government" (Nogsuan 2005, p. 51). The first-past-the-post system in single-member districts resulted in higher electoral competition and better electoral accountability since only the winner gets a seat. People thus had a better opportunity to punish candidates who perform poorly by voting for others. In the previous multi-member-districts, punishment was much more difficult since a second or third place would also result in a seat. The single districts (instead of multi-member districts) obviously favoured the candidates of the bigger parties, whereas the previous multi-member districts favoured those of the small parties since they could also win seats without having a majority in the constituency.

The elections system of the 1997 Constitution was an advantage for the two big parties (TRT and Democrat Party). Only the winners within a district garnered parliamentary mandates. The introduction of proportional elements further strengthened these parties because, due to their financial resources, only major parties have a chance to win proportional votes from the national level elections. The 5 per cent threshold for party-list elections also disadvantaged smaller parties. However, the introduction of national party lists strengthened political parties in general, as people were allowed for the first time in Thai history to vote directly for parties. The influence of local elites on voting behaviour declined to some degree and party affiliation became more important than in previous elections. Those candidates who entered either the Democrat or the TRT party had significantly better chances to get a parliamentary seat, since these two parties received more than two-thirds of the votes (Phongpaichit and Baker 2009, p. 88).

The proportional elements of the electoral system also gave party leaders more control over the candidate selection process. Prior to the introduction of party-list votes, the chances of gaining parliamentary seats in multi-member districts depended on the social status and influence of individual candidates among their constituencies, over which party leaders had little control. Instead, in the run-up to the 2005 elections candidates were more often picked by their party leadership. Consequently, opportunities for candidates depended more on their relationships with party leaders than their responsibilities of addressing the needs of specific localities (Nogsuan 2005, p. 62).

Electoral reform, including the proportional elements, also meant that the election campaigns and the party's platforms had to be nationalized. Increasingly, prominent party figures toured around the entire country while mass media conveyed the parties' national slogans. Electoral accountability thus shifted by some degree from voters of an individual electoral district to the national level. Previously, ordinary Thai voters were relatively uninterested in – and ignorant of – national politics. With the possibility of voting for national parties, an enormous wave of politicization reached even small villages (Nelson 2011, p. 62).

In the four years following 2001, the power of Prime Minister Thaksin grew enormously since his party, Thai Rak Thai (TRT), was able to convince smaller parties to join it: these were Seridham (Liberal Democratic) with 14 MPs, Tin Thai (Thai Motherland) with 1 MP, Kwam Wang Mai (New Aspiration Party, NAP) with 36 MPs, and Chart Pattana (National Development) with 29 MPs. Altogether the majority from TRT totalled 328 out of 500. Additionally, several members of the Chart Thai defected to TRT in the 2005 elections, leaving the Democratic Party as the only serious contender of TRT.

The elections in 2005 resulted in a landslide victory by TRT, which won 377 out of 500 seats (75.4 per cent). Table 3.2 depicts the election results:

Table 3.2
Result of the 2005 Elections in Thailand

	Constituency Mandates	Party-List Mandates	Total Number of Mandates
Thais love Thais Party/ Thai Rak Thai	310	67	377
Democrat Party/Prachathipat	70	26	96
Thai Nation Party/ Chart Thai	18	7	25
Mahachon	2	0	2
Total Number	**400**	**100**	**500**

Source: Election Commission of Thailand, quoted in Nogsuan (2005), p. 55.

It was for the first time in Thai history that a prime minister was re-elected for a second term. The 2005 elections also marked the first time a single party could form a government without needing coalition partners. The majoritarian bias of the electoral system proved successful. Indeed, little more than 60 per cent of the people voted for the Thai Rak Thai Party, but due to the first-past-the-post system they won 310 direct mandates and altogether 77.5 per cent of the mandates.

The election result came as a shock for the political establishment of Thailand, which prefers a greater dispersion of power, so that the elites can interfere in the process of political decision-making.[3] Fears over a parliamentary dictatorship were voiced. Yet, the result of the 2005 elections was exactly what a majoritarian election system aims at achieving, namely the creation of clearly responsible governments in which a single-party majority has a chance to implement its policies effectively. In the case of Thailand, the Thai Rak Thai Party certainly benefited from the electoral system, but the voters' decisions were clear. Furthermore, the election system gave stability to the political system because for the first time in Thai history a government stayed in power for a four-year term without the dissolution of the House of Representatives.

However, resistance against Thaksin was mounting. His opponents feared that his election victories were dangerous for Thai democracy, arguing that the prime minister was becoming too powerful. Charan Phakdithanakun, who later became a constitutional judge, said that "the party list element of Thailand's election system had been turned into a quasi-direct election of the prime minister, so that it now resembled a presidential system. This 'severely contradicts the parliamentary democratic regime of government that has the king as head of state'" (Nelson 2011, p. 64). Ong-art Klampaiboon, Spokesman of the Democrat Party, argued in similar terms that "the proportional election system with the 5 percent threshold in the 1997 Constitution produced too strong a government."[4]

Military Coup

By the end of 2005, massive street protests opposing Prime Minister Thaksin Shinawatra began in Bangkok accusing him of corruption and monopolizing power. Thaksin reacted by calling a snap-election for April 2006. However, the opposition boycotted the elections and the Constitutional Court annulled them for technical reasons, and since about 38 per cent of the voters made use of the "abstain" option on their ballot papers to reject TRT candidates. A high-ranking member of the opposition, Democrat Party (DP), later explained that "the DP boycotted the elections since Prime Minister Thaksin planned to use the elections only as a tool to demonstrate his power."[5]

The Thai government announced new elections scheduled for October 2006, but on 19 September the military initiated a successful *coup d'état* against the elected government and toppled Prime Minister Thaksin Shinawatra. The military takeover went relatively peacefully, since "many members of the Bangkok elite and middle class did not condemn this military coup as a destruction of democracy. Rather, they saw it as a defense of democracy and good governance against the provincial-based members of parliament, who had brought Thaksin to power" (Nelson 2011, p. 56). Veteran Asian expert Michael Vatikiotis interpreted the *coup d'état* as a "temporary pit stop for repairs. ... The democratic framework will be overhauled and hopefully streamlined, not abolished" (Vatikiotis 2006). This statement is definitively too euphemistic for the consequences of the military coup, it does show the main intention of the coup makers, namely to re-configure the political and electoral systems.

Electoral Rules in the 2007 Constitution

Soon after the bloodless coup, the military junta appointed a committee of loyal scholars to draft a new constitution. In December 2006, a 2,000-member strong National Assembly, which was appointed by the coup makers, elected 200 of its members as candidates for a Constitution Drafting Assembly (CDA) designed to create a new and permanent constitution. The members were handpicked by the military junta and, unlike drafting process prior to the 1997 Constitution, did not include individuals from different sectors of society. It remained doubtful if the candidates for the CDA were representative of the population. Prinya Thaewanarumitkul from Thammasat University commented: "We had already 18 constitutions since 1932 and they are getting more voluminous every time. This is a wrong development. A lot of people, including me, refused to work on a new constitution because of the coup, so only the 2nd row of experts were included."[6] The chairman of the then-ruling Council of National Security (CNS), General Sonthi Boonyakalin, said that the CNS selected able people who know how to draft the new constitution and is quoted to have stated that the CNS "can't force them to do things but responsible people will know what the constitution should look like" (The Nation Online 2006).

To give the new constitution at least some legitimacy, the military junta decided to organize a referendum. However, this target was reached only to some extent. On 19 August 2007, a referendum was held in which 57.8 per cent of the voters voted in favour of the new constitution. This result is rather low, considering that opponents of the new constitution were not allowed to voice their disapproval, and that the military government intensively campaigned for several weeks in all forms of national media. The military-supported new charter could be seen "as antithetical to its bottom-up, reform-driven 1997 predecessor" (Pongsudhirak 2008, p. 2). The constitutional drafters tried to find an antidote to Thaksin's massive electoral support. Thaksin's popularity and his unchallenged political power, which derived from his overwhelming electoral victories and "ultimately threatened the authority of the traditional centers of power in Thailand"

(Hicken 2008, p. 220). Hence, the 2007 Constitution was written "with the single-minded aim to prevent the return of Thaksin and the social forces he has come to represent" (Phongpaichit 2006, p. 4). The supporters of the coup feared that Thaksin could limit their powers and influence and transformed the new democratic rules in order to make the access to power more difficult for Thaksin and his party.

The military-led CNS tried to return to democracy by holding elections one year and 3 months after the *coup d'état*. In the meantime, it changed several provisions concerning the electoral system. The number of members of the House of Representatives was reduced from 500 to 480. Still, 400 were elected directly, but this time in 157 electoral multi-member districts, a smaller number than before. The number of legislative seats from party lists was reduced from 100 to 80. Additionally, the single national constituency as basis for the proportional distribution of seats was scrapped and replaced by eight electoral areas. The electoral rules prohibited candidates from running for election in a district and being on the national party list at the same time.

As in the 1997 Constitution, voting was compulsory in order to ensure a high turnout and make vote-buying so expensive as to be unfeasible (Punyaratabandhu 1998, p. 165). Chapter 4, Section 72 of the Constitution of 2007 states that every person "shall have the duty to exercise his or her right to vote at an election. The person who ... fails to attend an election for voting without notifying a reasonable cause of such failure shall ... lose such rights as provided by law" (Constitution of the Kingdom of Thailand 2007).

The new electoral rules, particularly the multi-seat constituencies and the lifting of the 5 per cent requirement of total votes for a party to be eligible to have MPs from the party list, favoured smaller parties to the detriment of the bigger ones (Sinpeng 2011). However, the Democrat Party prevented a higher number of seats distributed by proportional election mode and stuck to the 400 district seats, since they thought they would win the elections with this system.[7]

The Secretary General of the Election Commission of Thailand (ECT) Suthipon Thaveechaiyagarn commented on the drafting process of the electoral regulations in the 2007 Constitution:

> Some members of the election commission (ECT) were involved in drafting the election law, but politicians finally decided. The problem was that after the coup we were in a hurry to produce a new election law.

It was a very fast process. We drew on many things from the 1997 Constitution. Now we need to socialize the election law. Many people are still suspicious because the law was the result of the coup. It has legitimacy problems.[8]

Before the elections could take place, the military government installed an interim Constitutional Tribunal composed of nine handpicked judges (Nardi 2010) that dissolved the Thai Rak Thai Party (together with two other small parties) and banned 111 TRT executives, among them Thaksin Shinawatra, from contesting in elections for five years. However, those TRT members who had not been banned from politics soon regrouped in the People's Power Party (PPP), which was led by veteran politician Samak Sundaravej. Table 3.3 shows the election result of the elections, which took place on 23 December 2007.

Table 3.3
Result of the 2007 Elections in Thailand

	Constituency Mandates*	Party-List Mandates	Total Number of Mandates
People's Power Party/ Phak Palang Prachachon	199	34	233
Democrat Party/Prachathipat	131	33	164
Thai Nation Party/ Thai Chart	30	4	34
For the Motherland Party/ Puea Pandin Party	17	7	24
Neutral Democratic Party/ Matchimathipataya	11	0	11
Thai's United National Development Party/ Ruam Jai Thai Chart Pattana	8	1	9
Royalist People's Party/ Pracharaj	4	1	5
Total Number	**400**	**80**	**480**

Note: * Some candidates were disqualified by the Election Commission of Thailand and re-polls took place in these constituencies. Table 3.3 shows the final election result after these re-polls.
Source: Election Commission of Thailand, quoted in Phongpaichit and Baker (2010, p. 26).

The reincarnation party of the banned TRT, the People's Power Party, was the clear winner of the 2007 elections. In January 2008, it was able to form a government coalition with five small parties leaving the Democrat Party again the sole opposition party. Consequently, Samak Sundaravej (PPP) became prime minister.

Massive public protests led by the PAD (People's Alliance for Democracy) and other yellow-shirt organizations started soon after. For months, key public roads were blocked, major airports and the parliament occupied and the Government House compound seized. Political observer Michael H. Nelson commented: "Few governments in western democracies that had a similar degree of electoral legitimacy as the one led by Samak Sundaravej would have tolerated that a right-wing protest group prevented them from working in their respective seats of government by storming and occupying their premises" (Nelson 2011, p. 71f).

In September 2008, Prime Minister Samak Sundaravej had to resign from the premiership after the Constitutional Court disqualified him for receiving illegal remuneration for his appearance in TV cooking shows. Thaksin's brother-in-law, Somchai Wongsawat, was elected as new prime minister, only to resign a few weeks later as the Constitutional Court dissolved the ruling PPP for electoral fraud and banned its leading politicians for five years from politics, among them Somchai. These controversial decisions will be discussed in more detail in chapter 5.1 on horizontal accountability in Thailand. The Democrat Party finally took power when in December 2008 dozens of PPP members defected and joined the oppositional camp. Together with all of the small parties in the House of Representatives, which also changed sides, the Democrat party was able to form a new parliamentary majority, and Abhisit Vejjajiva (Democrat Party) was elected as the new prime minister.

Chaturon Chaisang, minister in the Thaksin governments, bitterly commented:

> The Constitution of 2007 built up a system in which the power no longer belongs to the people. Elections no longer have any meaning since those who have the power overturned the people's decision. Two prime ministers were disqualified for no good reason. The 2007 election result was not what they have expected. But those in power made some people switch sides.[9]

The legitimacy of the Abhisit government was strongly challenged by many parts of Thai society. The red-shirt movement and the National United Front of Democracy Against Dictatorship (UDD) staged countrywide protests, rallies and demonstrations. The situation escalated when in April/

May 2010, protesters occupied central intersections and erected barricades in downtown Bangkok, particularly in the Ratchaprasong area. Military units violently cracked down on the protesters, leaving around 100 people dead.

Those members of the PPP not banned from participating in elections regrouped in the Pheu Thai Party, which chose the sister of Thaksin, Yingluck Shinawatra, as their leading candidate for the 2011 elections which took place on 3 July. In the end, Pheu Thai clearly beat Prime Minister Abhisit's Democrat Party and Yingluck Shinawatra became the new prime minister in August 2011.

Table 3.4 depicts the election results:

Table 3.4
Result of the 2011 Elections in Thailand

	Constituency Mandates	Party-List Mandates	Total Number of Mandates
For Thais Party/Pheu Thai	204	61	265
Democrat Party/Prachathipat	115	44	159
Thai Pride Party/Bhumjaithai	29	5	34
Thai Nation Development Party/ Chart Thai Pattana	15	5	20
Power of the People Party/ Phalang Chon	6	1	7
Love Thailand Party/ Rak Thailand	0	4	4
Motherland Party/Matabhum	1	1	2
Others	0	3	3
Total Number	**375**	**125**	**500**

Source: Election Commission of Thailand (2011).

Compared to the 2007 elections, the number of constituency seats was reduced from 400 to 375, whereas the number of party-list seats was increased from 80 to 125. This considerable increase in the number of party-list seats is set to benefit large, well-established parties, which in the case of the 2011 elections were the Democrat Party and Pheu Thai Party. Smaller parties that rely largely on their leaders' personal networks or reputations in a given region do not profit from the seats distributed in the national party-list elections (Sinpeng 2011). In 2011, 105 out of 125 seats (84 per cent) went either to the Democrat Party or to the Pheu Thai Party.

Accordingly, the Democrat Party proposed a change in the number of party-list seats prior to the 2011 elections. Nataphol Teepsuwan, Director General of Democrat Party stated that "there were some discussions in the Democrat Party about changing the electoral laws in order to have more mandates from the party lists and fewer district mandates. Our district members of parliament, however, are very upset about this plan."[10] Additionally, all of the coalition partners opposed the change, but agreed to the compromise that the number of party-list seats be increased significantly.

A questionable component of the 1997 electoral law was that a university bachelor's degree be required to run as a parliamentary candidate. This condition was introduced in order to "encourage better-known and more respectable personalities to enter politics" (Chantornvong 2002, p. 203). This goes hand in hand with the view that many educated people hold: that Thaksin was only elected by villagers who have no understanding of politics and whose votes can be easily bought. In this view, the uneducated masses are prone to fall for populist policies and election gifts.[11] A law professor, for instance, argued that "most Thais don't understand intellectually what proportional election system means."[12] Even if this might be true in reality, this educational bias runs against the basic democratic principle of equality. If the large majority of the Thai population is excluded from the eligibility for office, active politics remain a business of the intelligentsia and a select elite while the lower social strata are unable to participate in democratic procedures in any meaningful way (Nogsuan 2005, p. 69). However, the bachelor clause was introduced by public demand and illustrates how democracy is seen by many Thais (Harding and Leyland 2011, p. 45f).

The question as to what constitutes a good and capable MP can be seen from two perspectives. On the one hand, the Bangkok-based establishment

> attaches great importance to formal education degrees, and expects the representatives to spend their time in Bangkok reading and debating draft legislation. The voters, on the other hand, want representatives who represent them, care for them, bring money to their constituency, and help them in a variety of everyday issues (Nelson 2007, p. 11).

The typical member of the House of Representatives in rural Thailand is very often the offspring of a political family which has occupied official positions for generations. He or she is wealthy, pragmatic, sometimes a *chao pho* (godfather), and surely knows what needs to be done to win the elections. He or she possesses a large network of vote canvassers (*hua khanaen*) in sub-districts and villages and has many business and private connections with smaller local elites. Since most Thai voters expect direct and personal help in the form of clientelistic transactions, being a successful patron is the best opportunity to become a successful politician (Bjarnegård 2013, p. 145). For this reason,

> there is basically no chance for any new and unknown – but supposedly good and capable – candidate to pop up a few months before an election and win a seat. Much long-term patronage work and network-building – both of which are quite expensive – are necessary for any candidate to construct his or her personal voter base and thereby be a serious contender in a national election (Nelson 2007, p. 13).

However, some changes occurred in recent years that move away from person-centred electoral strategies to party-centred strategies. The Thai Rak Thai Party and its successors tried to establish nationwide election campaigns. Their voters opted for the local candidate not because of his or her personality but rather due to his or her party affiliation.

Despite all institutional engineering, efforts to reduce vote-buying has continued to be a feature of Thai politics (Nogsuan 2005, p. 67f., Harding and Leyland 2011, p. 67). A member of the Democrat Party reported that "vote buying is still happening on a grand scale. Vote-buying is a well-organized system, which is based on a patron-client basis. The Thaksin party has computerized data bases for all villages which they use for vote-buying. It works like a well-oiled machine, which is hard to beat."[13] This statement, however, should not be seen as an neutral and adequate description but rather as a political argument of a member of the Democrat Party. Very often, this party misleadingly reduces the electoral wins of the other camp to vote-buying and money politics.

The 1997 Constitution introduced so-called "yellow" and "red cards" for cheating candidates issued by the national election commission (more in chapter 5.1). Those who receive red cards are directly disqualified and – in contrast to yellow cards – are not allowed to participate in by-elections. After the 2001 elections, the Election Commission ordered a repeat election in 62 constituencies (yellow cards) and disqualified eight elected candidates with red cards (Kokpol 2002, p. 297). This practice is controversial, however, in regard to electoral accountability. If a candidate who receives 90 per cent of the votes in his or her district is disqualified for unlawfully giving donations to a few villagers, the voters' will may be distorted. Such a system needs an absolutely impartial election commission.

Senate Elections

After the Senate was introduced into the political system in 1947, all senators were appointed by the King. The existence of such a second chamber "stocked with representatives of the military and bureaucracy meant that the parties that controlled the House and cabinet still did not hold all the reins of power" (Hicken 2009, p. 118). Hence, prior to 1997, the Thai Senate had no electoral accountability and defended the interests of the military and bureaucracy against initiatives from the elected House of Representatives.

This changed to some extent in 1997 when the People's Constitution established for the first time a fully and directly elected 200 member Senate for a six-year term. The constitution did not allow the 200 senators to be members of parties or have partisan connections, nor to hold a cabinet portfolio. The senators were restricted to two consecutive terms. The Senate, which was not allowed to be dissolved by the prime minister, had the right to amend or approve legislation, but not to propose it.

After the military coup the constitutional drafters opted in a first proposal for a Senate consisting of 160 members, all of them appointed by a five-person committee (Chambers 2009, p. 24), a highly undemocratic suggestion. In the end they opted for a half-way compromise between this proposal and the previous situation: a little more than half the Senate is elected directly while the other half is appointed by a Senators Selection Committee. Out of the 150 Senators, 76 are directly elected with a first-past-the-post electoral system in single member districts shaped in accordance with the 76 provinces of Thailand. The appointment of the 74 other senators is done by a committee consisting of seven persons, mostly from judiciary and independent government organizations. Chapter 6, Part 3, Section 113 of the 2007 Constitution states that the Committee consists of the President of the Constitutional Court, the Chairman of the Election Commission, the Chairman of the Ombudsmen, the President of the National Counter Corruption Commission, the Chairman of the State Audit Commission, a Supreme Court judge, and a judge of the Supreme Administrative Court (Constitution of the Kingdom of Thailand 2007). It is important to note that all the mentioned persons are appointed rather than elected. The task of this selection committee is to "select suitable persons from those nominated by organizations in the academic sector, the public sector, the private sector, the professional sector and other sectors, who are of value to the performance of duties of senators" (Constitution of the Kingdom of Thailand 2007).

These rather vague formulations give way to the personal preferences of the selection body, which may not necessarily consist of the favoured candidates of the people. The selection of senatorial candidates without consulting the general public is certainly a problem in regard to electoral accountability. The appointed senators are not directly accountable to the people and cannot be controlled by them. There is no regulation that restricts politicians or their relatives from becoming appointed senators. Of the 76 senators who are directly elected, there are much more detailed criteria. According to Chapter 6, Part 3, Section 115, Senate candidates must be at least forty years of age, must not be an ascendant, a spouse or son or daughter of a member of the House of Representatives, or a person holding a political position. Candidates are also not allowed to be a member or a holder of any position in a political party, nor a Minister or person holding a political position other than a member of a local assembly or local administrator (Constitution of the Kingdom of Thailand 2007). It is obvious that these regulations aim to prevent the 76 elected senators from being politicians or politically active people.

After the re-formation of the Thai Senate in accordance with the 2007 Constitution, appointed Senator Prasobsook Boondech became the first president of the half-appointed Senate. Approximately 10 per cent of of the appointed members were retired military officers. Boondech was replaced in 2011 by General Teeradej Meepien. Having the background of a high-ranking military and intelligence official, he was appointed senator in April 2011, shortly before the general elections for the House of Representatives. Some senators had earlier opposed the appointment of Teeradej Meepien since he still had a pending case against him for illegally increasing salaries in his former position (Narykhiew and Raksaseri 2011). A few days after his appointment, Senate members elected him as the new Senate President. General Teeradej Meepien commented that "he would promote the Senate as an agency of love and unity" (Narykhiew and Raksaseri 2011).

The fact that since 2007 the Thai Senate has not been fully elected, but instead nearly half-appointed, is a strong setback for electoral accountability. The decision that a fully elected Senate was not worth retaining did not come from the Thai voters but from the constitutional drafters. Consequently, "the decision to move some political offices beyond the reach of voters was made for them by individuals who are effectively unaccountable to those voters" (Hicken 2007*b*, p. 156).

Additionally, the intention of the constitutional drafters to keep the senators away from party politics seems to have failed. Nataphol Teepsuwan,

Director General of the Democrat Party, stated in an interview with the author that

> the senators, the elected as well as the appointed, have taken their sides as they became part of the political system. Now they are all close to the political parties. There are three groups of senators: Those close to the PAD, those close to the Democrat Party and those with Pheu Thai sympathies.[14]

In general, most observers tend to place the majority of the senators after 2006 more in the conservative camp or close to the Democrat Party.

Table 3.5 gives an overview of institutional changes affecting the electoral system for the House of Representatives and the Senate.

Table 3.5
Constitutional Reforms Concerning Elections in Thailand

	1978/1991 Constitutions	1997 Constitution	2007 Constitution
House of Representatives	1-3 seat constituencies Block vote	Mixed-member system 400 single-seat constituencies 100 national party-list seats	Mixed-member system 400 (375 in 2011) 1-3 seat constituencies 80 (125 in 2011) regional party-list seats
Senate	Appointed	Elected using SNTV, non-partisan	Elected/Appointed
Party Switching	Allowed	90-day membership requirement	90-day membership requirement 30-day exception if early election called
Party restrictions	Full team ¼- ½ of constituencies	5% threshold for list tier	none

Source: Hicken (2006*b*, p. 384) with modifications by the author.

Political Parties and the Party System

Thai political parties can be described as "either individual-centered vehicles, mechanisms for rural godfathers and their families, or 'clubs' for well-to-do notables" (Chambers and Croissant 2010, p. 16). Traditionally, they can be characterized as catch-all parties with little ideological differences, marginally developed party platforms, and with few connections to other groups and associations. Generally, political parties are poorly institutionalized and are usually made up of the personal followings of certain public figures (Harding and Leyland 2011, p. 50). As Thai political scientist Naruemon Thabchumpon explained, the parties "had no time to develop since there were so many coups. In Thai political culture, there is no support for parties/institutions, but rather for persons/leaders/patrons."[15] However, the situation has changed to some extent in recent years, not least due to institutional reforms, particularly the 1997 Constitution.

The introduction of majoritarian elements in the electoral system, such as plurality elections in single-member districts and the 5 per cent threshold for the party lists, led to a concentration of the party system. The 2001 and 2005 elections resulted in a strong decline in the number of parties represented in the House of Representatives. This national change in the effective number of parties was "a direct result of the constitutional changes Thailand adopted in 1997" (Hicken 2009, p. 127). Instead of a multitude of political parties, two strong political parties emerged: the Democrat Party and the Pheu Thai, and their banned predecessors, TRT and PPP. Naruemon Thabchumpon commented that "in the 1997 Constitution there was too much focus on a strong government. The drafters thought two big parties would solve all problems and therefore effectively eliminated many smaller parties."[16]

Traditionally, Thailand was ruled for decades by multi-party coalitions. In Lijphart's terms, these coalitions were an important feature of a consensus democracy (see chapter 2.4). Indeed, the political parties in various cases formed large alliances, often consisting of more parties than necessary. They did so because they were interested in a stable government and to be prepared for possible defections of smaller coalition partners. The largest party including the prime minister always had to give concessions, such as cabinet posts, to smaller parties. Therefore, the cabinet was generally made up of different party members, giving a disproportionate bargaining power to small parties far beyond their numerical strength in seats (Nogsuan 2005, p. 58). Additionally, Thai political parties were extremely fragmented. The power of party leaders was decreased by rival factions within their own political parties. Frequent cabinet reshuffles and short-lived governments were thus a typical feature of Thai politics prior to 1997.

The introduction of the 1997 Constitution, particularly the ban on party-switching and the single-member electoral districts, "contributed to centralizing control of party managers over their parties, ensuring greater cabinet durability" (Chambers and Croissant 2010, p. 20). Not surprisingly, the TRT, like the government it led, was an organization which centred entirely around a single man (McCargo and Pathmanand 2005, p. 110). The shift from multi-member districts to all single seat constituencies reduced the number of parties from an average of 6.2 before 1997 to 3.2 in 2001, and 2.0 in 2005 (Hicken 2005, p. 106, Hicken 2007b, p. 147). Together with this concentration of the party system, the political system prior to the coup adopted more and more features of a majoritarian democracy. Particularly after TRT's landslide victory in the 2005 elections, analysts questioned whether Thailand's traditionally fragmented multi-party system was at an end. They asked whether the electoral system turned the country into a two-party system or into a dominant party system (Nogsuan 2005, p. 58). As a consequence, the antagonism between the elected government and the powerless opposition grew enormously.

The 2007 Constitution reduced many of the incentives of the 1997 Constitution, which led to the concentration of the party system and to increased power of the prime ministers over rank-and-file MPs. It was intended to weaken the prime minister and the ruling political party and was specifically "designed to re-enfeeble parties and undermine parliamentary rule precisely so that strong parties (such as Thaksin's Thai Rak Thai) could never again threaten entrenched social forces and interests such as the monarchy, military and old established metropolitan businesses" (Chambers and Croissant 2010, p. 9). Therefore, the 2007 Constitution was aimed "for a return to the fluid coalition politics of the 1980s and 1990s" (Phongpaichit 2006, p. 3). Some scholars even predicted that Thailand "might be reverting back to its pre-1997 system of unstable, weakly cohering parties amidst competitive, powerful factions" (Chambers and Croissant 2010, p. 30).

However, the political reality developed differently. Two powerful parties continued to dominate Thai politics in the following years. A leading member of the Democrat Party commented that "Thailand is divided among party lines into two camps, such as in the USA. However, what is different is that the polarization leads to violence."[17] Both sides have their electoral strongholds. While the Pheu Thai Party wins almost every seat in the Northeastern part of the country (*Isaan*), the Democrat Party is unchallenged in the South of Thailand. Both sides are supported by mass organizations. The Pheu Thai Party can rely on the heterogeneous red-shirt movement, particularly the UDD (United Front for Democracy Against Dictatorship). In contrast, the Democrat Party is supported by the royalist yellow-shirts and to some extent by the PAD. The latter, who founded its own party, the New Politics Party, in 2009 has some leading members which are very close to the Democrat Party, but the PAD is far more right-wing, nationalist, and authoritarian than the mainstream in the DP.

The antagonism between the two big parties is still prevalent. A main dividing point is the dealing with the exiled former TRT leader, Thaksin Shinawatra. Kraisak Choonhavan, MP for the Democrat Party, explained that "a compromise with the Pheu Thai Party is very difficult. We must stick to the law. Thaksin was sentenced by the court and a release is not possible in a state ruled by the law."[18] Another MP added: "The Pheu Thai MPs always talk about the Thaksin issue. I don't greet them when I am meeting them, for example in the parliament's restaurant. Some have a totally different mind-set than me. Some are brain-washed. Thaksin is still the major reason for a failed reconciliation."[19] As for the other side Chaturon Chaisang made clear that "a coalition with the Democrat party is not possible. There is no point to a compromise and there is no opportunity for reconciliation."[20] After the electoral win of the Pheu Thai party in May 2011, the fierce antagonism between the two rival camps had somewhat decreased, as both sides made some conciliatory gestures towards each other and massive street violence disappeared. The previous stalemate between the Thaksin side and the Democrat Party had already been broken on a number of occasions (Farrelly 2012, p. 314), but both sides still remain bitter political opponents.

3.2 INDONESIA

National Elections in General

National elections have a long tradition in independent Indonesia. The first free and fair elections were held in 1955. After the military takeover and establishment of the authoritarian New Order (*Orde Baru*), elections were held in 1971, 1977, 1982, 1987, 1992, and 1997. However, these elections, despite being titled *pesta demokrasi* (democratic festival), were far from freedom and fairness. The number of participating political parties was limited by the authoritarian government, the opposition tightly controlled, the candidacy of undesirable candidates prohibited, and the voting results manipulated. The result was always an overwhelming victory of the regime's party, Golkar (*Golongan Karya*, functional groups).

After decades of authoritarian rule, Indonesia started a democratization process after the resignation of President Soeharto in May 1998. His successor, B.J. Habibie, initiated a series of political reforms, among them the holding of free and fair parliamentary elections in June 1999. Further elections for the national parliament (*Dewan Perwakilan Rakyat*, DPR) were held in 2004 and 2009. The president, as head of government, was not directly elected by the people until 2004. Prior to this, he was elected by the so-called People's Assembly (*Majelis Permusyawaratan Rakyat*, MPR), which was composed of the DPR and other representatives. Through incremental constitutional changes and the direct election of the president, Indonesia developed into a presidential system of government with many similarities to that of the United States. However, many particularities make Indonesian presidentialism a unique form of government.

Presidential Elections

The direct presidential election in 2004 was new for Indonesians, since previously they never had the chance to vote for individual leaders. Although Indonesia had a long series of elections since independence, none of these included the direct elections of the president or regional leaders. After the end of the authoritarian New Order of President Soeharto, Indonesia initially kept its constitution and thus a presidential form of government. The first democratic presidential elections in 1999 followed nearly the same procedure as those in the authoritarian era. The president was not elected directly by the people but from the People's Consultative Assembly (MPR). This institution consisted of 695 individuals. Five hundred from the previously elected members of parliament (DPR), 65 appointed functional group delegates and 130 provincial delegates. For the first time in Indonesian history, the MPR rejected a president's accountability speech (Habibie), and the presidential elections were held not by acclamation, but with more than one person competing.

Together with the fact that the president was now responsible to the MPR, the entire governmental system resembled a parliamentary system. According to the criteria of Steffani (1983), the latter system of government is defined by the appointment and dismissal of the head of government by the parliament. Such a development took place in 2001, when President

Abdurrahman Wahid lost the support of the large majority in the DPR and was removed from office by an "impeachment", due not so much to accusations of criminality as a politically-motivated vote of no confidence.

These political events influenced the ongoing negotiations concerning the restructuring of the constitution. The mode of the presidential election was changed. Instead of the MPR, the Indonesians could directly vote for a president for the first time in 2004. As a result, the president was no longer directly dependent on the political parties in parliament, strengthening the position of the president *vis-à-vis* the parliament. To counterbalance this gain in power, only presidential candidates from political parties participating in the parliamentary elections could run for president. Additionally, the previously unlimited re-election possibilities that former presidents enjoyed[21] were scrapped and replaced by a single re-election for another five-year term. According to the newly introduced Article 6A of the Indonesian Constitution, the president and vice-president had to be elected on the same ticket and would need at least 50 per cent of the votes with the additional requirement of more than 20 per cent of the votes in at least half of the provinces. If none of the candidates reach this target in the first round, a run-off election between the two candidates that received the most votes must take place. These provisions guarantee that the Indonesian president has a broad legitimacy.

However, the Indonesian presidential elections are different than that of other presidential systems, since the above mentioned Article 6A of the Constitution states that presidential and vice-presidential candidates must be proposed by a political party or coalition of parties that participate in the general election. There is no required minimum number of votes and seats in the parliamentary elections mentioned in the constitution. The law (UU 12/2003) which introduced a minimum threshold for the right to propose presidential candidates was passed by the political parties in the national parliament. In 2004, only parties with at least 5 per cent of the votes or 3 per cent of the seats were given the right to submit presidential candidates. Independent candidates, who are not nominated by the bigger political parties, are not allowed to run for president. To determine which parties are allowed, and to give some time for coalition-building, the Indonesian presidential elections are held three months after the DPR election.

In the 2004 elections, five presidential candidates were nominated by the political parties. Since no candidate could reach an absolute majority, a second round became necessary. In this run-off election, Susilo Bambang Yudhoyono (SBY) defeated then-incumbent President Megawati Sukarnoputri with about 60 per cent of the votes, becoming the first directly elected president of Indonesia.

In the election law for the 2009 presidential elections (Law No. 10/2008), the parliamentarians decided that all presidential candidates needed to be proposed by parties representing at least 20 per cent of the parliamentary mandates or 25 per cent of the votes. If a party did not reach this threshold, it could combine seats/votes together with other small parties in order to propose a common candidate. In 2009, due to the higher thresholds for the right to nominate candidates, only three candidates qualified themselves for a presidential bid. Incumbent President Susilo Bambang Yudhoyono was nominated by his party, the Democratic Party (DP) as well as by all Islamic parties represented in the DPR. His opponents were Megawati Sukarnoputri, proposed by the Indonesian Democratic Party — Struggle (PDI-P) and the Great Indonesia Movement Party (Gerindra), while the third candidate, Jusuf Kalla, was nominated by Golkar and the People's Conscience Party (Hanura). This time, a run-off election was not necessary since Susilo Bambang Yudhoyono won an absolute majority with more than 60 per cent of the votes in the first round.

With the relatively high requirement of 20 per cent of the seats or 25 per cent of the votes, political parties guarded their influence and limited the number of candidates. However, this provision was controversial. The Spokesman of the relatively small Hanura Party, Saleh Husin, stated in 2012 that in a democratic state there should be no limitations on proposing presidential candidates, as voters deserve to have options that may be different from that of the major political parties (Daslani 2012*b*).

This type of presidential election system is clearly to the disadvantage of popular candidates who lack support of one big or many small parties, but favours presidential candidates proposed by successful parties or by candidates who are able to form coalitions with many small parties. The chance of winning is increased for candidates who are familiar with party politics over political outsiders. The requirement that presidential candidates must be supported by at least a quarter of the DPR is advantageous in that a president must cooperate with parliament in order to prevent permanent gridlock. At the same time, the pre-condition of having support from members of the legislature for a presidential candidacy contradicts the principle of separation of powers. The legitimacy of the president thus not only derives from the majority of the votes in the election, but also from the political parties in parliament who picked him or her as presidential candidate. It follows then, that the electoral accountability of the Indonesian president is not only dependent on the voters but on the political parties in the DPR as well. This could even lead to the rather odd situation in which an incumbent president is not nominated by the major political parties in the DPR so that he or she cannot be re-elected or voted out of office by the citizens.

Law 10/2008 increased the president's dependency on political parties by drastically raising the required number of votes for presidential candidacy from 5 per cent to 25 per cent (while the required number of seats increased from 3 to 20 per cent) for the 2009 elections. This decision had various consequences for the presidential elections. Only one party – the Democratic Party – slightly exceeded the requirement of 20.9 per cent of the votes and 26.4 per cent of the seats. All other parties had to form coalitions in order to file a candidate. While parties with, say, 7 per cent could propose their own candidate in 2004, they had to start negotiations with other parties to find a common candidate in 2009. The provision on a minimum number of parliamentary support for presidential candidates thus – deliberately or not – leads to coalition-building and a more consensus-oriented democracy. At the time of writing, the mentioned requirements for presidential candidacy seem to be continued for the 2014 elections.

Parliamentary Elections

After the previously reserved seats for ABRI (military and police) were abolished with the implementation of the constitutional amendments in 2004, all seats of the national parliament became contestable. Parliamentary elections are traditionally held with a proportional election system in multi-member electoral districts. Under this system, political parties are represented according to the percentage of votes that they received. As has been described in chapter 2.4, proportional election systems are intended to create a parliament that mirrors the electorate. In a rather heterogeneous and young democracy such as Indonesia, this election mode resulted in a high number of political parties.

In 1999, hundreds of parties registered and 48 were admitted. In 2004, about 150 parties registered and 24 were allowed by the national election commission, KPU (*Komisi Pemilihan Umum*), to participate in the parliamentary elections. The excluded (usually very small) parties did not fulfill the organizational requirements of the Election Law demanding countrywide presence. For the 2009 election more than 60 parties registered and 32 of them were allowed to run in the national elections.

An effective threshold with the aim of restricting the number of parties represented in parliament is often used in other democracies with a proportional election system. The Indonesian threshold applied in the 1999 and 2004 elections proved ineffective, however. The stipulations concerning the threshold stated that political parties with less than 2.5 per cent were allowed to retain their seats, but were not permitted to participate in the forthcoming elections. Consequently, 21 parties in 1999 and 17 in 2004 were able to gain seats in the national parliament, several of them with only one or two seats. The prohibition to run again for parties with less than 2.5 per cent was circumvented. For instance, the Justice Party (Partai Keadilan) received only 1.4 per cent of the votes and 7 seats and was prohibited to run again in the next elections. However, the party simply registered under a modified name as Justice and Welfare Party (Partai Keadilan Sejahtera, PKS) and participated with more success in the 2004 elections.

Despite that many small parties agreed to work in joined factions, the extreme fragmentation of the national parliament – beside other factors – led to inefficient and time-consuming negotiation processes. Additionally, the proportional election system did not resulted in clear majorities for individual parties. In 1999, the strongest party, the Indonesian Democratic Party-Struggle (PDI-P), had 30.6 per cent of the seats, whereas in 2004 the Golkar Party was strongest with 23.3 per cent of the seats, and in 2009, the Democratic Party (Partai Demokrat, PD) won with just 20.9 per cent. Thus, there were no clear majorities in parliament and the building of coalitions with at least two or more factions became a necessity in order to reach regular parliamentary majorities. The multitude of parties results in a greater degree of representativeness but a complicated situation for governability (Hadiwinata 2006, p. 140).

The perceived problem of the proliferation of parties has been debated since 1999 and many local and international experts and media lament the mentioned negative effects alongside the major political parties in the DPR. While the former want to avoid political fragmentation and confusion among voters, the latter aim at restricting competition from new players (Sherlock 2009, p. 11f.).

After lengthy debates, Law No. 10/2008 (UU 10/2008) paved the way for incremental revisions of Law No. 12/2003 on elections. For the first time, decisions concerning electoral accountability reform were not the sole task of the DPR. The newly created Constitutional Court now shared this responsibility. The latter was for the parliamentarians "a somewhat unpredictable factor" (Crouch 2010, p. 71). The above mentioned election law (UU 10/2008) changed several provisions, which had far-reaching impacts for the 2009 elections. It allowed, for instance, all parties to participate in the general elections, even those who failed to reach more than 3 per cent of the votes in the last elections. The Constitutional Court invalidated this decision, but since the KPU had already announced the final list of eligible parties one day before, the court's decision did not go into effect (Crouch 2010, p. 74). The main innovation of Law No. 10/2008 was the introduction of an effective 2.5 per cent threshold. This meant, in contrast to the previous thresholds that parties under this percentage were not allowed to receive any seats. This regulation reduced the number of political parties in the DPR from 17 to 9 in 2009. Nine is still a high number in a national parliament by international standards, but the working efficiency could be improved without losing the inclusiveness ideal of the proportional election system. In the first elections with the effective 2.5 per cent threshold in 2009, nearly 18 per cent of the votes were used for parties that later did not get a single seat. This distortion, however, was balanced with the positive effect of a concentration of the party system, which can be expected in the forthcoming elections in 2014.

Politicians from the major parties, particularly PDI-P and Golkar, demanded an even higher threshold of 5 or more per cent. Puan Maharani, one of PDI-P's leading figures, argued that

> it is impossible for Indonesia to treat legislative elections as a free market that allows all parties to compete and to send their representatives to the legislature. We should learn from the last three general elections that the more parties there are, the more chaotic the elections will be, the more confused voters will be, the more factions will appear in the legislature and the more ineffective the government will be (Sijabat 2011a).

In April 2012, the major parties were successful in their lobbying in the DPR to pass a new election law that raised the effective vote threshold to 3.5 per cent compared to the previous 2.5 per cent. Seventeen smaller parties filed a judicial review with the Constitutional Court over these stipulations, arguing that they were discriminatory and thus would prevent them from competing against more established parties. Constitutional Court Chief Justice Mahfud MD argued that "newly-established political parties must not be treated differently, as their rights are also guaranteed by the Constitution" (Aritonang 2012). Another judge, Ahmad Fadlil Sumadi, maintained:

Demokrasi harus mampu memberikan jaminan sebesar-besarnya untuk perlindungan kebebasan mengeluarkan pendapat, berserikat, dan berkumpul. Pembatasan yang ketat atas perlindungan kebebasan tersebut merupakan pemberangusan terhadap nilai-nilai demokrasi [Democracy must allow the greatest possible potential for the protection of freedom of speech, association and assembly. A strict threshold limits the mentioned freedoms and is not in accordance with democratic values] (Revianur 2012, translation by the author).

Whereas the constitutional court seemed to prioritize freedom over practical concerns, the national election commission in late 2012 was more in accordance with the interests of the major parties. For the parliamentary election scheduled to be held in April 2014, a total of 46 parties registered to take part. After thoroughly checking the required pre-conditions, the national election commission allowed only 10 parties to participate for the 2014 elections. It stated that only the 9 parties which were already represented in the DPR as well as the well-sponsored National Democrats could fulfill all necessary requirements (Maharani 2013). However, some of the parties not admitted filed protests and two of them were finally successful in obtaining access to elections months after the first announcement of the KPU.

The primary objective of the various thresholds for parliamentary elections in Indonesia was to limit the number of parties taking part in elections and receiving seats in parliament. Accordingly, the existing parties were indirectly strengthened and the incentives for the creation of new parties reduced. However, the efforts in stabilizing the party system in the parliamentary elections stood in sharp contrast to the requirement for presidential candidates to be proposed and backed by political parties. This resulted in the formation of new parties by influential persons with presidential since the election law required them to have support from a party represented in the DPR while pursuing their presidential candidacy.

Open Party Lists

Until 2004, parliamentary elections were held with a closed-list proportional election system. The closed-list system is often criticized since it places a great deal of power in the hands of the party leadership, who then determine the rankings on the lists, particularly since "it makes MPs answerable to the party but not to the electors" (Sherlock 2009, p. 4).

This means that in Indonesia, as well as in other countries with a closed-list proportional election system, elected members of the parliament had to fear punishment not by the voters but rather by the party leadership. Consequently, maintaining close relations with the central party leadership became more important over the desires of the constituency.

The weak link between citizens and their representatives led to a multitude of academic and political debates, in which mainly two solutions were proposed: the introduction of a plurality system and the transformation of the closed lists into open lists within a proportional election system. In Election Law No. 12/2003, the DPR members agreed on a partial opening of the closed-list system. The voters were for the first time allowed to choose a certain candidate from the party list and could thus change its order. The motivation for this "reform – common in Europe, but unique in the Asia-Pacific – was to give voters more influence over which candidates from a given party list would be elected, thus in theory strengthening the link between voters and politicians" (Reilly 2006, p. 106).

However, in practice this system failed to work since the percentage of personal votes required for getting to the top of the list was too high. In 2004, only 2 candidates over all of Indonesia were able to obtain a parliamentary seat due to the open party list. The other 548 seats went to candidates in the order of the list prepared by the political parties. The disadvantages of introducing an open party list outweighed the benefits. Ballots now listed all of the candidates running under a given party beside the party's name, turning ballots into a relatively voluminous and labyrinthine document for ordinary voters, especially in comparison to the prior ballot list of 24 parties. Accordingly, the number of invalid votes rose from 3.4 per cent in the 1999 elections to 8 per cent in the 2004 elections. In contrast, in the less complicated presidential elections, only 2.1 per cent of voters cast invalid votes (IDEA 2011).

The failure of introducing open party lists in the 2004 elections led to modifications for the forthcoming elections. Election Law No. 10/2008 reduced the probability of invalid votes by allowing votes to be cast for either an individual candidate or a party. Additionally, the percentage of personal votes required to reach the top of the electoral district's party list was reduced significantly. This reform aimed at giving candidates with a low position a chance to be elected with personal votes while at the same time retaining the power of political parties to determine their top candidates for the list.

This compromise, however, did not hold long. In March 2009, only a few weeks ahead of the 2009 parliamentary elections, the Constitutional Court annulled Article 214 of Law No. 10/2008, and decided that those candidates on the party list get a seat in the DPR, which received the largest number of personal votes, regardless of their position on the party list (Crouch 2010, p. 74f.; Sherlock 2009, p. 6). Consequently, the voters, rather than the party leadership, determine who will represent them in the national parliament, or, to put it more directly, the introduction of the full open party list "intended to break the power of party leaders, who under the previous 'closed-list' system could place their cronies on the top of their lists (and thus ensure their election), and thwart the ambitions of other, worthier party members by placing them at the bottom of their lists" (Harvard Kennedy School Indonesia Program 2010, p. 86). Hence, electoral accountability was strengthened by the above mentioned institutional reform.

The effects became noticeable in the 2009 parliamentary election when several important and well-known party politicians failed to be re-elected in their electoral districts, losing to more popular candidates or to politicians with genuine grassroots support (Sukma 2010, p. 59). Even the speaker of parliament, Agung Laksono (Golkar), was not re-elected, losing in district Jakarta I to the comedian and actor Mandra from the National Mandate Party (Partai Amanat Nasional, PAN). Nearly 70 per cent of the DPR seats went to newcomers who entered the national parliament for the first time. This enormous turnover rate of national legislators is much higher than in Thailand and the Philippines, and is also extremely high when compared to most Western democracies.

However, there were some noticeable side effects of the open party-list regulation. Candidates were now in competition not only with those from rival parties, but also with candidates from their own ranks. This has increased the costs of election campaigns. The intra-party competition fostered by the open-list system resulted in a reduction of party cohesion (Harvard Kennedy School Indonesia Program 2010, p. 86f.). Nevertheless, the introduction of the open party list brought candidates and legislators closer to their constituents. Prospective candidates and incumbent legislators learned that constituency work counts and that patronage by party leaders is not sufficient to be (re-)elected. Closer relations with constituents could result in an improvement of the channels for public input into the work of the DPR and make the legislators more responsive to public demands (Sherlock 2009, p. 8). DPR member Nurul Arifin (Golkar) argued in a similarly way by stating that with the open-list system "any lawmakers who fail to fight for their constituents' aspirations will risk being unpopular and miss out on being elected in 2014". Legislator Saan Mustopa (Democratic Party) was quoted as saying that "the open-list system was not without weaknesses as it was prone to vote-buying, but was still better than the closed-list system" (Sijabat 2012*a*). Most parties represented in parliament publicly voiced their support for the open-list system, only PDI-P and Gerindra still prefer a closed list (*daftar tertutup*).

Debates on a Majority Election System

The replacement of the proportional election system by a plurality system (*sistem distrik*, district system, as it is known in Indonesia) was and is a frequent topic of political and academic debate in Indonesia. As has been described in chapter 2.4, a plurality system, in which voters can directly reward and punish their district candidates, would clearly enhance electoral accountability. Additionally, proponents argue that Indonesia, as the third most populous democracy worldwide, should take the two largest democracies, India and the United States, as examples of plurality election systems that have operated for decades/centuries in a way that is simple to understand for the public.

So far, these proposals to introduce a first-past-the-post election system in single-member districts "have always been rejected, often on the grounds that such an approach would introduce a winner-take-all attitude that could endanger Indonesia's ethnic and religious pluralism" (Aspinall 2010, p. 26). A plurality election system would endanger the consensus style of democracy that shaped Indonesia's democracy since 1999. The inherent distortion effect of a plurality system would artificially increase the power of the bigger parties to the detriment of smaller ones. Like in India, small parties with strong regional bases profit from a plurality system, but since in Indonesia (with the exception of Aceh) regional parties are not allowed to run in national elections the smaller parties which represent millions of voters would sooner or later disappear or merge with the bigger ones, leading to a situation in which minority groups would not be represented at all.

I would consequently argue that the introduction of a plurality system in Indonesia would lead to the "philippinization" of electoral accountability. It would make the political parties more or less obsolete, since Indonesian citizens, who already have a very low esteem for political parties, would prefer individual reputation over party affiliation. Elected candidates would be those that appeal to voters with promises of targeted goods that they will deliver to the district instead of broad national goals that will benefit all Indonesians. Moreover, campaigns under these systems tend to require lots of money, and … the burden of financing campaigns falls on the candidates themselves. As a result, those who run for office must either be wealthy, or have wealthy patrons to whom they are expected to render services once elected (Harvard Kennedy School Indonesia Program 2010, p. 86).

Restrictions on Electoral Accountability

Effective electoral accountability requires that all adults and mentally healthy individuals have the right to cast their vote and to run for office. In Indonesia, there are still some restrictions which can be regarded as weaknesses in terms of the quality of democracy. For example, military personnel (a population of more than 400,000 people) and police (also over 400,000) do not have the right to vote. In 2012, defense ministry spokesman Hartind Asrin argued that with the current level of democratic maturity, it is still too risky for military and police personnel to vote or be nominated in elections since there could be a civil war if military and police troops disagree over different political views (Daslani 2012*a*).

Whereas the exclusion of active military and police officers for political candidacies makes sense, the lack of voting rights does not. Many high-ranking army members turned into politicians (among them most prominently SBY, Wiranto, and Prabowo Subianto) after their obligatory retirement of 55 years. The question of civil supremacy over the military and the police in Indonesia cannot be discussed here extensively, but military and police officers are also citizens who deserve the right to vote for their representatives.

Another group that has been disenfranchised for a long time from voting or running for office were members of the former Indonesian Communist Party, which was banned in 1965 after the military coup of General Soeharto. This relic from Indonesia's authoritarian past was carried over to the democratic order. Article 60g of Election Law No. 12/2003 continued the anti-communist voting ban. However, the Constitutional Court decided in 2004 that this regulation "clearly contains the nuances of political punishment against certain groups" and "a denial of the human rights of the citizens or discrimination based on political beliefs, and therefore it is contradictory to human rights protection guaranteed by the 1945 Constitution" (Mahfud 2009, p. 14). Consequently, this formerly excluded group of elderly people can now exercise their democratic voting rights.

Flaws regarding electoral administration can also infringe on electoral accountability. Whereas the KPU coped relatively well with the huge logistical and technical challenges in the vast archipelago in the 1999 and 2004 elections, "the KPU team responsible for administering the 2009 elections was hampered by its own sheer incompetence" (Sukma 2009, p. 318). The worst problems concerned the absence of millions of registered voters on the voter's list (*daftar pemilih tetap*), the very slow vote counting process, and the following seat allocation for DPR which took weeks. These administrative weaknesses are a threat to the credibility of the democracy even in the absence of systematic fraud or manipulation. In the 2009 elections, persons and parties who lost in the elections filed a series of protests and judicial processes due to these administrative flaws, but, in the end, all accepted the decisions of the Constitutional Court. Fortunately, in the presidential elections, SBY's margin of victory was wide enough that all the errors in the electoral process did not pose a serious threat to his legitimacy. This is unlikely to be the case in the 2014 elections, "when there will be no incumbent candidate, and probably a more hotly contested race for the presidency as a consequence" (Diamond 2009, p. 340). Under such circumstances, flaws in the electoral process could lead to a more violent scenario. In the presidential election in Kenya in 2007, for example, a weak electoral administration caused controversies as to who won the very tight election race, bringing the country to the edge of a civil war and heavily compromising the democratic system. Administrative reforms such as improving the capacity of the electoral administration namely the KPU, and the creation of reliable and accurate voter lists "may not appear to be particularly exciting, but it is precisely these kinds of boring, technical reforms that have the greatest potential to improve the durability of Indonesia's democracy" (Harvard Kennedy School Indonesia Program 2010, p. 89).

Other major constraints to electoral accountability are due to practices in the Indonesian parliament. Citizens are in most cases unaware whether or not a given representative supported a bill. Voters have little opportunity to discern which representative has acted in what way, since decisions on legislation are usually made by consensus (more on this issue in chapter 5.2). Additionally, verbatim transcripts from committee sessions, a basic instrument of transparency and accountability of parliaments, are not produced systematically and are not accessible for the general public (Sherlock 2010, p. 172f.). Another peculiarity which is in contrast to the principle of electoral accountability is the recall mechanism, which allows political parties represented in parliament to replace individual legislators, who no longer follow the party line (Ziegenhain 2008, p. 125f.). Whereas this practice might have some positive effects in terms of party cohesion, the prevention of turncoatism (see chapter 3.3) and effective decision-making in parliament is in sharp contrast to the principles of representative democracies, wherein elected representatives should be more accountable to the citizens they represent than to their political parties. In 2006, the Indonesian Constitutional Court nevertheless allowed the recall mechanism, what could be characterized as "the party holds the seat and the individual who occupies it does so at the party's discretion" (Sherlock 2007, p. 43). In recent years, however, recalls of individual legislators did not occur for having different opinions on policies, but rather in several cases when members of the DPR left the party under which banner they won in the elections to join other parties (Sherlock 2010, p. 175).

Parties and Their Function in the Political System

It is quite a common assumption that political parties are less important in presidential systems of government since the direct election of the chief executive and his independence from parliament implies that persons matter more than parties. In Indonesia, however, political parties play a very important role in national politics for two reasons. First, as mentioned before, only parties which have a certain number of seats in the DPR are entitled to select presidential candidates, and second, the proportional election system, despite the open list, results in strong political parties that act as gatekeepers for entrance into parliament.

Additionally, political parties are important factors of political decision-making in Indonesia since the DPR is a powerful veto-player to the presidency in nearly all policy areas. If any president wants to implement his or her agenda, he or she needs the backup of a majority within the DPR. The Indonesian president has to deal with many political parties, since the daily work in the DPR is divided among factions formed along party lines. The parties and factions represented in the DPR are also the main initiators of institutional reforms concerning electoral accountability. While the political parties in the DPR tried to maximize their role in all of their decisions concerning electoral accountability (election laws, electoral thresholds), the Constitutional Court tried to downsize their role (open-list system, nullification of thresholds).

Parties are not too different from their platforms but there are still social, ethnic, religious and professional cleavages in relation to the different political parties. The main division is between religious (Islamic) and the so-called secular part of the population. However, one has to be aware that those in the so-called secular camp are usually still religious people, but they set other priorities over and above those related to Islamic parties. Additionally, both sides are extremely heterogeneous. Voting behaviour is still influenced by pre-democratic traditions. Loyalities of kin, religious affiliation and community play a major role in voting decisions. However, political parties try to neutralize these effects in direct votes for individual leaders by putting candidates with different backgrounds on the same ticket. By doing so, they cross-cut ethnic or religious loyalties.

In the 2004 elections, former general Susilo Bambang Yudhoyono (Java) chose businessman Jusuf Kalla (Sulawesi) as his running mate, while Wiranto (a rather secular former general) decided to take Salahuddin Wahid (religious figure with a strong Islamic background). In the same election Muslim politician Amien Rais (Java) had rather secular businessman Siswono Yudohusodo from Kalimantan as his running-mate. In the 2009 presidential elections, the differences were less pronounced, as five of the six presidential and vice-presidential candidates came from Java, three of which had an army background. A peculiarity at the time was that no presidential candidate was proposed by the Islamic political parties, since they all threw their support behind incumbent President Susilo Bambang Yudhoyono. Such cross-cut candidate pairs refer to a type of catch-all strategy of the candidates. It is an attempt to attract potential voters from different social, ethnic and religious backgrounds and not to rely on a specific group entirely.

The prohibition of local political parties (except Aceh since the Peace Agreement in 2005) is another feature of Indonesian politics. All electoral laws allow only parties to participate in elections, which have a broad presence in all parts of the country. The effective exclusion of parties representing specific ethnic or regional groups is part of the ideology of the unitary state (*negara kesatuan*). On the one hand, "the exclusion of local parties has prevented Indonesia's national institutions from becoming a battleground for organized regional and ethnic interests, and limited the extent to which local institutions can be captured by ethnically exclusivist movements" (Aspinall 2010, p. 26). On the other hand, political parties which do not represent the heterogeneity of the multi-ethnic archipelago decrease the electoral choices of the voters and hence electoral accountability.

Another trend, which is caused by electoral reforms, particularly the requirement to have party support in order to run for the presidency, is the emergence of person-centred political parties. The most significant example was

> President Yudhoyono himself, who formed the Democrat Party in 2001 because it was necessary to have a party backing in order to stand for election in 2004. It seems clear that SBY personally would have won the election regardless of party backing, but he saw it desirable to found a new party because of the electoral law (Sherlock 2009, p. 13).

The emergence of Hanura and Gerindra as electoral vehicles for the retired generals Wiranto and Subianto Prabowo are other cases in point. These parties are not based on the above mentioned social, ethnic, and religious cleavages, but are rather constructed top-down by influential and wealthy individuals.

Political parties and legislators generally have a bad reputation among the general public. Hundreds of corruption scandals and the alleged self-interests of politicians led to a very low public image. Not only the general public but also political analysts blame political parties for the myriad of shortcomings of Indonesia's democracy. However, as Mietzner and Aspinall (2010, p. 9) show, the disregard for political parties and politicians is rather a global problem in nearly all democracies than a specific Indonesian phenomenon.

3.3 PHILIPPINES

Presidential Elections

After the ouster of authoritarian ruler Ferdinand Marcos in 1986, the new constitution[22] continued the tradition of a presidential system, which was in place since the country's independence. The Philippine presidential system has several references to the US model. However, significant differences, which arose in the process of drafting the constitution, were included. The drafters of the 1987 Constitution sought to provide the necessary legal preconditions for free and fair democratic elections. As a lesson from the Marcos era, several provisions were introduced in order to decrease the possibilities of a president becoming too powerful. In light of the experience under Marcos, who was a democratically elected president–turned–authoritarian ruler, the drafters of the Constitution included the provision that a president cannot be re-elected, but is granted a significantly longer term than a US-American president (six years opposed to four).[23] The method of presidential election is an important criterion for electoral accountability, since the president's legitimacy depends on it. Analogous to the US presidential election system, an absolute majority of the votes is not necessary to win in a single round of elections in the Philippines. The candidate who receives the relative majority of the votes becomes president. Thus, a Philippine president does not necessarily need to have the support of a high number of voters. Accordingly, the legitimacy of a Philippine president can be lower than that of presidents in countries where absolute majority is needed to become president.

The first post-authoritarian president, Corazon Aquino, was declared winner by the Supreme Court after the so-called People Power Revolution that followed electoral fraud by then incumbent President/Dictator Marcos in 1992. Fidel Ramos won the following election with 23.58 per cent of the votes in 1998, Joseph "Erap" Estrada with 39.86 per cent in 2004, Gloria Macapagal-Arroyo (GMA) with 39.99 per cent, and Benigno "Noynoy" Aquino III with 42.08 per cent in 2010.

It can thus be observed that no elected president has ever received an absolute majority after the re-introduction of democracy in 1986. Fidel Ramos notably won with a meager 23.5 per cent. Though the last three victories had a relatively high legitimacy, with around 40 per cent, the electoral system does not guarantee such outcomes. Run-off elections would enhance the legitimacy of the winning candidate in the Philippines, but have never been considered seriously in public or academic debates.

Another problem of one-round presidential elections is the possibility of small margins between the winner and the second-ranked candidate. Some ten or hundred thousand votes can decide victory or loss. In developing countries like the Philippines, where infrastructural deficiencies, remote areas, and a vote counting process plagued with irregularities exist, such an electoral system for the top executive position is particularly questionable. Case in point: after the 2004 elections, a recorded phone call conversation from President GMA was publicly circulated, in which she asked the chairman of the national election commission (COMELEC) Virgilio "Garci" Garcillano to rig the vote counting in such a way that she would win the presidential elections by a margin of a million votes. In the official COMELEC election result, she won indeed by about one million votes ahead of her contender, Fernando Poe Jr. When the wire-tapped recording became public in June 2005 there was a huge public outcry. GMA's famous greeting at the beginning of the conversation, "Hello Garci", became synonymous with the biggest election scandal of the country. The affair severely compromised both the impartiality of the election commission and the electoral process itself (Dressel 2011, p. 534). Fallout from the scandal included a massive public protest that tried to nullify the 2004 election results, the resignation of several secretaries from GMA's administration, and an unsuccessful impeachment process by the congress. The political legitimacy of GMA was severely damaged until the end of her presidency in 2010.

The constitutional provision that prohibits re-election for a president can be seen from two perspectives. On the one hand, it provides the president with a higher independence from outside interference. Six years allow the president enough time to pursue his or her policies and to initiate reforms. The fact that the president cannot be re-elected allows him or her to come up with rather unpopular (but maybe necessary) decisions or appointments. This could have both positive and negative consequences. Without the prospect of re-election, Philippine Presidents are free to directly bring sensitive issues onto their agenda that might affect vested interests and could cost them support, while those presidents who are re-electable tend to avoid tackling unpopular topics which might endanger their re-election chances.

On the other hand, critics argue that the fixed term is too long a period when the president is underperforming, and too short if he or she genuinely endeavours to deliver on his or her promises (Rüland 2003, p. 479). Additionally, a president who does not stand for re-election is often considered to be a "lame duck". In the United States, presidents in their second and final term are expected to refrain from ambitious policy initiatives and generally have less political power. Often, Congress and other important players within the political system, such as lobby groups, pay less attention to them and are less willing to cooperate. Additionally, the presidential influence in its own party decreases if there is no re-election possibility. In the Philippines, GMA became such a "lame duck" president ahead of the 2010 elections. Many former political allies, seeking to save their own re-election chances distanced themselves from the incumbent president and left the governmental camp. For example, her party's presidential candidate, former Defense Secretary Gilberto Teodoro Jr., dissociated publicly from her (Abinales 2011, p. 164). Since GMA's popularity rating shortly before the 2010 elections was the lowest for any president in Philippine history, "her endorsement [was] as welcome as leprosy. Political analysts say identification with her [was] a 'kiss of death' for candidates running in the 2010 elections" (Laguatan 2010).

In terms of electoral accountability the Philippine's presidential election system is far from optimal, because it is prone to manipulation and vote rigging, what in turn diminishes the electoral accountability of a Philippine president. The missing possibility for re-election gives the voters no choice to pass a judgement upon his or her performance. They can neither reward the president by extending his or her time in office nor punish him or her by refusing to give their votes.

Vice-President

According to Article VII, Section 3 of the Philippine Constitution, the vice-president is "elected with and in the same manner as the president". However, different from the US model, the Philippine vice-president is elected with a separate vote. The drafters of the 1987 Constitution did this for various considerations. They wanted to let the people have their own direct choice and additionally guarantee a relatively independent vice-president in order to balance the power of the presidency. In order to prevent presidential power abuse, such as that of dictator Marcos, the vice-president was intended to be independent of the president. Whereas the separate vote for the vice-president is positive in terms of electoral accountability, such a model has some weaknesses, as recent history shows. If the president and vice-president come from two different political camps, conflicts between the two are highly probable. The more ambitious and powerful the vice-president is, the more he or she will undermine presidential policies. Even as a central part of the government, such vice-presidents can regard themselves as oppositional towards the head of government. A vice-president may even try to contribute to the downfall of a president, such as in 2001, when Vice-President GMA actively supported efforts to impeach then-President Estrada in order to succeed him (Kasuya 2003). Vice-presidents such as Joseph Estrada and GMA used the vice-presidency as a springboard for the presidency in the following term. GMA, for example, replaced Estrada and became president in 2001 for the rest of his term. In 2004, she won the presidency for a complete term, in a sense finding the loophole to escape the rigid six-year ban on re-election.

The phrase "united versus divided government", which is usually applied to executive-legislative relations, can also be transferred to the presidential–vice-presidential relations in the Philippines. Under these conditions, the Philippines experienced a "united government" with the duos Corazon Aquino–Salvador Laurel (1987–92), GMA-Guingona/de Castro (2001–10) and a "divided government" with Ramos-Estrada

(1992–98), Estrada-GMA (1998–2001), and Benigno Aquino–Jejomar Binay (since 2010).

In the 2010 elections, Benigno "Noynoy" Aquino's high popularity did not ensure his running-mate Manuel Roxas' election victory in the vice-presidential race. Instead, Jejomar Binay from the oppositional Estrada camp became the new vice-president. Therefore, a fissure currently exists in the presidential palace (*Malacañang*) itself.

House of Representatives

The Congress of the Philippines is – similar to the US model – divided into two chambers: the House of Representatives and the Senate. The House of Representatives in the 15th Congress (2010–13) was composed of 229 members, which are elected in as many electoral districts by a first-past-the-post election system, and 57 additional representatives, elected from so-called party lists. Article VI, Section 5 (1), of the constitution states that

> the House of Representatives shall be composed of no more than two hundred and fifty members ... who shall be elected from legislative districts, apportioned among the provinces, cities, and the Metropolitan Manila area in accordance with the number of their respective inhabitants and on the basis of a uniform and progressive ratio (Constitution of the Philippines).

The plurality election system for the large majority of the members reduces the influence of political parties, since the voters decide on personalities rather than on party platforms. In the Philippines, the plurality voting system favours affluent local elites, which are the only ones who can afford the high expenses for campaigning with little party support (Rüland, Nelson, Jürgenmeyer, and Ziegenhain 2005, p. 170f.). The House of Representatives in the Philippines is thus often described as a "millionaires' club" (Coronel 2007*b*, p. 22). The social profile of the Philippine House is as a result highly distorted in favour of the rich and powerful. Like the Thai parliament, the Philippine Congress acts "more like a business club where deals [are] cut than a modern legislature for the representation and aggregation of various movements, interests, and social groups" (Phongpaichit and Baker 2005, p. 60).

However, one has to keep in mind that in other established democracies such conditions prevail in plurality systems as well. If there are no strong political parties and the election campaign has to be financed by the candidates themselves or by their private sponsors, the electoral chances for less affluent candidates are limited. To say in more realistic words, people

without wealth or support from wealthy companies are effectively barred
from winning electoral districts in first-past-the-post election system of the
Philippines. The single-member district electoral rule benefits well-established
and powerful local strongmen who are able to deliver material goods to
their constituents (Shin 2013, p. 105). Congressman Nereus "Neric" Acosta
stated that

> the Philippine House of Representatives is a mirror of the inequalities
> of Philippine society and fits perfectly to the prevalent political culture.
> In a weak state, which is held hostage by some oligarchies and where
> everything is negotiable, Congress cannot act completely independent.[24]

Due to the social and historical background of the country, nearly all district
seats in the House of Representatives are regularly won by the same clans
and families. Butch Abad, then former Secretary of Education, concluded
that the economic oligarchy and the political aristocracy have captured the
institutions.[25] Irrespective of committed crimes or an authoritarian past, the
same clans can still win their districts. In 2010,

> among those elected to the lower house were former First Lady Imelda
> Marcos; Romeo Jalosjos, Jr., a former congressman and pardoned rapist;
> Ruben Ecleo, Jr., a leader of a cult group on trial for murdering his wife;
> and Luis 'Chavit' Singson, one of the country's most notorious warlords,
> as well as his son, who is currently detained in a Hong Kong jail after
> being arrested for carrying 26.1 grams of cocaine by airport authorities
> (Abinales 2011. p. 167).

The drafters of the Philippine 1987 Constitution tried to prevent
the continued dominance of certain dynasties in Congress, who have
traditionally held power since colonial times. Article II, Section 26 states
that the "state shall guarantee equal access to opportunities for public
service and prohibit political dynasties as may be defined by law". If
properly implemented, such a provision could significantly improve electoral
accountability. However, the law which the Constitution demands has
never been agreed upon. In 1987, the Senate passed an anti-dynasty bill
and sent it to the House of Representatives. Former Senator Guingona
recalled that shortly afterward,

> someone from the rules committee of the House of Representatives
> came to see me and explained that there were so many inter-relatives
> among the congressmen that it would be next to impossible to have it

successfully approved in the House so they would have to just put it aside (Bordadora 2012).

It has stayed there for over twenty-five years.

Despite many efforts of some Congressmen and civil society organizations, the anti-dynasty bill is still ignored by the majority of the members of the House of Representatives. In November 2012, Vice-President Jejomar Binay himself was quoted as saying "that the anti-political dynasties measures were only being pushed by people who are perennial losers in elections" (Sy 2012).

Beside the anti-dynasty provision, another attempt to break the dominance of political clans was the provision in Article VI, Section 7 of the Philippine constitution. It states that members of the House of Representatives are not allowed to serve more than three consecutive terms of three years. This stipulation is quite unusual in established democracies in which certain legislators represent a district for decades. A term limit implicates a certain mistrust against the voters' will. However, it makes sense in overcoming the so-called "incumbency effect", when incumbents are favoured over newcomers. In the US elections for the House of Representatives, which take place every two years, more than 90 per cent of representatives in office have won re-election in the second half of the twentieth century (Jacobson 1997, p. 22; Abramowitz, Alexander, and Gunning 2006, p. 75). In terms of electoral accountability, the term limit in the Philippines was intended to break with the incumbency effect and to give other candidates a chance to win. However, in practice, incumbents do not run again for office after three terms, but very often field their wife/husband, children, or close relatives with the same family name as candidates. By doing so, the office is kept in the family.

Party Lists

In order to counterbalance the dominance of dynasties and to reduce the upper class bias of the House of Representatives, the Philippine Constitution of 1987 provided in Article VI, Section 5 (2) the requirement to also include socially disadvantaged groups in the House of Representatives, whose total number should make up to 20 per cent of the seats in the House. The groups were defined in the mentioned article of the constitution as "the labor, peasant, urban poor, indigenous cultural communities, women, youth, and such other sectors as may be provided by law, except the religious sector".

This provision shows that the constitutional drafters were well aware of the dangers of a distorted social profile of the people's representatives and tried to increase the inclusiveness of the House. Reserved seats broaden the social base of a parliament and grant access for disadvantaged societal groups, which have otherwise no chance to enter the national assembly. While the idea of strengthening these underprivileged groups might have a positive impact on political decision-making, the practical effect of such reserved seats depends on the circumstances of their elections or selections (Rüland, Nelson, Jürgenmeyer, and Ziegenhain 2005, p. 103) and their ability to influence the legislative processes in the House of Representatives.

In the Philippines, it took until 1999 for the above mentioned constitutional provision to be put into practice and for the first party-list representatives to enter the House of Representatives. Despite all positive intentions by the constitutional drafters, the party-list system in the Philippines is fraught with many problems.

Until 2009, however, due to a questionable election system, no more than 26 representatives of the socially disadvantaged groups were granted seats in the House (Co, Tigno, Lao, and Sayo 2005, p. 89f.). This number was far lower than the constitutionally mandated 20 per cent of the seats. The reason for this was a two-per cent threshold for party lists to get parliamentary representation. The party-list election system, which was prevalent until 2009, allowed additionally a maximum of three seats for each party list, irrespective of their election result. Even if a party-list group would have received 50 per cent of the votes, it would get the same three seats as a party-list group with only 5 per cent. These regulations led to a very high fragmentation of the party-list groups in the House. Political scientist Jürgen Rüland presumed that "the political class sought to prevent the rise of a reformist party that could effectively challenge vested interests" (Rüland 2003, p. 479).

In April 2009, the Supreme Court declared as unconstitutional the existing 2 per cent threshold in the distribution of additional party-list seats and granted 29 additional seats to party-list groups. However, it retained the maximum number of three seats (three-seat cap) for each winning party list. The latter decision is doubtful in terms of electoral accountability, since more popular party lists are disadvantaged by a three-seat cap, which is in contradiction to the principle of proportional representation. Additionally, the three-seat cap has much more effects in expressing the voters' will than the lifting of the two per cent threshold. The Supreme Court decision did contribute to an even bigger fragmentation of the party-list seats.

In many regards, it would have been better to reform the electoral rules of the party-list system exactly the other way around: to retain a reasonable threshold to control the excessive party fragmentation, but to abolish the seat caps to allow popular party lists to have their rightful share of seats.

In the 15th Congress, elected in May 2010, about 30 different groups with one or two representatives each were elected. Voters had the choice among nearly 200 different party-list groups on their voting ballot. Since most of them are hardly known to the general public, the whole election process became rather byzantine for the ordinary voter. In the words of Philippine academic and presidential adviser Joel Rocamora "so many party lists are just crazy".[26]

Since the party groups usually come from very different backgrounds, regions and social groupings, there is no overarching sense of togetherness in order to challenge the dominance of the traditional political elites. Therefore, having in mind that party lists comprise of only 20 per cent of the House of Representatives members, the high fragmentation of this percentage leads to a very low importance of the party-list groups. Each of the party-list groups as well as all of them together thus play a minor role in the daily work of the House of Representatives. Philippine political scientist Ronnie Holmes commented: "The whole party list system is not effective. With 20 percent of the seats and maximum 3 seats they will always be a powerless minority."[27]

Another problem of the party-list groups is whom they represent. If one takes a closer look at the party-list representatives, it is questionable if they really represent the disadvantaged classes of society, particularly the huge masses of the poor. Sons and daughters of rich businessmen and politicians quite often found such party groups in order to strengthen their power. Juan Miguel "Mikey" Arroyo, son of former President Gloria Macapagal-Arroyo, for instance, had to give up his safe district seat in Pampanga's 2nd district to be succeeded by his mother before the 2010 elections. In order to keep his parliamentary seat, he decided to create Ang Galing Pinoy, a party-list group supposedly representing the interests of ordinary security guards and entered the House of Representatives in this way. NGO activist Renato M. Reyes, Jr. commented that Mikey Arroyo

> does not come from the ranks of the marginalized. He is the incumbent congressman of his district, a member of the dominant political party Lakas-Kampi, and the son of the [then-] incumbent president. By no stretch of the imagination can he be considered marginalized or fit to represent the marginalized for which the party-list system was meant to serve (Reformina and Cruz 2010).

Other questionable examples of party-list representatives were Lourdes Arroyo, sister-in-law of former President GMA, who entered Congress as the representative of party list Kasangga representing self-reliant Filipino micro-entrepreneurs. Asked whether the Arroyo clan is not overrepresented, a then-speaker of the presidential palace simply stated: "It is part of the democratic process. These people have been elected. The party-lists were elected by the people and it just so happens Ms. Arroyo was the nominee to that seat" (Sy 2009).

Another very doubtful figure among the party-list representatives is retired army general Jovito Palparan of Bantay, a political party that advocates anti-communism. During his active military service under the presidency of GMA, Palparan was allegedly involved in extrajudicial abductions and killings of government critics. In December 2011, Palparan was finally indicted, fled the country, and went missing. President Aquino offered 2 million Philippine Peso (approximately US$50,000/37,000 Euros) for information leading to the arrest of the absconder.

The participation of party lists, which are not in accordance with the constitutional prerogative of representing marginalized social groups, is dependent on the accreditation of the Commission on Elections (COMELEC). Ahead of the 2013 elections, the COMELEC leadership, which was appointed by Noynoy Aquino, was more strict in checking links with politicians and other powerful groups. It disqualified, for instance, the Alliance for Nationalism and Democracy (Anad), an anti-communist group said to be linked to the military (Uy 2012).

COMELEC chairman Sixto Brillantes Jr. stated that he strongly supports that wealthy individuals be barred from participating at the party-list elections. He highlighted COMELEC's responsibility in accrediting party lists by stating that, "we have to make our own definition of what is marginalized unless we are overruled by the Supreme Court. *Yun ang aming* (That is our) definition unless the law is passed to amend the partylist system" (Ager 2012). From 289 applicants, only 79 managed to get accreditation for the 2013 elections (Esmaquel 2012), which underlines that the COMELEC took the screening process more seriously than in previous elections.

Another small but also meaningful institutional reform was that the list of party-list groups will no longer be in alphabetical order. In the 2010 elections, 103 of the 187 party-list groups chose names that started with either A or AA, while 11 of them either affixed "1" or "1st" to their names, so that they could be on the top of the voting list and get ahead of their poll rivals (InterAksyon.com 2013).

Senate

Second chambers often represent regional interests. This is not the case in the Philippines. The Senate is composed of 24 senators, which are elected for six-year terms by relative majority, with the whole country acting as election district. Every three years half of the senatorial seats are contested. In order to be re-elected, senators usually try to appear regularly in the national media. The chances for re-election depend less on performance than on popularity. Thus, their electoral accountability is limited. Virtually no senator "has a real policy platform and they are not accountable to any party or platform".[28] Unlike the US Senate, Philippine senators represent their own agendas rather than the different regions of the country.

This is understood by the Philippine Senate to be positive. It is proudly stated on the official homepage of the Senate that "the members of this chamber are elected at large by the entire electorate. The rationale for this rule intends to make the Senate a training ground for national leaders and possibly a springboard for the presidency" (Senate of the Philippines 2013). From this argumentation it is quite logical that senators are often more guided by their personal political career ambitions rather than by representing people's interests. This is cast in a positive light as "the Senator will have a broader outlook of the problems of the country, instead of being restricted by narrow viewpoints and interests" (Senate of the Philippines 2013). From this perspective, the senators are intentionally distanced from the problems of the ordinary electorate.

Belonging to an exclusive round of the national political elite is the most important goal for any politician, but this is very difficult to achieve. The doors for the Senate open easily only for those who belong to traditional influential families. Ordinary politicians need to be extremely popular since the 12 senators are elected in a nationwide constituency. This means that a candidate must make himself or herself nationally known, which necessitates excessive media coverage or widespread advertisements. The electoral system for the Senate, including the national (instead of a regional) constituency, results in social exclusion. Only very rich persons can afford to run election campaigns on a national level. It is no wonder then that the Senate is often seen as the "club of billionaires". Only well-known personalities, most of them from established dynasties or show business, have chances to become senators.

In the current Senate from 2010 to 2013,[29] as of this writing, contains many examples. For instance, the sons of former Presidents Marcos and

Estrada, Ferdinand "Bongbong" R. Marcos Jr. and Ejercito "Jinggoy" Estrada were elected. In the previous term, Benigno "Noynoy" Aquino III, son of former President Corazon "Cory" Aquino, served in the Senate. Senators Alan and Pia Cayetano followed in the footsteps of their senatorial father as well as Aquilino "Koko" Pimentel and Teofisto Guingona. Other senators like Sergio R. Osmeña III, Ralph G. Recto, Ramon "Bong" Revilla, and Francis "Chiz" Escudero have extensive family background in the history of Philippine senators. Vicente C. Sotto III, Loren Legarda, Manuel "Lito" Lapid, and Kiko Pangilinan were well-known enough nationwide due to their extensive TV engagement.

Some senators have a rather dubious record. Panfilo "Ping" Lacson started his police career under the authoritarian Marcos regime. While still keeping his senatorial post, he left the Philippines in January 2010, shortly before charges against him for the double murder of a political rival and his driver in 2000 were filed in court. In February 2011, the Court of Appeals withdrew the murder charges against Lacson and the senator returned to take up his position again (Abinales 2011, p. 167). Philippine voters also have no hesitation to elect prominent figures of the authoritarian era. Beside the son of Dictator Ferdinand Marcos, Ferdinand "Bongbong" R. Marcos Jr., Senate President Juan Ponce Enrile was the "right hand" of Marcos and worked as his Justice Secretary and Defense Minister.

Two senators with military backgrounds are also lacking democratic credentials. Senator Gregorio "Gringo" Honasan launched several deadly coup attempts against the Corazon Aquino administration between 1987 and December 1989 with his army units, only to later use his rebel infamy, after being pardoned, to enter politics and win a senate seat from 1995 to 2004, and another since 2007. Senator Antonio "Sonny" Trillanes IV became a senator by direct election on the anti-government Genuine Opposition ticket in 2007, "running" his campaign from prison. He served a prison sentence for his involvement in the Oakwood Mutiny in 2003, when he and a group of 321 soldiers took control over the Oakwood towers in Manila's business district Makati City. In November 2007, he walked out of his own trial and, together with other soldiers occupied the Peninsula Hotel in Makati, demanding the ousting of President GMA.

The representation of the three major regions of the country – Luzon, the Visayas and Mindanao – in the Senate is distorted since the latter two are notoriously under-represented leading to a huge bias towards the capital region of Metro Manila, from where the majority of the 24 senators came in recent years. It is obvious that the social profile of the Senate is not the image of the Philippine people. One could argue that this might be the case in any democratically elected parliament in the world. However, the social profile of the Philippine Senate is particularly elitist and homogeneous. The typical senator is male, comes from Metro Manila, has studied law and has a congressional history. Of the 22 senators in the 15th Congress of the Philippines (2010–13), 18 came from Luzon (among them 11 from Metro Manila), 10 of whom have university degrees in law, mostly attained at the prestigious University of the Philippines (Mang 2011, p. 99ff.). Except for Senators Trillanes and Pimentel, all the other 20 senators have been either a senator or congressman before. Women are under-represented with only three (Loren Legarda, Miriam Defensor, and Pia Cayetano) out of 22 senators.

The Philippine model of a second chamber thus does not reflect the regional, ethnic, and linguistic diversity of the country. The Muslim minority which makes up around 5 per cent of the population has not been represented in the Senate since 1995 (Priwitzer and Ziegenhain 2009, p. 97). The acting governor of the Autonomous Region of Muslim Mindanao, Mujiv Hataman, therefore complained that "the senatorial election system is to the disadvantage of the Muslims, because we have difficulties to build up national figures such as former Senator Rasul. Nobody can become a senator with the Muslim votes alone."[30]

Given such an inaccurate social profile, the Philippine Senate is hardly able to fulfill the representational function accorded to it by theories of electoral accountability. If the electoral districts were regional ones, the access possibilities for Senate would be less elitist. However, in reality it would be likely that the dominance of the family clans still prevails. Nevertheless, senatorial candidates would not be required to finance a nationwide media campaign to have at least some chances to succeed.

Clan/Family Dominance

The electoral system design, the classical first-past-the-post-system,

> encourages politics based on personalities and patronage rather than platforms and parties, to inequities in financing political parties and candidates. As a result, the national legislature is still firmly controlled by traditional Filipino elites, which often also rotate through local positions (Dressel 2011, 534).

Accordingly, the electoral accountability of the Congress members is limited, since in many districts members from influential political families dominate politics and there are no political alternatives which have realistic chances to win in this constituency.

These dynasties are full of so-called traditional politicians (often jokingly abbreviated to *trapos* in Filipino what can be translated as dishrags) and often hold various government and legislative positions within their families. They control their districts for decades in a relationship that fits well with the patron-client scheme. Ordinary voters thus deliver their vote for the same oligarchs in order to keep their job and retain the protection of their patrons. These

> constraints on voters' electoral choices are all too real in societies where power relationships are acutely unequal as seen in deeply rooted patronage-client ties or in the use of force and coercion by powerful elites to elicit desired political outcomes. Hence, elections may in fact function primarily to legitimize the rule by powerful elites skilled in the use of material incentives, co-optation and coercion (Rivera 2011, p. 51).

Additionally, Philippine voters expect their representatives to deliver practical and visible improvements for their area. The more national money is transferred to projects for the district, the higher the reputation for the representative. While this is quite a common feature in many democracies, the Philippines aggravate the negative side effects of this mechanism with the so-called pork-barrel system.

In the national budget of the Philippines, a high amount of money is allocated to improve the overall living conditions at the local level. Congress members are entitled to distribute the state's money to various projects in their constituencies, which they regard as valuable for the development. The district representatives are then perceived as the benevolent arbiters of much needed financial resources for district development. House of representative members frequently display their engagement for certain projects by placing easily noticeable plates, such as "This road was sponsored by Congressman XY." By doing so, the Congressman hopes to convince potential voters of his ability to improve the living conditions of 'his' people. Of course, the money comes from the national budget and not from the Congressman's own pockets. Very often, the national development funds are abused by irresponsible projects undertaken for private benefits and tactics aimed at the re-election date.

House of Representatives members are expected to deliver feasible results to their constituencies. Voters do not expect their congressman to argue on an abstract level or care about foreign policy, for instance, but rather focus on "bringing home money" from Manila. According to Dr Francisco Magno from the Institute of Governance of De La Salle University in Manila, "about 50 percent of Filipinos think in traditional and undemocratic ways and expect something from the candidates before they vote for them".[31] Scholar Alma Salvador added that "there is no connection between good governance and electoral win. Filipinos are not rational, when it comes to voting. Most of them think only in short-term gains."[32]

On the one hand, it is good in terms of electoral accountability that congressman care for the material welfare of their constituents by focusing on acquiring money from Manila. On the other hand, electoral accountability declines if there are structures of dependency between voters and candidates. Particularly in rural and less developed areas, feudal social structures persist, wherein the congressman is sometimes the employer of thousands of farm workers or other workers dependent on his patronage. In these patron-client relationships, voters that are clients have no other choice than to vote for their boss.

Political scientist Temario C. Rivera conducted a study about turnover rates for governors and representatives between 1987 and 2010 (Rivera 2011) and revealed extremely low figures across all provinces. He concluded that elections do not serve well as an accountability mechanism, since Philippine voters were both not able to select "good policies or policy-bearing politicians and to use elections as an instrument to hold governments responsible for the results of their past actions" (Rivera 2011, p. 73). The reason for

the ability of incumbent political families to win even in the provinces with the worst governance and socio-economic outcomes stress the fact that there are deep-seated structural problems (such as poverty and lack of education) and backward political-institutional practices (such as patronage networks, unregulated use of violence and coercion, and electoral manipulation) that systematically undermine the potential of elections to serve as accountability mechanisms (Rivera 2011, p. 73).

Vote-Buying/Manipulations

That the voting process itself not be flawed by manipulations and irregularities is a precondition for electoral accountability. One common technique of manipulation is vote-buying, which occurs regularly in remote and/or poor areas in the Philippines. Those who accept money from vote-buyers usually do not care about politics and have little hope that any of the candidates will improve their situation. Some hundred pesos (a few Euros) for a vote is an attractive offer. Of course, they know that the money comes from candidates with populist rhetoric who promise to fight poverty and, ironically, corruption. They are also aware that the campaigners, after being elected, do not always follow the interests and needs of the millions of impoverished people of the Philippines. Candidates are often sponsored by private businessmen, who try to gain some influence on political decisions and the protection of the political elite. In the Philippines, candidates are sponsored by rich individuals and corporate sponsors, but also tap into their private fortunes (Ufen 2008, p. 339). Financial reports have to be presented only during election times. Like in the United States, there is no ceiling for donations and contributions to candidates, but they must afterward be made public.

A difference must be made between free market votes and command votes (Perron 2008, p. 362). The former are gained – as in other democracies – by advertisements, speeches, slogans, and media presence. Just as in other democracies, TV advertisements are the most influential form of advertising in the Philippines. Even candidates who were less known, "obtained excellent results thanks to well-orchestrated and well-executed television campaigns" (Perron 2009, p. 633), while other candidates with less TV time lost ground in the polls.

The other form of votes are command votes won by previous arrangements. Senators, and to a lesser extent congressmen, face the difficulty of reaching voters in remote rural areas. They often rely on the help of local allies who promise to deliver votes from particular villages or districts for financial rewards (Reilly 2006, p. 100). These vote canvassers are often dubious figures, but nearly every Congressman has to resort to working with them. Congressman Nereus "Neric" Acosta from the Liberal Party described the situation during the election campaign as follows:

> In order to get elected as a district member of the House of Representatives you have to be Machiavellian, otherwise you will not get elected. You have to accept command votes, you have to work together with the local patrons, and with shady business figures. They all expect you to pay back. This is very hard for me to live with. In Philippine politics, it is very difficult to act in a right way but very easy to be a *trapo*.[33]

As Acosta explained, candidates must hire vote canvassers and bribe local strongmen for block votes from villages in order to have realistic chances to win elections. Jose de Venecia, former chairman of the House of Representatives, once stated that "it is the drug lords and the gambling lords ... who finance the candidates. So, from Day One, they become corrupt" (quoted in Hutchcroft 2008, p. 151).

Election related violence has constantly been declining in the last decade. However, in some cases, candidates of established political clans who are confronted in elections by feisty upstarts, still "tend to recruit the goons and gunmen who are so disastrously in Philippine political life" (Case 2011, p. 19). An infamous incident was the so-called Ampatuan Massacre in November 2009, when a private army of the Ampatuan clan in Maguindanao killed 58 people who were on their way to the province capital Shariff Aguak to file a certificate of candidacy for the political rival of the Ampatuans, gubernational candidate Esmael Mangudadatu.

Synchronized Elections

One of the peculiarities of the Philippine democracy is that elections for all public offices take place simultaneously. The presidential and vice-presidential elections are held on the same day as the elections for the House of Representatives, for half of the Senate, for the province governor, for the provincial legislature, for the mayor, and for the municipal council. Since 1998, the party-list representatives in the Congress are also elected on the same occasion.

The 1987 Constitution states in several articles that the elections shall be held on the second Monday of May. In these synchronized elections, Philippine voters are left with a huge number of decisions to make since so many public offices have to be filled on one occasion.

There are several arguments in support of synchronized elections. The government argues that this measure reduces public expenditures. Additionally, considering the infrastructural problems of many regions of the Philippines and the inconveniences caused by long travel and waiting hours, the mobilization of voters might be higher if all elections are on the same day. Furthermore, national politics can concentrate on a fixed term and do not have to care for electoral results in regional and local elections. Often, national governments hesitate to take unpopular actions in order not to lose support in disputed states that face elections. In countries where political parties are important players in national politics, regional and local elections are often used as a means to "punish" national government policies.

However, the synchronized election date also has some disadvantages, particularly in terms of electoral accountability. As many Philippine voters told the author, they are unaware of many of the candidates who run for executive or legislative positions except the presidency and to a lesser extent the Senate. This means that on voting day, the presidential election draws too much attention away from other elections which are perceived less relevant by the general public.

In order to enhance their own visibility, candidates for governor and mayor positions as well as national and regional council candidates plaster cities and villages with their banners and other advertising material, stage rallies and push their candidature by more or less extensive media campaigns. The simultaneous national and local elections "overload the capacity of political machineries, and often result in local party bosses paying more attention to local than national candidates" (Aguilar 2007, p. 79). Ordinary voters are usually very confused about which candidate is running for which position. This is a clear constraint to electoral accountability, since no voter can at the same time remember all together. In an attempt to address these issues, political networks create sample ballot papers which voters can use as a template to fill their ballots. If voters are eager to support one presidential candidate, they can see on the sample ballot papers which candidates are connected to the presidential candidate for governor, mayor, provincial, and municipal council. The frequent use of such sample ballot papers does not come as a surprise since it cannot be expected from an ordinary Philippine citizen to keep track of all the candidates in the different levels of government at the same time.

Ballot Paper and Automated Counting Machines

The ballot paper itself has been a barrier to electoral accountability. Until 2007, voters had to fill out a blank ballot paper, where only the positions to be elected were already visible. Since all votes are synchronized in the Philippines, every voter had to write in the names of a presidential candidate, a vice-presidential candidate, twelve senatorial candidates, a House of Representatives candidate, a gubernatorial candidate, several provincial council candidates, a mayor candidate, and several municipal council candidates at the same time on the ballot paper. It is obvious that the ordinary voter cannot easily cope with this task, since he or she has to remember all the names of the candidates at the various electoral levels.

Additionally, it was always a difficult task for the election authorities to decide on the correctness of handwritten names, particularly nicknames and abbreviations of names. This led to often enormous time delays for counting the votes, since polling officials had to decipher the handwriting of all voters, "including some less than fully literate, all the while dealing with complaints from watchful party officials who were 'certain' that the illegible scrawl was a vote for their candidate" (Meisburger 2010). It was also a common practice to launch so-called nuisance candidates with similar or identical names with that of the political opponent. A nuisance candidate is expected to create confusion among the voters by running against candidates with similar names. In some cases, COMELEC failed to quickly resolve disqualification cases against these nuisance candidates so that votes for the proper candidate were lost (Palatino 2010).

In the 2010 elections, two major reforms concerning voting were eventually implemented. Initially they look rather technical, but their effects contributed positively in increasing electoral accountability. For the first time in the national electoral history, the printed names of all candidates replaced blank lines, solving both the problematic task of learning and memorizing candidate names and the illegibility of handwriting. The pre-printed ballot papers were a useful measure both for giving voters more overview of whom they actually elect and for reducing possibilities to cheat in the vote counting process. The infamous method of electoral fraud in the Philippines was for a long time *dagdag-bawas* (add-subtract), wherein votes were subtracted from the opposition candidate and added to a favoured candidate by corrupt election officials during the vote counting process. A recent example was the 2007 senatorial elections in the Maguindanao province. Lintang Bedol, the former election supervisor of the province, admitted in 2011 that former President GMA had then instructed the local COMELEC officials to ensure that the votes garnered for the three opposition candidates, Panfilo Lacson, Alan Peter Cayetano, and Benigno Aquino, should be redirected to administration candidate Juan Miguel Zubiri (Holmes 2012, p. 83).

Another novelty in the 2010 elections was the countrywide introduction of automated counting machines. Despite all previous criticism about alleged bugs in the system and widespread fraud suspicions, the automated polling system helped for the speedy and accurate count of votes and effectively reduced the above mentioned *dagdag-bawas* practices (Abinales 2011, p. 165f.). The long time period between voting and the official announcement of results which raised concerns over the election's credibility was significantly reduced. The introduction of automated counting machines "represented a distinct improvement over the past. 65 percent of citizens felt that the use of the ... machines lessened cheating in the counting of votes" (Rood 2010). In the above mentioned province of Maguindanao, local clan boss Datu Andal Ampatuan lost the vice-gubernatorial elections against neophyte Ismael Mastura who later stated that "he would never have beaten Datu Andal without the speed of electronic counting of votes and transmission of votes, which prevented all post-election cheating" (Rood 2010).

Parties and Their Function in the Political System

Political parties are relatively weak in the Philippines. This is due to various reasons. One is the plurality election system, which was and is applied in all major elections with the exception of the mentioned party-list seats in the House of Representatives. Individual persons run for office and very often their party affiliation is unknown to the public. Like in the United States, congressmen are not known by their party but by their regional constituency. In the Philippines, people vote for persons and not for parties. Accordingly, on the ballot papers only the names and not the party affiliation are depicted.

The weakness of political parties does not stem only from the plurality election system, but from the combination of this electoral system with a presidential system of government. In a parliamentary system (like in the UK or Thailand), political parties are required to have at least some coherence and discipline in order to stabilize the government. In a presidential system of government, political parties are generally of less importance.

Another reason for the relative weakness of the political parties in the Philippines is their similarity and their short-livedness. Most political parties do not have meaningful party platforms. Additionally, all major parties are catch-all parties meaning they do not focus on a specific target group nor pretend to represent the interests of certain groups. Political ideologies do not develop into party platforms. A party system dominated by catch-all parties has some advantages. For instance, a radicalization of certain parties is unlikely and compromise and consensus are much easier to achieve. The danger, however, lies in the relative similarity of all major parties resulting in blurred contours.

Philippine political parties "lack cultural underpinnings, constitutional basis, public funding, and any organizational scaffolding at the branch level" (Case 2011, p. 13). Most parties are no older than 25 years. This is partly due to the return to democracy in 1986, but also due to the fact that nearly every presidential candidate functioned as founder of a political party. In December 1991, Fidel Ramos founded Lakas after not being nominated by LDP (*Laban ng Demokratikong Pilipino*, Struggle of Democratic Filipinos), the party of then-incumbent President Corazon Aquino. Before the 1998 elections, then Vice-President Joseph "Erap"

Estrada built up with LAMP (*Lapian ng Masang Pilipino*, Organization of the Filipino Masses) a powerful party supporting his successful presidential bid. At the same time, vice-presidential candidate GMA founded KAMPI (*Kabalikat ng Malayang Pilipino*, Partner of the Free Filipino) after leaving the LDP.

The Liberal Party, the party of President Noynoy Aquino, is an exception in the Philippine party system, since it was founded shortly after the country's independence in 1946. Even older is the Nationalist Party (*Nacionalista Party*), which was founded in 1907 and dominated politics in the colonial times, but has held importance until today.

Another aspect that contributes to the relative weakness of political parties within the political system of the Philippines is the frequent turncoatism of its party members. Since the parties do not reflect ideological differences or other cleavages, they serve merely as electoral vehicles. It occurs quite often that senators, congressmen, governors or mayors move to other parties. The reasons are usually of pragmatic nature, be it ambition, vested interests or political survival. These turncoats are often called "political butterflies" or *balimbing* (starfruit) in Filipino and describe a politician who switches parties for his own personal interests. In her long-term study that examined the period from 1946 to 2004, Yuko Kasuya found that roughly 40 per cent of incumbent House members, and roughly 25 per cent of the senators switched their party affiliation after elections (Kasuya 2009, p. 121). The stability of political parties is therefore relatively low. Political analyst Joel Rocamora commented: "Developed parties are not possible in the Philippines, since MPs do not want to follow a party line."[34]

Additionally, voters should know the political camp their representative belongs. It can make a difference if the candidate supports one presidential candidate or another one. Elected members of the House of Representatives, however, very often change their positions and party affiliation after the elections and turn to the camp of the winning presidential candidate. In 1992, for instance, the party of newly elected President Fidel Ramos, Lakas, won only a few seats in the House of Representatives. Soon afterwards, however, it became the biggest party due to a high number of other MPs joining the winning party. The same happened after the 1998 elections, when the party of winning candidate Joseph "Erap" Estrada soon became the dominant party group in Congress. Thus, one can conclude that "party affiliation is hardly existent in the Philippines. Sometimes it can be bought. This became evident during the ousting process of Estrada, when a 70 percent majority of Estrada's party turned into a 30 percent minority in the House of Representatives within a few weeks."[35] After the presidential elections in 2004, as well in 2010, the parties of the new president always received a high influx of MPs from other parties. The reasons for these party changes are clear. If they belong to the presidential followers, they increase their chances of accessing government funds, which in turn secures the support of their voters (this issue will be covered further in chapter 5.3).

The weakness of political parties and the frequent turncoatism of elected parliamentarians has several consequences for electoral accountability. Voters cannot predict their candidate's behaviour after becoming a Congressman. In a political system with a high party discipline, voters usually know in advance whether their candidate supports or will be in opposition to a certain government. In the Philippines, they very often have to learn that after the entrance into Congress, their candidate follows only his personal ambitions irrespective of his voters' attitude towards the administration. A shift from opposition to government support might not only be profitable for the MP but also for the whole constituency. Still, turncoatism can distort the voting intentions of the people electing a certain candidate.

This much criticized behaviour of politicians is in real danger, however. In 2010 and 2011, several senators started initiatives to prohibit political turncoatism demanding a ban for changes of political party affiliation within one year immediately preceding or following an election (Esguerra 2011). In December 2012, the House of Representatives passed the Political Party Development Act. If members change party affiliations, except within six months prior to the end of their term, they will lose their elective post, will be disqualified from running in the next elections, and prohibited from being appointed to any government office for three years (Calonzo 2012). This bill must be passed by the Senate to become effective.

Notes

1   The CDA for the 1997 constitution consisted of 99 members, with 76 elected by provincial assemblies and 23 appointed academics by the Parliament.
2   Interview with Naruemon Thabchumpon, Faculty of Political Science, Chulangalongkorn University, Bangkok, 14 August 2009.
3   Interview with Michael Nelson, Faculty of Political Science, Chulalongkorn University, Bangkok, 18 August 2009.
4   Interview with Suthipon Thaveechaiyagarn, Secretary General of the Election Commission of Thailand, 17 August 2009.

5   Interview with Ong-art Klampaiboon, Democrat Party, Minister to the Prime Minister's Office, Bangkok, 14 October 2010.

6   Interview with Prinya Thaewanarumitkul, Thammasat University, Bangkok, 18 August 2009.

7   Interview with Kittisak Prokati, Faculty of Law, Thammasat University, Bangkok, 13 August 2009.

8   Interview with Suthipon Thaveechaiyagarn, Secretary General of the Election Commission of Thailand, 17 August 2009.

9   Interview with Chaturon Chaisang, Former MP, Thai Rak Thai, Bangkok, 17 August 2009.

10 Interview with Nataphol Teepsuwan, Director General of Democrat Party, Member of the House of Representatives, Bangkok, 11 October 2010.

11 Interviews with several academics in Bangkok 2009 and 2010.

12 Interview with Kittisak Prokati, Faculty of Law, Thammasat University, Bangkok, 13 August 2009.

13 Interview with Kraisak Choonhavan, MP, Democrat Party, Bangkok, 17 August 2009.

14 Interview with Nataphol Teepsuwan, Director General of Democrat Party, Member of the House of Representatives, Bangkok, 11 October 2010.

15 Interview with Naruemon Thabchumpon, Faculty of Political Science, Chulangalongkorn University, Bangkok, 14 August 2009.

16 Ibid.

17 Interview with Nataphol Teepsuwan, Director General of Democrat Party, Member of the House of Representatives, Bangkok, 11 October 2010.

18 Interview with Kraisak Choonhavan, MP, Democrat Party, Bangkok, 17 August 2009.

19 Interview with Boonyad Sukthinthai, Democrat Party, Member of the House of Representatives, Bangkok, 14 October 2010.

20 Interview with Chaturon Chaisang, Former MP, Thai Rak Thai, Bangkok, 17 August 2009.

21 Authoritarian President Soeharto was re-elected six times between 1966 and 1998.

22 The Constitution of the Philippines (Filipino: *Saligang Batas ng Pilipinas*) was enacted in 1987 and is popularly known as the "1987 Constitution".

23 Ibid.

24 Interview with Nereus "Neric" Acosta, former member of the House of Representatives, Liberal Party, Manila, 6 September 2007.

25 Interview with Florencio "Butch" Abad, Former Secretary of Education, Manila, 12 September 2007.

26 Interview with Joel Rocamora, Director, Secretary of the National Anti-Poverty Commission, Quezon City, 5 October 2010.

27 Interview with Ronald "Ronnie" Holmes, Department of Political Science, De La Salle University, Manila, 24 August 2009.

28   Interview with Djorina Velasco (Institute for Popular Democracy), Quezon City, 22 August 2007.

29   Instead of the usual 24 senators, the Philippine Senate between 2010 and 2013 comprised only 22 senators. Elected senator Benigno Aquino was elected as President in May 2010 and elected senator Juan Miguel Zubiri, accused of electoral fraud, resigned in August 2011.

30   Interview with Mujiv Hataman, Member of the House of Representatives, party list A-MIN, Quezon City, 13 September 2007.

31   Interview with Francisco Magno, Executive Director, Institute of Governance, De La Salle University, Manila, 1 September 2009.

32   Interview with Alma Salvador, Assistant Professor at the Department of Political Science, Ateneo University, Quezon City, 6 October 2010.

33   Interview with Nereus "Neric" Acosta, former member of the House of Representatives, Liberal Party, Manila, 6 September 2007.

34   Interview with Joel Rocamora, Secretary of the National Anti-Poverty Commission, Quezon City, 5 October 2010.

35   Interview with Herwig Mayer, Program Manager, Decentralization Program of GTZ, Makati City, 2 September 2009.

4

THE VERTICAL
ACCOUNTABILITY DIMENSION

As explained in chapter 2.5, vertical accountability in this study refers to an accountability mechanism between central and local levels of a political system. Citizens and institutions at the local level are important by exercising accountability towards local governments and at the same time by exerting control over national politics.

In order to analyse institutional engineering in regard to vertical accountability, I will assess what kind of institutional reforms concerning local democracy and centre-local relations were undertaken in the three countries under research. I will start with the Philippines, followed by Indonesia, and then Thailand and an assessement of the respective legal frameworks in order to determine the level of autonomy and powers of local governments. Following, I will then examine the working of democracy at the local level. In a next step I will analyse the degree to which ethnic conflicts and separatism in the troubled regions of the three countries were impacted by the course of the decentralization process. Finally, I will take a closer look at the interactions between central and local governments and examine in which ways the accountability mechanisms are structured and work in practice.

4.1 THAILAND

Thailand had traditionally been ruled by bureaucratic elites, whose political struggles took place almost exclusively within the bureaucratic institutions of the centralist state. Frequent military coups and decades of authoritarian rule further strengthened the centralist tradition. Until today, the dominant legacy of centralized governance, which is deeply embedded in Thai society and politics, has been a major barrier to decentralization (Haque 2010, p. 686).

Thailand's political and economic power was and is concentrated in the capital, Bangkok. The next state sub-division is the provinces (*changwat*). Due to their relatively high number (about 80), in addition to the Bangkok Metropolitan Administration, the provinces have little importance in national politics. Traditionally, the role of each governor was to carry out the orders of the national government and to coordinate the work of the other sub-divisions. Among them are about 900 districts (*amphoe*), more than 7,000 sub-districts (*tambon*) and about 75,000 villages (*muban*). Before 1997 more than 90 per cent of the sales and excise taxes collected by local governments were transferred to Bangkok (Hunsacker, quoted in Hicken 2009, p. 117). Consequently, subnational government expenditures were less than 10 per cent of the national GDP prior to 1997.

The 1990s saw growing demands for more power by local groups outside Bangkok. At the same time, Thai politicians from various camps had to recognize that they "had to champion the notions of expanded democracy, one of which was greater self-government at sub-national levels along with the necessary decentralization of financial and human resources" (Mutebi 2005, p. 18). In the 1990s, Thailand witnessed a "gradual, but steady decentralization of the country's broader political system to allow for a growing number of social groups to gain access to the levers of power" (Mutebi 2008, p. 154).

Decentralization was a major issue during the negotiations of the 1997 Constitution, in which an unprecedented number of representatives of civil society took part. The 1997 Constitution, Chapter V, Section 78, made decentralization a directive principle of fundamental state policies by declaring that "the State shall decentralize powers to localities for the purpose of independence and self-determination of local affairs." Accordingly, Chapter IX, Section 282, stated that "the State shall give autonomy to the locality in accordance with the principle of self-government according to the will of the people in the locality" (Constitution of the Kingdom of Thailand 1997). In Section 284, all local government organizations were given autonomy in laying down policies for their governance, administration, personnel administration, and finance.

The decentralization initiative laid down by the 1997 Constitution turned away from the long tradition in Thailand of a unitary administrative system with a strong centralized government. Furthermore, "several clauses direct[ed] the central government to grant greater authority and autonomy to local level government organs so as to permit greater grassroots pluralist participation and input" (Chambers 2002, p. 21).

The Decentralization Act of 1999 donned further autonomy to local governments, the financial decentralization benchmarks being particularly remarkable. They mandated "that local revenues shall be at least 20% and 35% of the government's total revenue in the fiscal years of 2001 and 2006, respectively" (Amornvivat 2004, p. 6). This was in accordance with the re-shifting of tasks personnel from national agencies to local governments. The number of local government officials grew more than 100 per cent (Wongpreedee 2009, p. 4).

Decentralization took influence away from the former centralized bureaucratic elites and gave it to more powerful positions and personalities from outside the bureaucracy, such as local entrepreneurs and traditional local leaders. Among these new local economic and political elites were also a number of "Sino-Thai businessmen and the so-called *chao-poh*, or provincial, mafia-like bosses" (Mutebi 2008, p. 154). The beginning of the democratization process led to a situation in which the former all-deciding bureaucratic and military elites had to deal with these new emerging civilian politicians. Political power and rents had to be shared with and among them.

In accordance with Section 285 of the 1997 Constitution, local executives, such as mayors and members of local councils were directly elected by local citizens. Section 286 was particularly important in terms of electoral accountability. It deemed that mayors and local councilors could be voted out of office by a three-fourths majority of the voters.

The 2007 Constitution promulgated after the military coup kept the essence of the decentralization provisions of the previous constitution. Most parts remained untouched. Some articles were given more detail. For example, Chapter IX, Section 284, determined that local administrators, local assemblies, and local administrative committees must be directly elected by the people in a secret ballot. Chapter IX, Section 284, did not allow local administrators to hold another permanent government or state enterprise position. Section 288 stressed – as demanded by the coup-makers – the importance of building up systems for the protection of virtue and ethics. In the same article the previously mentioned possibility of voting administrators out of office was removed.

Level of Autonomy and Quality of Democracy at the Local Level

The level of autonomy for local governments in Thailand can best be seen by its percentage of the total national revenues. Table 4.1 depicts the effects of fiscal decentralization in proportion of LAOs (local administrative organizations) revenues from the total national revenues in million baht.

Table 4.1
Revenues of National and Local Governments in Thailand

Fiscal Year	LAOs Revenues	National Revenues	Proportion of LAOs of Total Revenues
1996	60,663	850,458	7.13 %
1999	105,036	708,826	14.82 %
2002	176,803	803,651	22.00 %
2005	293,750	1,250,000	23.50 %
2008	376,740	1,495,000	25.20 %
2009	400,338	1,550,496	25.82 %
2010			25.26 %
2011			26.14 %

Sources: Wongpreedee (2007. p. 7), Tanchai (2010, p. 12), and Mansrisuk (2012, p. 93).

As can be seen, local revenues increased steadily since the mid-1990s. The total number of LAO's revenues is now more than six times that of 1996. Similarly, their proportional share from all national revenues strongly increased, particularly until 2002, and then grew at a slow pace. The level of 35 per cent, which has been a target of fiscal decentralization in the Decentralization Act of 1999, has, however, not yet been reached.

Since a high number of services were devolved to the local level without adequate funding from the national government, LAOs are financially dependent on the national government (Mansrisuk 2012, p. 93). The possibilities for their own income-generating measures, such as local taxes, are limited. The grants from the central government are often not predictable and lead to financial uncertainty at the local level. Additionally, the local administrative structures do not have financial autonomy since the budgets of local governments are subject to approval from the governors.

These governors are bureaucrats appointed by the Ministry of Interior (MoI) and are hence under the control of the national government. The only exceptions are the Bangkok Metropolitan Administration and Pattaya City, where the governor and the mayor respectively are publicly elected. The governors monitor and coordinate the activities of the elected local governments in their respective provinces and report to the MoI. Political scientist Naruemon Thabchumpon explained: "The removal of [non-elected] governors for political reasons is very difficult, since they are elite bureaucrats, who made their career in the Ministry of Interior. In the ongoing conflict between red and yellow the governors play safe and stay in power."[1]

However there are indications that – not in complete contrast to previous times – politically motivated removals and relocations of governors took place after the military coup in 2006. In March 2009, 22 province governors were replaced by the MoI under Minister Chaovarat Chanweerakul from the Democrat Party. When asked, the minister nevertheless denied that this step was intended to remove officials close to former Prime Minister Thaksin Shinawatra, but insisted rather that "when provincial governors are getting too familiar with their areas, they should move on" (The Nation Online 2009).

In 2010, several province governors, particularly in Northern and Northeastern provinces – the electoral strongholds of the then opposition – were replaced by the national government. Deputy Interior Minister Boonjong Vongtrirat explained that some of them were sent to other provinces since they "failed to prevent city halls from being burned by protestors of the United Front of Democracy Against Dictatorship during the political unrest" (Saelee 2010) in May and June 2010. However, some former governors complained that their transfer was unfair and politically motivated (Bangkok Post Online 2010). In Thailand's second biggest city, Chiang Mai, the Ministry of Interior appointed Panadda Diskul, "known for his royalist stand ... [and] an opponent of ex-PM Thaksin. His move to Thaksin's home-town at the time of polarization between red and yellow shirts might signal a campaign to subdue red 'influence' in the northern province" (The Nation Online 2010). The governors are treated as a proxy of the national government at the province level. They depend on the support of the government party-controlled Ministry of Interior. Thus, they are not accountable to the local citizens but rather to the central government.

If governors were to be directly elected by their constituents, there would be a different kind of provincial administration. Instead of bureaucrats, politicians who could prove themselves to be capable political leaders would enter the scene. Additionally, some provinces would be led by governors who might strongly oppose the national government in Bangkok. Until now, the national government in Bangkok "exercises direct control over policy for the entire nation, including those regions where it enjoys little support" (Harding and Leyland 2011, p. 134). Devolution would result in a weakening of the power of the national government. This meets heavy resistance from the national elites despite the statement of a Democrat Party MP who said that, to him, "it would be no problem if the red groups control several local governments."[2] The direct election of governors is not the main target of further decentralization, despite then Minister Ong-art Klampaiboon's statement that "after the direct election of mayors, we can think also of a direct election of the governors in a next step."[3]

In contrast to the governors, mayors and members of the local councils are usually politicians with party affiliations. Since 2000, all local administrators, such as mayors and councilors at the sub-district, municipal, and village levels, have to be elected in their respective constituencies. To some extent, local accountability has been improved with increased public participation at the community level (Suwanmala and Weist 2009, p. 216). However, in many cases local elections did not work effectively as accountability mechanisms because the "functions of local elections have been distorted by local elites, who ... [abused decentralization] as a means to access devolved authority and financial resources" (Mansrisuk 2012, p. 73). It must be recognized though that the decentralization-led reforms deepened the appreciation of the people's representation through elections at the local level, generated a sense of accountability among local government representatives, and expanded the scope for interaction among diverse stakeholders (Haque 2010, p. 682).

Additionally, decentralization led to a politicization of ordinary Thai citizens. Until the start of decentralization, people living in the villages were often not much interested in politics. The local patron was responsible for keeping ties with the provincial and the national level, and the local bureaucrats followed their orders from Bangkok. Today, local people care, at least to some extent, about local politics since they are allowed to cast their votes. Additionally, the two major national parties, the Democrat Party and the TRT (and its successor parties) have started to extend local party branches, which were financially supported by the Political Party Development Fund from the national government (Sirivunnabood 2013).

In Thai local politics, mayors try to get as many council members in their camps in order to secure support for their policies. Usually, a mayor has broad support from the voters as well as from the council members. However, there are still possibilities for a gridlock at the local level. In times of high tension between political camps, for instance the yellow-red split in society, opposition council members will try to undermine the mayor's policies. Opposition assemblymen also often question municipal executives, if their personal business interests are not served adequately (Wongpreedee and Mahakanjana 2006, p. 69), but they have no right to remove them.

Gridlocks and power struggles at the local level often attract the attention of national elites who prefer local affairs to run smoothly. The centralist past creates deep-rooted negative attitudes of national politicians and bureaucrats towards local autonomy and devolution. In interviews with these people from the national arena, many arguments can be heard opposing further decentralization in Thailand. One of the most frequently stated arguments is of a financial nature: "In rural areas, there are not enough taxpayers and the local government needs too much money from the central government."[4] This might be true for less developed areas that would be financially dependent on Bangkok even with greater autonomy. Other better developed regions, however, would have no problems to finance themselves.

Another argument is that "for further decentralization, Thailand does not have enough professional politicians"[5] and "capable persons at the local level".[6] There is a grain of truth in these assessments, since indeed in some areas local politicians are linked to powerful local clans, or pursue their own interests as the top prerogative. As an MP from the Democrat Party stated,

> so many of the local government leaders are in the construction business, since they hope they can make personal profit from their government jobs. There are also some mafia clans, who control certain districts (e.g. Chonburi, Rayong, or Pattaya) and are less suited as local government heads.[7]

There are many people, particularly in the conservative camp, who do not believe in the benefits of decentralization. They argue that a well-educated, independent, non-politicized, non-corrupt central bureaucracy with high ethical standards can better deal with government affairs than ordinary rural folks, who are politicized, corrupt, dependent on their patrons, and have dubious moral standards. The Secretary General of the

Election Commission of Thailand (ECT) simply stated: "Decentralization does not work since the people are not ready for this."[8]

A more detailed analysis, which nevertheless goes in the same direction, comes from an MP in the Democrat Party:

> A serious problem of decentralization is that the local people with power, such as mayors, might abuse this power. Decentralization can work in Bangkok, since the people understand local politics, but in the provinces, there are not enough qualified people. Additionally, at the local level, ordinary people are often attached by relationships to those in power. They vote for who benefits them personally and not for who may be the best for the city.[9]

Though one should be careful when generalizing about experiences in some regions, it seems quite logical to assess that "if there is real decentralization, then there would be more corruption at the local level."[10] The more financial resources a local government receives, the higher the opportunities for abuse. In many cases, "elected local government representatives had favored their families and cronies to get government contracts" (Haque 2010, p. 684). However, there are also good examples of local governments spending their revenues in a transparent and effective manner. Corrupt and criminal individuals are not only active at the local level.

Statements, such as that of an MP who claimed that "in the countryside, there is more corruption than in big cities" and concludes that "[d]ecentralization must therefore be implemented step by step"[11] are typical of those who delay further decentralization. The motivation of national politicians is not only the fear of misuse of public money but also their own decline of power if local autonomy were strengthened. Consequently, much resistance against a further devolution of power and money is still prevalent among the national elite. Nataphol Teepsuwan, director general of the Democrat Party, admitted: "The attempt to strengthen the local level was not successful as was originally intended. There was a lot of resistance from those who have the benefits from the central state structure. If the local governments become powerful, they would have to divide the cake into pieces."[12]

Conflict in Southern Thailand

A recent academic debate arose as to whether Thailand is a homogeneous or pluralistic country. If the latter is the case, some mechanism of power-sharing between the majority population and the various minorities could lead to better conflict management between these social groups. However, this topic is very sensitive for those who demand further decentralization. Duncan McCargo, professor of Southeast Asian politics commented:

> If you talk to people on all sides of the political divide they recognize the need for decentralization of power, but it is unspeakable. Admitting you need to decentralize power in the south is to admit there is a problem with the legitimacy of the Thai state. And to admit that is to go back to what the Thai state is based on, which is arguably the shibboleth of the nation, religion, king. Once you start to admit there is a problem with that, you are in danger of treasonous sentiments (quoted in Szep 2011).

The Southern provinces of Thailand are of particular importance for reforms aiming at decentralization and local autonomy. In the provinces of Pattani, Yala, and Narathiwat, the majority of the population are ethnic Malays with an adherence to Islam. A resistance movement became very active and demanded far-reaching autonomy or an independent (Islamic) state. Since 2004, violence has further escalated. In a huge number of small-scale incidents more than 5,000 people have been killed and roughly 10,000 wounded between 2004 and 2012. How many of these victims are directly attributable to separatist militancy is not yet clear. Common criminality and extrajudicial killings by state (or state-backed) forces must also be considered (International Crisis Group 2012, p. 4).

The escalation of the conflict arose during the government of Prime Minister Thaksin Shinawatra (2001–06), who pursued a centralist course and imposed martial law for the Southern provinces in 2004. A politician from the Democrat Party noted: "Thaksin had a very bad approach to the conflict in Southern Thailand. He wanted to wipe out the insurgents."[13]

A National Reconciliation Commission, under former Prime Minister Anand Panyarachun, criticized the military aggression and demanded a dialogue with Islamic forces. The Commission proposed to allow parts of the Islamic law as well as that Malay be an official second language in the Southern provinces. These proposals have not yet been realized, as they met opposition from the military and nationalist politicians in Bangkok. Kraisak Choonhaven, an MP from the Democrat Party, stated that he wants peace through dialogue, "but unfortunately there still are so many colleagues in my party who agree with the militarization in the South. I am against it, like 30 percent of my party's MPs, mostly heads of Southern members of the Democrat Party."[14] The South of Thailand is strongly dominated by the Democrat Party (Askew 2008).

Prime Minister Abhisit Vejjajiva (2008–11) often stressed that he would look for a peaceful solution for the conflict and channelled additional financial resources in the conflict area without ending the bloodshed. An MP from the Democrat Party explained that "if Abhisit would have had a more stable coalition, he would have agreed with the demands of the Southerners. But he was dependent on military support."[15]

Despite the ongoing conflict, no specific institutional reforms in favour of local autonomy have been undertaken. After the military coup in 2006, the new government re-installed the Southern Border Provinces Administration Center, which Prime Minister Thaksin had previously dissolved. Since then, many conflict mediation attempts by the international donor community as well as by neighbouring countries such as Malaysia, Indonesia, and the Philippines, brought no substantial results. The failure of all the initiatives has to do with the attitude of the central governments in Bangkok but also by the lack of interest in the general public. As an MP from the Democrat Party stated, "many Thais don't care about the problems in the South. The central Bangkok elitism is difficult to overcome, which has to do with Thai nationalism, including the monarchy."[16]

Many Thais have a strong nationalism expressed in the official state ideology "Chat, Satsana, Phra Mahakasat" (ชาติ ศาสนา พระมหากษัตริย์, Nation, Religion, King), which was already mentioned previously. Many Muslims in the South cannot identify themselves with these three principles, particularly since religion in the above mentioned state motto is translated as Buddhism. If the interests and demands for autonomy of the Muslim population in Southern Thailand are not taken seriously, a resolution seems unlikely. In the long run, a form of devolution with power-sharing features and greater autonomy, as in Aceh, might be the only viable solution to end the violent conflict (Harding and Leyland 2011, p. 154f.). However, considering the general reluctance of Thai national elites for further decentralization, this will still need quite some time.

Interaction between Centre and Periphery

During the rule of Prime Minister Thaksin Shinawatra, the devolution of tasks to the local level was impeded by his centralist CEO-style of government, which he enforced on the subnational levels. Governors were no longer under the tutelage of the Ministry of the Interior but were instead under the direct command of the office of the prime minister. By doing so, these CEO-like governors effectively became the "lieutenants of Thai Rak Thai" in the provinces, providing a much greater degree of control for Thaksin across the nation, and thus helping him to extend his tenure in power (Chambers 2002, p. 31; Mutebi 2004, p. 46). Thaksin thus assumed the governors to be his assistants in the provinces, which had the power to punish or promote other lower-level local officials under their jurisdiction (Painter 2005, p. 12). New CEO governors for all provinces across the country were appointed by the Thaksin government until 2003.

These governors started to no longer simply pass national funds on to local governments, but rather exercised direct control over their expenditure plans (Painter 2005, p. 13). The practiced CEO-style policy was not in accordance with the principles of decentralization as demanded by the 1997 Constitution. Power and financial autonomy were not devolved to local authorities. In contrast, the powers of representatives of central authorities at the provincial level were enhanced. Additionally, the Thaksin government bypassed all subnational organizations and transferred remarkable financial means under the so-called "village fund scheme" directly to the village level. Until the military coup in September 2006, the implementation of the decentralization reforms were obstructed and delayed by these measures (Mansrisuk 2012, p. 85).

After the *coup d'état* in 2006, the conflict between the red and yellow shirts has drawn public attention away from the issue of decentralization. In the years after the introduction of decentralization in the 1997 Constitution, local autonomy and government were frequently debated in the political and academic sphere. This has changed to some degree. A minister of the Abhisit government explained in 2010 that "currently, the Thai society doesn't talk very much about decentralization. So, the Democrat Party has other priorities than to push for more decentralization."[17] The government under Prime Minister Yingluck Shinawatra did not prioritize decentralization among its policies as well after the election victory of the Pheu Thai Party in 2011.

It therefore comes as no surprise that although decentralization was demanded by the 1997 Constitution, the implementation has been rather half-hearted and with much foot-dragging. Bureaucrats at the national level "opportunistically thwarted and distorted the reform in the implementation process, frustrating many of the reformers' original goals" (Mansrisuk 2012, p. 73). National politicians and bureaucrats continue to affect the decisions of elected LAOs through different forms of pressure or influence (Haque 2010, p. 685). The local governments thus enjoy no full autonomy and have to accept too many directions from their superior bureaucrats instead of listening to their constituents (Wong 2007, p. 177).

The dependence on support from above becomes particularly feasible in financial matters. Whereas some grants are automatically transferred to LAOs for service delivery, specific grants require written project proposals, and "are often used by the approving political authorities to expand their political control and influence over the local government" (Haque 2010, p. 683). A major incentive for local businessmen to spend expensive campaigns for local office elections is that this local government position gives the holder access to district and provincial bureaucrats and opportunities to establish mutually helpful relations with them (Arghiros 2001, p. 223). A mayor from a Northern province explained: "if we have a good connection with those national politicians who supervise the Department of Local Administration, we have a better chance to get specific grants comparing to those who do not" (quoted in Chardchawarn 2010, p. 31).

Not only in this case are local politics closely tied to national politics. Instead of formal political structures or citizen-directed political activities, informal, mostly invisible, local political groups or cliques called *phakphuak* or *phuak* in Thai dominate local politics (Nelson 2005, p. 8). Members of the House of Representatives often act as patrons in their constituencies. This patronage is exercised in such a way that relatives, friends, and business partners of the national MPs run as candidates for positions in local governments and often get elected. In turn, these local officials help the House member in the national election campaign and vice-versa (Bowornwathana 2006, p. 31).

The House members thus have an interest in creating dependencies with local government officials. Until 2007, "the MPs were regarded as legislator on the national level and problem solver in his or her constituency."[18] The 2007 Constitution, however, tried to stop this long-lasting tradition. Chapter XII, Section 266, ruled out that MPs interfere or intervene in matters concerning the local administration. Courts and the upper levels of bureaucracy should have control over them, not politicians.

The intention of this constitutional provision was to have neutral and non-politicized government structures at the local level. In practice, however, the power of local patrons seems to be unbroken. Many national MPs "exert influence to create local-level spoils, and plunder projects to channel money to their own pockets" (Haque 2010, p. 684). The result of local elections depends on the candidates' connections with national level politicians, particularly MPs. Political cronyism and family ties have led members of powerful local clans to lead nearly all local governments (Wongpreedee 2007, p. 462).

Both sides, the local as well as the national elites, profit from close cooperation. An obstacle for the continuity of national-local relations was the two-term maximum of office for the elected executives of LAOs. After persistent efforts by local politicians, the national parliament skipped the term limits for local government executives in 2009 (Chardchawarn 2010, p. 37).

Some reforms towards decentralization have been undertaken in Thailand, but the question remains whether they can be rated as real devolution or rather a deconcentration. The dual system of elected local governments and appointed central government officials at the provincial level contradict each other. The struggle between supporters and opponents of further local autonomy and vertical accountability between the central and the local levels will continue in the forthcoming years. The further development of decentralization in Thailand, with its "deeply engrained cultural acceptance of a highly centralized administrative system" (Wong 2007, p. 176), is more difficult than in other countries in Southeast Asia.

4.2 INDONESIA

Under the authoritarian New Order (1966–98), Indonesia was one of the most centralized countries in the world. Like other authoritarian regimes, the national government pursued a practice of mass de-politicization. In Indonesia, the so-called "floating mass policy" did not allow any political or party activities below the provincial level. As a result, local policies were dominated by appointed bureaucrats who implemented decisions from above.

The start of the democratization process in 1998 also marked the beginning of a decentralization process. Soeharto's successor, B.J. Habibie, made decentralization one of the major focus points on his political agenda. The attempt to introduce democracy at various local levels, rather than only at the national level in the capital, Jakarta, was one of the main incentives for such an ambitious undertaking. Decentralization and reform was thought to "open more space to nurture the emergence of local democracy" (Sulistiyanto and Erb 2009, p. 3), which had been denied to the people during the authoritarian period. Habibie ordered a team of bureaucrat-academics around Ryaas Rasyid to come up with a draft for a legal framework that would decentralize the country. They opted for a "big bang" solution, which would introduce new administrative structures as fast as possible in order to make them irreversible. Rapid introduction was also necessary since the new freedom after the demise of the authoritarian regime revitalized various ethnic and regional conflicts all over the archipelago, which had previously been suppressed by force. Various separatist movements gained momentum, inspired by the precedent set when East Timor left Indonesia after a referendum in August 1999. President Habibie responded to these movements by arguing that with decentralization the possibility of micro-nationalism, which could sow the seeds of disintegration, would be eliminated (Habibie 2006, p. 278). In order to keep the unity of the country, a reform was inevitable.

At this time, the constitutional changes that reduced the powers of the president were not yet implemented characterizing Habibie's presidency by an enormous power of discretion which none of his successors would have. The short time between the resignation of Soeharto (May 1998) and the election of Abdurrahman Wahid as the new president (October 1999) represented a window of opportunity for radical change. If decentralization would have been initiated afterwards in cooperation with the parliament and the numerous political parties and interests, a "big bang" solution had never been possible.

So, a complete fiscal and political decentralization process was started. Laws No. 22/1999 (on Regional Governance) and No. 25/1999 (on Fiscal Balance between the Center and the Regions) led to an enormous restructuring process. With the exception of a few tasks (foreign policy, defense and security, monetary policy, judicial system, and religious affairs), all public tasks were transferred to the local level. Sixty per cent of government revenues were diverted within a few years from the centre to regencies and cities (Harvard Kennedy School Indonesia Program 2010, p. 74). Approximately 2.6 million public servants were transferred to local administrations. While in 1999, 3.5 million government officials worked for the central government, this number was reduced to only

0.9 million by 2002. The inverse occurred at the local level; the number of civil servants in local governments rose from 0.5 million to 3.1 million (Rohdewohld 2003, p. 260).

The two laws of 1999 re-organized the internal power relations between central and local level and led to a vertical power-sharing constellation between these two layers of government. In striking contrast to the decentralization processes in other countries, however, was the fact that power was devolved to the third tier of government; the regencies (*kabupaten*) and urban municipalities (*kota*). The second tier, the provinces, were given only limited powers because of "historical and re-emergent challenges to the nation state and separatist threats from some disaffected provinces" (Morrell 2010, p. 51). After the end of authoritarian rule many decision-makers feared that "Indonesia might be pulled apart by strong regional interests" (Harvard Kennedy School Indonesia Program 2010, p. 90). Insofar, the dispersion of power among several hundred regencies and municipalities seemed to be less dangerous to the integrity of the state than did the decentralization of power to some provinces.

Another aim was the deepening of the democratization process. In this regard, the Indonesian government has "crafted and implemented administrative and political decentralization as a way of consolidating their new democracy at local levels" (Choi 2011, p. 20). President Habibie stated that democracy should be reflected "through the way in which governance was practiced in the regions" (Habibie 2006, p. 275). The decision to particularly strengthen the regency level was also influenced by the argument that shifting authority to the local level would promote democratization, since local communities were regarded as having a greater awareness of local needs. Citizens were seen as showing more commitment to local politics than with provincial or national affairs. The Indonesian model of local autonomy should thus "bring decision-making to a level where communities were more inclined to participate and where they could hold politicians accountable for their actions" (Aspinall and Fealy 2003, p. 4). However, one should be aware that the political and personal objectives of various stakeholders still typically dictate the nature and implementation of decentralization, rather than democratic ideals (Seymour and Turner 2002, p. 48).

The Indonesian government avoided calling the decentralization programme a transfer to a federal state, since the term "federalism" has negative connotations due to a history of Dutch colonial power, which prevented the creation of a unitary Indonesian state. Instead, the term "regional autonomy" (*otonomi daerah*) was coined for the decentralization process. The constitutional changes from August 2002 introduced the legislation on regional autonomy in the national constitution. According to the constitution, Indonesia remained a unitary state (Article 11, Section 1), but in Article 18, Section 5, it also states that regional administration shall exercise the broadest possible autonomy. To appease those who feared the end of national unity, the concept of Indonesia as a unitary state (*negara kesatuan*) was underlined with its prominent position as the first sentence of the constitution after the preamble. The alleged contradiction between far reaching local autonomy and a unitary state was solved by placing these two principles in a sort of coexistence. The "father" of decentralization in Indonesia, Ryaas Rasyid, described the measures as a compromise between highly centralist and federal systems and an acceptable middle-way solution (Rasyid 2003, p. 63f.). From a global perspective, the Indonesian approach is unique in that it is more decentralized than federal democratic states.

In the first years of decentralization, local governments made full use of their newly acquired powers. Confusion about competences, lack of experience as well as in some cases plain mismanagement of local governments led to adjustments by the central government. The lack of legal coherence led to various attempts to improve the cooperation between central and local governments. These reforms tried "to balance the initial moves to sub-national autonomy with better oversight and coordination from higher level government agencies" (Harvard Kennedy School Indonesia Program 2010, p. 90). Law No. 32/2004 on Regional Administration and Law No. 33/2004 on Fiscal Balance between Central and Regional Governments modified and specified the existing regulations on decentralization. Province authorities were given monitoring and coordinating functions for local governments on behalf of the centre. Law No. 32/2004 was "the result of a complex series of compromises involving not only the government and the political parties in the DPR but also bureaucrats at the national and regional levels" (Crouch 2010, p. 341).

Level of Autonomy

Law No. 32/2004 curtailed some rights of the local government, such as the rules for hiring and dismissing local civil servants. In addition, the national Ministry of Finance gained more authority *vis-à-vis* local governments since the ex-ante approval of local budgets became obligatory. Hence, the years of complete budget autonomy for the local governments were over (Harvard Kennedy School Indonesia Program 2010, p. 90). However, they still had "a degree of financial freedom which allows them fundamental independence when making political decisions for the regions within the framework of existing legislation" (Lustermann 2002, p. 15). The degree of financial independence of the regencies and cities is, however, dependent on the existence of natural resources and tax revenues. East Kalimantan, for example, can generate relatively high tax revenues through the availability of timber, oil, natural gas, coal and gold. These regencies and cities are financially autonomous and not at all dependent on government. Others that lack these opportunities have to rely on national government subsidies. Law No. 33/2004 provided for a fiscal equalization scheme, named DAU (*dana alokasi umum*), which is the main source of income for several less developed regencies, particularly in the Eastern parts of the country.

The national Ministry of Finance is responsible for overseeing local budgets and distributing financial transfers from the national to the local. In the initial years of decentralization, local governments had enormous difficulties delivering their budget records to the Ministry of Finance in a proper form. The Secretary of the Directorate General of Fiscal Balance in the Ministry of Finance of Indonesia explained that he received a huge amount of printed data which were of very low quality ("it was a nightmare"[19]). In the meantime, the data communication is digitalized and the Ministry of Finance has the right to sanction late or incorrect data delivery from local governments by cutting financial allotments. Regencies and cities can establish public policies by issuing local regulations (*peraturan daerah*), which impact political, economic and social life in the respective community to a great extent. Usually, these local regulations are checked by the Ministry of Home Affairs for conformity with constitutional principles.

There are few examples in the world in which regencies and cities enjoy such enormous autonomy and scope of action as those in Indonesia. It is highly attractive in terms of power and the production of income for local elites to create their "own" regency/city and to become a *bupati*, or mayor, to run a local administration. Not only local politicians, but also national elites had an interest in gaining regional influence and seats for their respective political parties (Kimura 2007, p. 95). Between 1996 and 2007, the number of regencies and cities grew from 297 to 456. Increases have occurred in all parts of the country, but most significantly in the rather sparsely populated outer islands. Kalimantan witnessed an increase from 29 to 53 *kabupaten*, Sulawesi 40 to 69, while in Maluku and Papua the number of regencies grew from 18 to 45 (McWilliam 2011, p. 152). The official reasons for encouraging this substantial rise in administrative units (*pemekaran*) are typically expressed in terms of two main objectives, namely, to improve the welfare of citizens in the new areas and the related goal of encouraging development to reduce the economic disparities between new and original (*induk*) regions (McWilliam 2011, p. 152).

However, the newly created regions added more problems than they solved. As a high-ranking official from the national Ministry of Finance explained: "*Pemekaran* is a bad practice, since local leaders are driven by short-time financial gains."[20] A study from the National Planning Board revealed that the divided regions are generally not in a better situation compared with the initial situation and undivided regencies (Bappenas 2008, p. 31). In fact, the creation of new regions caused an increase in regional inequality (Brata 2008, p. 9). Consequently, the national Ministry of Interior has become more and more reluctant to allow the splitting of regencies.

At the local level, there are also strong barriers to further implementation of the decentralization process. Problems often occur since the legal framework is inconsistent and not clearly defined. In many cases, local administrations hesitate to spend money for public service delivery because they doubt the legality of their actions. Some mayors and regency leaders (*bupati*) have been convicted of illegal spending of public money, though sometimes they acted unintentionally. However, the corruption at the local level has risen enormously. Since local elites can decide on large amounts of money, they are more tempted to do favours or to put cash in their own pockets. While the national government was previously the centre of bribery attempts, since they decided on public contracts, it is now the local level which takes precedent.

In some regencies and municipalities, decentralization has been accompanied by the rise of local *preman* (gangsters) (Hadiz 2010, p. 119ff.). Local bosses, corruptors and thugs "have been innovative in capturing the new democratic spaces provided by the dismantling of the Soeharto empire and the centralized state" (Antlöv 2003, p. 72). Money politics and corruption have spread to nearly everywhere in local politics. Since it became so attractive in terms of power and money, squabbles and fights to influence the local administration and exploit (natural) resources turned into a frequent feature of local politics.

Since local governments can also appoint several well-paid permanent or temporary positions, there is also the danger of patronage. It is a common practice that frequent changes (*mutasi*) between the local areas of responsibility lead to a loss in capacity. The decentralization of political decision-making has also led to a decentralization of corruption. At least 60 per cent of the local budget is spent for personnel, so that there is often a lack of money for the delivery of a minimum of service standards and poverty alleviation. Local authorities often lack a solid professional qualification and have many difficulties in fulfilling their new responsibilities. Particularly, in many cases they are not able to fulfill their constitutional tasks due to a lack of competence, skills, and financial resources. In general, however, the problems of local administrations are not caused by a weak financial framework but rather by difficulties during the implementation process.

Reforms Concerning Democracy at the Local Level

After the introduction of decentralization in 1999, Law No. 22/1999 ruled out that the regent/regency leaders (*bupati*) and mayors (*walikota*) were elected by the local parliaments (DPRD), which in turn were directly elected every five years. The right to elect the local leader gave the DPRDs a "tremendous amount of power" (Sulistiyanto and Erb 2009, p. 18). Local councilors and their respective political parties often demanded money from potential candidates for the position of regency leader or mayor. In turn, candidates tried to outbid each other in the amount of money designated for DPRD members and often the candidates who spent the most money on the local legislators became regency leaders or mayors.

Every year the *bupati* or mayor had to present an accountability report (*laporan pertanggungjawaban*) of his or her activities, which had to be approved by the DPRD. It soon became evident that DPRDs all over the archipelago used this right for personal rent-seeking purposes. As a compensation for their approval, many DPRD members throughout Indonesia asked for money. If a *bupati* or mayor wanted to be elected and/or have his or her annual accountability report accepted, he or she had to bribe the legislators. If they did not get enough, they refused to grant discharge to the local leader. Local governments were thus often held hostage by powerful DPRDs. Since these practices spread all over Indonesia and discredited the whole decentralization process, the national government soon opted to reform the procedure of electing local leaders.

The above mentioned Law No. 32/2004 removed the DPRD's right to select local government heads. The local regent/regency leaders and mayors were now elected directly by their constituents. This direct election for all executive positions in local government termed *pilkada* (*pilihan kepala daerah*) transformed local politics in many regards. The accountability reports, which were previously often misused by DPRDs to extort heads of regions, were transformed into mere progress reports of which the local legislators had only to take notice. Since the heads of local government are now directly elected by the people the balance of power between executive and legislative has become more even (Kumorotomo 2009, p. 5f.).

Starting from mid-2005, Indonesia effectively has a presidential system not only at the national level, but also at the local level, with a clear separation of powers between the executive and legislative branches at the local level. The reformation led to a situation in which local parliaments no longer had the function of picking regional leaders. Rather the vote is in the hands of the local people. The direct election gives more legitimacy and a stronger popular mandate to local leaders. Proponents of the direct local elections further argued that this form of election would reduce corruption, as local parliaments could no longer blackmail candidates (Buehler 2010*b*, p. 271).

However, another form of "money politics" emerged, since Law No. 32/2004 stated that a pair of candidates for governor and vice-governor, *bupati* and vice-*bupati*, mayor and vice-mayor must be proposed by political parties with 15 per cent of the votes or seats in the DPRD. The idea of allowing independent candidates to run for local government leadership, which was suggested by the Ministry of Home Affairs and supported by diverse civil society organizations, was dropped by the national parliament (DPR) in 2004. For obvious reasons, the political parties in the DPR voted to credit political parties as the major mechanism for recruiting local political leaders and officials. Political parties thus played an important role as gatekeepers for the access to local leadership. At several occasions, however, political parties misused this role by demanding money from potential candidates in order to become the "vehicle" or "boat" for the candidates to carry them through the election process (Sulistiyanto and Erb 2009, pp. 20, 22). In many cases, nominations were simply bought by incumbents and wealthy contenders.

In July 2007, the Constitutional Court (*Mahkamah Konstitusi*) decided, with much support from civil society organizations (Gross 2007), that independent candidates were allowed to run for office. This decision meant an end to the monopoly of political parties on the selection and nomination of candidates at the local level. Since then, political parties play a less important role at the local than at the national level. This practice is in contrast to the election of the national President, who must still be nominated by the political parties represented in the national parliament (see chapter 3.2).

For the local level, the acceptance of independent candidates led to a contest of personalities rather than of party platforms. Since the first direct elections of local leaders were allowed in 2005, most of these elections were generally free and fair. However, frequent disputes occurred on the validity of election results. In many cases, the loser of the local election accused the winner of using "money politics" and cheating. Many cases had to be settled in court. Nevertheless, so far, "the *pilkada* have generally taken place without serious crises that might have undermined the whole [democratization] process" (Sulistiyanto and Erb 2009, p. 31).

Particularly after the introduction of *pilkada*, local candidates from various backgrounds came to local power. Former bureaucrats, business people (Hadiz 2010, p. 105ff.), military officers, religious leaders, academics, community leaders, NGO activists, and media personalities competed for the office of *bupati* or *walikota*. This marks a major contrast to the authoritarian period, when military leaders were often appointed as local leaders. At the end of the *Orde Baru*, all local leaders had to be from Golkar, and more than 80 per cent of all governors were from the military. Nowadays, Indonesia sees a colorful and heterogeneous local political leadership. Frequent elections have led to an increased circulation of local elites, which since 2005 removed many remnants of the authoritarian order, which were then appointed by then-President Soeharto. About 40 to 50 per cent of the incumbent governors, mayors, and regency leaders were not re-elected in 2005 and 2006 (Hadiz 2010, p. 161). The ratio for re-election of the appointed members of the local parliaments was less than 30 per cent.[21]

The intensification of competition for local power led to an "overall trend towards greater ... inclusiveness in local executive elections" (Buehler 2010*b*, p. 271). The direct local elections also allowed middle-class citizens to enter the political scene. Wealth did not guarantee success at the local level. Often, the delivery of good public services and policies in the previous term was a decisive voting factor for constituents.

Additionally, candidates with the support of some political parties and grassroot support groups were more successful. Incumbent local leaders who failed to deliver were often not re-elected as a punishment. Australian scholar Ed Aspinall reported that local elections have a "high turnover rate of about 40 percent, with voters showing that they will not hesitate to oust local government heads whom they view as corrupt or incompetent" (Aspinall 2010, p. 33). This is a very high rate, particularly compared to Thailand, the Philippines, and even established Western democracies. Corruption allegations and scandals with incumbents very often resulted in electoral defeat. Ismeth Abdullah, for instance, was elected governor of the Riau province in 2005 and later involved in a corruption case. His wife, Aida Ismeth, ran for the gubernatorial position in 2010 but failed to win the election.

People generally voted in a rational and pragmatic manner and did not follow party lines nor ideologies. They were rather focused on personality and quality of governance. A good example of this assumption was the election of Joko Widodo, commonly known as Jokowi, as governor of Jakarta in October 2012, who won the elections due to his credibility and previous successes as mayor of Surakarta. Party support plays a minor role, since local parties generally do not have wealth or a working party machinery. As in established democracies, Indonesian "local voters tended to vote for local leaders whom they knew best and who had delivered something back to society" (Sulistiyanto and Erb 2009, p. 20). The decentralization process led to "an unprecedented level of public scrutiny being imposed on Indonesian local governments and legislatures" (Buehler 2010*b*, p. 283).

However, in other cases, traditional factors of power "such as patronage networks, social prestige and wealth still matter more than ideas and programs in the selection of local leadership" (Choi 2011, p. 106). Despite the entry of new faces in many local governments, patrimonial relationships and practices still dominate in other regions. Whereas "voters have been given more power to throw out corrupt officials, their replacements have been recruited from the same pool of elite politicians" (Buehler 2010*b*, p. 269). Similar to the Philippines, but to a lesser extent, there are several regencies which are dominated by local elites, who are powerful and wealthy enough to ensure electoral victory. These "little kings" (*raja kecil*) are "unaccountable to their citizens … and, due to decentralization, no longer constrained in their confiscatory impulses by a strong central government either" (Pepinsky and Wihardja 2011, p. 361). Particularly socioeconomically backward regencies tend to have less responsive local governments which are not held accountable by their citizens. In turn, these local governments often implement policies that benefit themselves at the expense of the community at large.

A different phenomenon was the re-emergence of traditional elites such as local nobles as a consequence of the introduction of local autonomy in many parts of the country. A case in point is local politics in Yogyakarta. Being a long-established monarchy under a sultan with a specific role in the Indonesian war of independence, the special province (*daerah istimewa*) of Yogyakarta refused to accept elections as a tool to determine the governor. Instead, Sultan Hamengkubuwono X insisted that his administration had adopted democratic principles with the appointment of himself and the King of Paku Alam as governor and vice-governor (Sijabat 2011*b*). President Susilo Bambang Yudhoyono, however, voiced his opinion that Yogyakarta cannot have "a monarchy system that contradicts our constitution or democratic values" (Sihaloho, Nanginna and Rachman 2010). After strong pressure from local citizens and associations, the national parliament eventually passed a law (UU) in August 2012 affirming that the sultan of Yogyakarta would automatically be the governor of the province (Sihite 2012). This case shows long-established feudal traditions still persist in a democratic country. If the sultan would run as a candidate in the governor elections of Yogyakarta, he would most likely win overwhelmingly. For a democratic state, however, unelected and inherited lifetime rule is not in accordance with the principles of accountability.

The multitude of regencies and their different experiences make it very difficult to generalize the quality of democracy at the local level. A study of Kumorotomo (2009) compares various governance aspects, among them accountability, in the local governments of Ambon (Moluccas), Palembang (South Sumatra) and Sleman (Special Region of Yogyakarta in Central Java). The author concludes that the mechanisms of checks and balances are strong in Ambon, moderate in Sleman, and weak in Palembang. The misuse of executive power is, according to Kumorotomo, high in Palembang and Sleman, and moderate in Ambon. Responsiveness to people's needs was rated moderate in Ambon and low in the two other regencies. Table 4.2 depicts the results in detail.

Table 4.2
Different Outcomes in Terms of Accountability at the
Local Level in Indonesia

No.	Characteristics	District		
		Ambon	Palembang	Sleman
1.	Dominant political parties	PDIP, Golkar	PPP, Golkar	PDIP, PAN
2.	Leadership	Strong	Moderate	Moderate
3.	Participatory planning	Weak	Weak	Moderate
4.	Mechanism of checks and balances	Strong	Weak	Moderate
5.	Compliance with professionalism	Low	Moderate	Relatively strong
6.	Executive power misuse	Moderate	High	High
		Corruption is deterred	Collusion and nepotism	Indirect but extensive
7.	Responsiveness to people's need	Moderate	Low	Low
8.	Media coverage	Partisan, somewhat exclusive on certain issues	Extensive coverage but the information is asymmetric	Extensive, relatively impartial

Source: Kumorotomo (2009), p. 19.

Ethnic Conflicts

Indonesia is the fourth most populated country in the world, with over 230 million inhabitants. It is an extremely diverse country in which hundreds of different ethnic and linguistic groups live dispersed between thousands of islands. Existing beside one another are different historical experiences and cultural characteristics in various parts of the country. Though roughly 88 per cent of the population identifies with the Muslim community, other religious minorities are of regional relevance, particularly in the Eastern parts of the country.

The resistance to Dutch colonial rule in the early twentieth century was based on a feeling of togetherness between these different ethnic and religious groups. The only chance to gain freedom was to unify against the common enemy. In 1928, the youth pledge, "one motherland, one nation and one language" (*satu tanah air, satu bangsa, satu bahasa*), was of utmost importance for the eventual success of the independence movement.

During the war for liberation from the Dutch colonial rulers, negotiations led to the creation of a loosely connected construct called the Federal States of Indonesia in 1949. The young state, under then-President Sukarno, a fervent nationalist, saw the federal system as an instrument of the Dutch to weaken the authority of the central government. Consequently, a unitary system of state (*negara kesatuan*) was introduced only a year later in 1950. The term "federalism" is still today connected with an attempt by external forces to play the different ethnic groups against each other and to endanger national unity.

Under the rule of President Soeharto from 1965 until 1998, Indonesia became one of the most centralized states in the world. A small elite in Jakarta made decisions for the whole archipelago and local officials were dependent on them. They had no autonomous scope of action and only executed orders passed down from the national capital.

Soeharto's authoritarian rule propagated a uniform concept of Indonesian citizenship according to the Pancasila ideology.[22] Disputed neighbouring areas such as West Papua (1969) and East Timor (1976) were annexed and brought under the tight control of Jakarta. Local resistance against the centralist, Javanese-dominated, uniform policies were brutally suppressed. Indonesia had the semblance of a stable country in which the national language, Indonesian (*Bahasa Indonesia*), was widely spoken, and local differences were downplayed. It was strictly forbidden during the New Order to discuss racial, ethnic, and religious issues, the so-called "SARA"[23] issues.

However, under the surface of political stability, two areas of conflict emerged during Soeharto's rule: self-determination and communal conflicts (Gershman 2002). The first type refers to regional groups who demanded independence or significant autonomy from the Indonesian nation state. Particularly, the conflicts concerning Aceh, Papua, and East Timor belong to this category. The second type refers to "virtual small-scale civil wars between rival religious and ethnic communities" (Aspinall 2010, p. 25) in various regions such as West and South Kalimantan, Central Sulawesi, and the Moluccas.

Grievances over the distribution of economic resources were among some of the major reasons for these conflicts. In the highly centralized New

Order, locals rightly claimed that elites from Jakarta were exploiting the natural resources in their regions for their own benefit. While economic development in Java was booming, the regions were left behind despite their richness in resources. This sense of economic injustice was compounded with a feeling of political heteronomy, since nearly all provincial governors and many mayors and *bupati* were appointed by the president and ministers in faraway Jakarta.

While the mentioned conflicts were suppressed during the New Order, they erupted with full force at the end of Soeharto's reign. Loss of military control and the resulting power vacuum led to the re-emergence or outbreak of dozens of new and old conflicts. The violence was always localized and also caused by "vigorous competition among local elites to capture state power, often accompanied by a revival of local ethnic consciousness" (Aspinall 2010, p. 25). The referendum and the following secession of East Timor from Indonesia in 1999 seemed to heighten the possibility of a "Balkanization" of Indonesia. In 2000, fears were "mounting that the Yugoslav-type ethnic and sectarian violence that has wracked Indonesia for more than a year could escalate even further" (Hadar 2000, p. 4). Comparable to post-Tito Yugoslavia, Indonesia's forced cohesion began to unravel after the resignation of a strong authoritarian central government.

The decentralization process assuaged the main reasons for the various self-determination and communal conflicts. The right of various regencies to keep a major part of their economic resources reduced the resentments against the national elite in Jakarta. Some regions such as many regencies in East Kalimantan witnessed an economic boom and now belong to the fastest economically growing areas in the country. Conflicts over distribution with the centre have decreased to a normal level.

Additionally the political devolution of tasks to locally elected governors, mayors, and *bupati* resulted in far-reaching autonomy for the local units, reducing separatist tendencies. Locals, who are not satisfied with political, social and economic developments at their local level, now first blame their elected local representatives rather than the central government. Thus, in many troubled spots of the years between 1998 and the early 2000s, such as Poso, the Moluccas, and West and South Kalimantan, decentralization led to an end of communal violence. Ethnic conflicts that were caused by local elites in search of power and material gains could be abated since many of these elites could achieve their goals without having to resort to violence (Aspinall 2010, p. 28). Instead, they took over local government positions which enabled them to rule and to enjoy material benefits.

The most pressing conflicts within the Indonesian state, in Aceh and Papua, needed more efforts to be contained. A special peace agreement between the Indonesian government and the Acehnese separatist movement, GAM (*Gerakan Aceh Merdeka*, Movement Free Aceh), in January 2005 ended the armed conflict. Aceh was given a special autonomy and considerably more rights for self-determination than comparable provinces and regencies in the rest of Indonesia. Crucial for the success of the Aceh peace agreement was allowance of local Acehnese political parties, which compete for power at the local level. Former guerrilla leaders and jungle fighters have now been elected as governors and *bupati* all over Aceh. Now, the local elites struggle for political power and access to resources among one another rather than with the central government. Interestingly enough, "some former guerrillas since coming to [local] power have been implicated in the predatory practices that they had previously condemned" (Aspinall 2010, p. 28).

It might not be too far-fetched to say that East Timor is still an Indonesian province, if the referendum for independence would have taken place not in 1999, but ten or more years later. In a democratized Indonesia, where the influence of the military has been enormously reduced and the protection of human rights improved since 1998, an Indonesian province of East Timor might not suffer the brutal repression as in the authoritarian past. Additionally, its regencies and cities might enjoy a higher degree of autonomy so that elected local leaders and groups determine local politics and finances. Under such conditions, a referendum for complete independence would be a serious and viable alternative with a high degree of autonomy.

Thus, decentralization was (among other factors) responsible for a strong reduction of ethnically or religiously motivated violence in recent years. The balkanization of Indonesia, which some authors predicted to occur around the millennium (Hadar 2000), was prevented not least due to increasing political and financial powers for local leaders. However, decentralization cannot be successful "if the social and economic grievances that lie at the hearts of the conflicts are not addressed. After all, it was not only … the repression of the military and the central government that fueled armed violence in Aceh and Papua, but economic exploitation, poverty and unemployment" (Heiduk 2009, p. 311). Insofar, the relative success of decentralization in containing local conflicts must not only be attributed to the new financial possibilities of local governments but also to the overall economic improvements of the country.

Interaction between Centre and Local Levels

As has been described earlier, national elites initiated the decentralization process from above and at a very fast pace. Until 2004, many regencies and cities conflated regional autonomy with complete freedom.[24] They no longer followed orders from national ministries and replaced national regulations with local ones. At the same time, other rather underdeveloped regencies lacked the necessary capacities to cope with the huge amount of new tasks and lacked financial means for administrating their regency. Law No. 32/2004 and other regulations with a slight centripetal tendency further balanced central-local relations.

Several national ministries in Jakarta engage with hundreds of local governments. The Ministry of Home Affairs regulates local legislation and administrative issues, while the Ministry of Finance is responsible for fiscal decentralization. The State Ministry of Administrative Reform (MenPAN, *Kementerian Pendayagunaan Aparatur Negara dan Reformasi Birokrasi*) and the National Planning and Development Board (*Bappenas, Badan Perencanaan dan Pembangunan Nasional*) are further institutions guiding and structuring the decentralization process.

Unfortunately, cooperation between these national ministries is suboptimal. Bills and decrees originating from one of these ministries often contradict another. A high-ranking Bappenas staff commented that "the cooperation of the various ministries is indeed low."[25] Concerning the national level, an incomplete, and in some parts contradictory, legal framework makes it very difficult to fulfill the governments' tasks adequately. This also leads to unclear competencies for the various national ministries which have to deal with decentralization. The Ministry of Home Affairs claims leadership ("decentralization is the primary task of the Ministry of Home Affairs. Bappenas and the Ministry of Finance should accept this"[26]), but since inter-ministerial cooperation and coordination are not yet fully developed, many administrative weaknesses exist. Decentralization has not been "complemented by a systematic effort to overhaul the often unwieldy and byzantine central administration, where departments continue to be poor in functions, but rich in structures" (Rohdewohld 2003, p. 259).

The Ministry of Home Affairs has to supervise the compliance of local laws with national laws. Local regulation (*peraturan daerah, perda*) could be declared invalid, but this does not happen very often. Local shari'ah laws concerning dressing and moral conduct, male and female interaction, drinking of liquor and obligatory alms giving, are all very sensitive issues.

Certain by-laws are openly discriminative against women (curfew in some areas) or religious minorities (obligation to Islamic dress code). These religious by-laws "have created problems not only with regard to Indonesian culture and tradition but also to the constitution" (Bünte 2009, p. 118), which states the equality of sexes and religious beliefs. In 2006, 56 members of the DPR asked the president to remove all the regional regulations concerning the implementation of Islamic law because they were unconstitutional, but SBY refused (Legowo and Djadijono 2007, p. 87). On this case, the Ministry of Home Affairs has so far taken no action, since they argue that this is a political decision under the President's discretion.[27]

The interactions between the national and local levels are manifold. Often, Indonesian local government officials contact members of the national parliament (DPR) to provide assistance for getting state funds or projects. The parliament members then act as *calo* (broker) and receive money from local government funds. In June 2011, a number of NGOs reported to the National Corruption Eradication Commission that nearly 7,700,800,000,000 Rupiah (about 630 million Euros) have been deducted from the Local Infrastructure Funds (DPID, *Dana Penyesuaian Infrastruktur Daerah*) with the help of brokering legislators (Rastika and Wahono 2011).

Local politicians also often use their political relations with national ministries in order to gain popularity at the local level. If they have connections to politicians and bureaucrats in Jakarta, who decide upon various state-funded assistance, they used them as a bait to win the loyalty of potential voters. In one case, farmers from Subang in West Java reported that they would get funds from the Agricultural Ministry only if they vote for the party of the national minister. A farmer was quoted as saying, "If we take the assistance, we must support the party in the next election, including its campaign" (Afrida 2011). National political leaders meddle into local government affairs, particularly in resource-rich regions, while less developed regions are left to local power holders, who exercise power without much interference from the national level (Morishita 2008, p. 107).

In June 2010, the powerful Golkar party proposed to give legislators the power to allocate state funds directly to their constituencies. According to Golkar, this scheme dubbed *dana aspirasi* ("aspiration funds") was intended "to respond to constituents' requests and to accelerate the equal distribution of development projects across the country, particularly in remote and rural areas" (Afrida 2011). The plan, which would be similar to the so-called pork barrel of the Philippines, would give each legislator the right to spend 15 billion Rupiah (about 1.2 million Euros) from state funds in their constituencies as they saw fit (Kimura 2011, p. 189).

The proposed pork-barrel scheme would have a negative impact on national-local relations. Instead of more or less transparent funds management by the national ministries, politicians could use their power to channel state funds for patronage and corrupt practices. It would also have consequences for the legislators' accountability, since it would "downgrade the meaning of legislator accountability as the citizens' representative. An aspiration fund would likely make the performance accountability of legislators be exclusively addressed only to the loyal supporters" (Sobari 2010). Scholar Iwan Gunawan argued that "The pork barrel scheme proposed by Golkar politicians is ... against the spirit of regional autonomy. .... House of Representative members are not representing regions, although they are elected by political districts" (Gunawan 2010). President Susilo Bambang Yudhoyono said that "if the House members want their regions [namely those who've elected them] to be given attention for, let's say, project A or B, they can suggest this to regional administrations or through the national development planning conference" (Maulia 2010). In the end, nearly all other parties in the DPR objected the Golkar proposal, arguing that pork-barrel politics could open the door to all kinds of corruption (Kimura 2011, p. 189). Hence the pork-barrel scheme was not further debated in parliament. In contrast to the Philippines (see chapter 4.3), the role of national legislators as important deal-makers for local governments was not strengthened in Indonesia.

Altogether, decentralization supported the deepening of the democratization process. The social base of political decision-making was broadened enormously. While ordinary people could previously only look at the processes in the capital Jakarta, they can now see how decisions, which have a direct impact on their daily lives, are decided in their city or regency. The chance to participate and to influence politics has increased to a great extent. Political leaders at the local level had to re-adjust their policies in such a way as to be re-elected. A successful improvement of the local economic and social infrastructure is now seen as the best means for re-election.

Decentralization has also led to a strong increase in political activism at the local level. This has led to a vibrant civil society, which comprises many social and political organizations and cares about matters of local interests. The political awareness of ordinary people has also increased.

Local authorities are now monitored more strictly, not only by the elected local council (DPRD), but also by civil society organizations who act as watch dogs of good governance. The transparency and accountability of local administrations has risen enormously in recent years. Representative contestation has extended to a broader range of both bureaucrats and local leaders (Carnegie 2010, p. 131).

Decentralization was an important part of the reform agenda to transform a highly centralist and authoritarian regime to a more democratic one. In the beginning, the responsibility for the overall process rested in the hands of the central government, which started a top-down and at the same time "big bang" decentralization process. Within a few years after the implementation, the result was a state that is not at all centralist, but rather one of the most decentralized political systems in the world. Decentralization has had many effects on the democratization process, not least since it "has allowed the discussion and debate on the idea of 'democracy' to flourish" (Sulistiyanto and Erb 2009, p. 4). According to one of the fathers of Indonesian decentralization, Ryaas Rasyid, the process was fundamental and an important precondition for the development of democracy in Indonesia (Rasyid 2003, p. 64).

The high significance of decentralization lies in the dissolution of the centralist power monopoly and in triggering social and political power diffusion. Consequently, the whole political system became more flexible and thus more stable. Regional and local grievances are now addressed to the local government and not, as previously done, to the central government. The local level thus has taken over the role of a shock absorber.

4.3 PHILIPPINES

Legal Framework

During the authoritarian rule of Ferdinand Marcos (1972–86), the Philippines were transformed into a centralist state. Local governments lost their autonomy while local leaders were appointed only by the next highest level in the strict administrative hierarchy. After the removal of Marcos in 1986, decentralization was explicitly introduced as a measure to disperse power and to stabilize the new democracy.

Article X, Section 3 of the 1987 Constitution demanded that a local government code be provided by Congress in the following years to serve as a solid basis for decentralization. The Constitution further specified that this decentralization law should provide

for a more responsive and accountable local government structure
instituted through a system of decentralization with effective mechanisms
of recall, initiative, and referendum, allocate among the different local
government units their powers, responsibilities, and resources, and
provide for the qualifications, election, appointment and removal, term,
salaries, powers and functions and duties of local officials (Constitution
of the Philippines).

The implementation of this demanded decentralization process started with
the Local Government Code of 1991. The Philippines officially kept a
unitary form of government, but introduced a multi-tiered structure. Below
the central level, the country is divided into 17 administrative regions,
which with the exception of the Autonomous Region of Muslim Mindanao
(ARMM) are administrative subdivisions without elected regional officials
and a separate local government.

The regions form a convenient basis for statistical analysis, but, with
the exception of the ARMM, do not have any political authority (Balisacan,
Hill, and Piza 2006, p. 300). The administrative regions are divided into
provinces and independent cities, which are at the top of the local government
units (LGUs) and are headed by an elected chief executive (governor in
the case of provinces, mayor in the case of independent cities) and elected
legislative body called *Sangguniang Panlalawigan* (composed of elected
council members and an elected vice-governor/vice-mayor who serves as
the presiding officer). The next levels of government are the municipalities
and component cities, which are further subdivided into *barangays*, the
smallest political unit. Municipalities, component cities and *barangays* also
possess an elected mayor or barangay captain and an elected city council
(*Sangguniang Panlungsod, Sangguniang Bayan* and *Sangguniang Barangay*).
All elected local officials have a three-year term of office and are subject to
a three-term limit, meaning that after three consecutive terms they are not
allowed to run for office again in the next term (Manasan 2005, p. 32f.).

Starting in 1991, many government tasks were delegated from the
central to the local level, particularly in the areas of health, agriculture,
environment, social welfare, and public works. The devolution programme
transferred over 70,000 personnel from selected national government
agencies to LGUs (Manasan 2005, p. 35). According to Article 2,
Section 25, of the Philippine Constitution, the State shall ensure the
autonomy of local governments. However, due to the unitary government
framework, local governments are not fully autonomous, but rather operate
under the supervision of the national government through the Department
of Interior and Local Government (DILG) (Malixi 2008, p. 46).

According to former GTZ and country expert Herwig Mayer:

> the national administration interferes too often in local affairs. Mayors often complain that the national government imposes certain police chiefs, treasurers, and even school directors on them. Though this goes against the Local Government Code, it can in practice lead to positively democratic results, as many mayors tend to appoint unqualified individuals due to reasons of patronage.[28]

Despite local government units being given the right to raise taxes, they have become increasingly dependent on state subsidies (Manasan 2005, p. 72; Malixi 2008, p. 49; Hill, Balisacan, and Piza 2007, p. 42). Alma Salvador, Philippine political scientist, stated that "only some innovative local governments (e.g. Naga, Puerto Princesa) have real fiscal autonomy due to the leadership qualities of their local leaders."[29] In most LGUs the financial constraints for local governments are too high. Revenue generation at the local level is "limited by and large to taxes on real property, charges on business licenses and the imposition of various fees" (de Dios 2007, p. 190). Though local governments are allowed to increase property taxes, thus forcing the rich to pay their share, many local authorities refrain from doing so (Diokno 2009, p. 181). Highly urbanized cities ease the process of taxation with computerized databases. However, in rural areas such technologies are unavailable.[30]

According to political analyst and presidential adviser Joel Rocamora, local governments receive approximately 6 per cent of the national budget but spend about 24 per cent of all national expenses.[31] Data from 2006 show that local expenditures make up 20.7 per cent of all government expenditures, yet the revenues of local governments are only 7.0 per cent of total revenues (Uchimura and Suzuki 2012, p. 54f.). Decentralization thus "devolved spending functions without a similar devolution of taxation" (de Dios 2007, p. 196). The difference between income and expenses must be made up with resources from the national budget and the pork barrel from Congressmen. Rocamora therefore argued that "local politicians must invest considerable time in fetching national resources in order to get their rightful slice of the pie."[32]

The most important transfers from central to subnational governments are formula-based block grants (i.e., internal revenue allotment or IRA). The legal right to receive this allocation, which is shared with a fixed formula, "strengthens the hand of the local governments (and the political groups that control them) relative to national-level institutions, since it removes the longstanding and ultimately executive discretion over the budgetary assistance to local governments" (de Dios 2007, p. 190f.). However, whereas the Local Government Code of 1991 stipulated the automatic release of the IRA, financial transfers have become an often unpredictable source of financing for LGUs since different central governments in various cases tried to reduce the amount of intergovernmental transfers to LGUs. Since the IRA depends on the total tax collection of the government at the national level, the total financial amount for the individual LGUs can be unpredictable (Manasan 2005, p. 68, Malixi 2008, p. 49).

In 1997, the Ramos administration issued Administrative Order 372, cutting the LGU's IRA by 10 per cent as an austerity measure for the state budget. The Supreme Court, however, ruled in July 1999 that this administrative order was unconstitutional and demanded that the national government automatically and regularly releases IRAs (Villanueva 2000; Diokno 2009, p. 176). Despite the decision of the Constitutional Court, all national governments – among them most notoriously GMA – continued to withhold the financial transfers to local government, particularly to those who opposed the president. In the same manner, local governments were forced to side with the president (Abinales 2008, p. 297f.). The president's "power over the release of discretionary congressional allocations to local governments proved pivotal in garnering local government support" (Ramos 2007, p. 113). Particularly under President GMA, IRAs to uncooperative LGUs were delayed while those loyal to the president received generous funding. The central government thus used the IRA release as a bargaining chip with local officials in order to gain their support for the programmes and candidates of the national government (Villanueva 2001). In 2008, 16 senators in opposition to GMA criticized this practice, claiming in the Joint Resolution No. 10/2008 that "the highly centralized system of government has brought about a spotty development of the nation where preferential treatment has been given to localities whose officials are friendly with or have easy access to an incumbent administration" (Senate of the Philippines 2008, p. 1).

If a local politician defies the president and the national government, he or she can get into serious trouble. In Pampanga, the home province of GMA, the priest Eddie Panlilio, a staunch critic of GMA's policies, was elected as governor in May 2007. Panlilio became one of the whistle blowers when President GMA presented "Christmas gifts" to Congressman and local government heads in October 2007.[33] Academic Francisco Magno reported that the president directed all the money to the mayors and not to the governor of Pampanga province.[34]

Under such circumstances, it comes as no surprise that a large majority of governors and mayors are turncoats. During GMA's presidency, most of the local government heads supported her. After the electoral victory of Noynoy Aquino in 2010, majority of them switched to his camp.

Democracy at the Local Level

The quality of democracy varies considerably between hundreds of municipalities and provinces. In some LGUs, independent mayors or governors are not corrupt and follow a comprehensive development agenda. In other cases, local elites which are "the best at fetching national resources and those who control illegal economic activities, such as *jueteng*"[35] dominate local politics. There are many encouraging signs that several LGUs used their devolved powers to advance democracy (Cariño 2010, p. 199).

Compared to other countries in Southeast Asia, civil society organizations have a better chance at participating in local politics. The Local Government Code provided three official possibilities for the people's direct participation at the local level. First, local non-governmental organizations (NGOs) can exert influence via the local development council, where sectoral groups are represented. Second, a certain quorum of people is required to start so-called local people initiatives. In such a way, local people can pass ordinances on a variety of issues without the formal support of the local council. The generally vibrant NGO community at the local level thus has a chance to impact local politics. Due to these activities, the overall support for democracy is strengthened in the Philippines. Many citizens feel that their activities can contribute to improvements at the local level. The multitude and the activism of local civil society organizations thus play a crucial role in increasing the overall level of democracy in the Philippines.

The third possibility for citizens to impact local politics is the initiation of a recall election for local officials. The Local Government Code explicitly provided the right for citizens to hold their local heads of government accountable by initiating a recall election. This mechanism, adopted from the United States,[36] allows the removal from office of public officials deemed incompetent or corrupt before the end of their term.

At least 25 per cent of registered voters of an LGU is required to initiate a recall election. The signature lists are checked by the COMELEC and, if proved valid, a recall election begins. However, the regulations prescribe that recall proceedings can only be initiated one year after the local official has been elected and at least one year prior to the next election cycle. Since local elections are held every three years, the timeframe for recall elections is thus limited to one year.

Some examples show the ambiguous democratic value of recall elections at the local level. In 2001, the mayor of Puerto Princesa on the island of Palawan, Victorino Dennis M. Socrates, was replaced after the local *barangay* assembly initiated a recall election. In this case, there were indications, however, that the *barangay* captains "might have been intimidated"[37] by Socrates' predecessor, Edward S. Hagedorn, who under normal circumstance would have ended his service after three consecutive terms. Here, the recall elections, which Hagedorn won, were used as a backdoor to resume office.

Another interesting case was the recall initiative against the above mentioned Eddie Panlilio, governor from Pampanga between 2007 and 2010. In this case, local government officials of Pampanga loyal to then-President GMA, headed by Vice-Governor Joseller "Yeng" Guiao, petitioned for a recall of Panlilio in October 2008 and gained a sufficient amount of signatures from local citizens. Panilio, in his defense, questioned the legitimacy of the recall, claiming that recall elections should be the initiative of the people of Pampanga and not that of the province's public officials (ABS-CBN News 2008). In the end, bureaucratic procedures and the COMELEC delayed the dealing of the case until it was too late for a recall election, since the next regular elections were only one year ahead. This practice of dealing with recall initiatives is not the exception but rather the rule.

Another recall was initiated against Governor Abraham "Baham" Mitra of the province of Palawan in 2011, this time by his political opponents. In response, Mitra's adviser, Raji Mendoza, stated that "recall procedures can be easily abused … as a way for sore losers to try to overturn a valid election result". He further added "recall is a double-edged sword. Rightly used, it can promote the greater good. Wrongly used, it can result in greater evil" (GMA News 2011).

Further examples from other Philippine provinces and cities abound. These three examples demonstrate that the recall elections at the local level were supposed to strengthen the quality of democracy and the accountability of local officials. In practice, however, they are often abused in political power struggles either at the local level or through interference from the national level.

There is another design feature of the institutional arrangements at the local level that does not promote good governance. The fact that the vice-mayor or vice-governor is the head of the local council violates the principle of separation of powers between executive and legislative. It was introduced to prevent gridlock and for the better functioning of the local government. At the same time, however, the local executive thereby dominates the local councils. In times of dispute, the mayor has a veto right over the councilors. Decentralization expert Francisco Magno therefore stated: "In the countryside the councilors are often not capable and the mayors can do what they want."[38]

A good illustration of this statement is the local politics of Davao, the biggest city of the Philippines outside of Metro Manila. Rodrigo Duterte was city mayor from 1988 until 1998. Then, the term limit forced him to run for the House of Representatives, where he won the position of Congressman of 1st District of Davao City. From 2001, he was re-elected as mayor. Again, the term limit did not allow him to run as mayor again, and so he successfully ran for vice-mayor, while his daughter Sara Duterte-Carpio replaced him as mayor. In 2013, Duterte announced his bid for mayor with his son Paolo as running mate for vice-mayor.

Rodrigo Duterte has the reputation of an iron-fisted dictatorial leader. Nicknamed "the Punisher" by Time Magazine in 2002 (Zabriskie 2002), under his rule, hundreds of alleged criminals have been extra-judicially killed. In February 2009, Duterte declared: "If you are doing an illegal activity in my city, if you are a criminal or part of a syndicate that preys on the innocent people of the city, for as long as I am the mayor, you are a legitimate target of assassination" (quoted by Human Rights Watch 2009).

Beside the questionable attitude of the mayor on constitutional rights and the popularity of local strongman, who know how to use violence (Kreuzer 2009, p. 19), the case of Duterte also illustrates another feature of Philippine local politics: the dominance of political families and clans which rule their provinces, districts, and cities often for decades. These dynasties try to run for as many elective positions as its members can and bequeath the won positions to clan members upon reaching the term limit (Teehankee 2013, p. 207). Despite obvious cases of power abuse, human rights violations, and unjust enrichment, many political families have dominated their regions for decades. The notorious Ampatuan clan responsible for the November 2009 election-rated massacre (already mentioned in chapter 3.3) fared well in the 2010 elections. Despite the imprisonment of patron Andal Ampatuan and some of his sons, 15 relatives won various local seats in Maguindanao, thereby retaining control of the province (Abinales 2011, p. 168). Eight members of the Ampatuan clan were elected as mayors and six as vice-mayors. Despite the clan's

> global infamy, the multiple victories of the Ampatuans in post-massacre Maguindanao were not unexpected. The results reflect their hold on Maguindanao's political machinery, their control of much of the wealth in the province, and a wily electoral strategy (aside from the outright, alleged murders of their opponents' allies) (Tiongson-Mayrina 2010).

In the 2010 elections, Luis "Chavit" Singson, one of the country's most notorious warlords and underworld figures, managed to get himself and his son elected as members of the National House of Representatives, matching the Ampatuans' record, with 10 members elected to various local government posts in Ilocos Sur Province in the northern Philippines (Abinales 2011, p. 168). These two cases are no exceptions. In the 2010 elections, 34 out of 77 provinces, or 44 per cent, had the same political family winning the governorship and at least one congressional district (Rivera 2011, p. 69). Table 4.3 illustrates the dominance of dynasties at the local level.

The feudal political culture that still prevails over large parts of the rural Philippines is one explanation for the continued dominance of powerful political families. As in Latin America, the dominance of local leaders often reaches quasi-monarchic levels, such that outgoing governors/mayors are able to pass their office to family members. These local clan leaders exert control over the access to state institutions, public offices, franchises, and business opportunities in a quasi-monopolistic fashion (Ardanaz, Leiras, and Tommasi 2010, p. 14; Kreuzer 2009, p. 9). Local government positions are often used to redirect or gain privileged access to local public resources and to control the bureaucracy (de Dios 2007, p. 169).

Patron-Client relationships in which ordinary citizens expect benefits in return for their loyalty towards a patron are widespread, particularly in rural areas. Francisco Magno described in an interview a typical situation in small towns and villages:

> If a mayor has a people's day, many poor people come and ask for financial help. Although there is a social welfare department in every LGU, people prefer to seek assistance in crisis situations directly from the highest approachable official. If he does not give them cash and refers them to the administration, they feel offended. The feudal system, particularly in rural areas, is deeply rooted in ordinary people's mind.[39]

These described patron-client relations hinder democratic political procedures and accountability at the local level.

Table 4.3
Political Families with Gubernatorial and Congressional Positions in the Philippines, 1987–2010

Province	Political Family	Province	Political Family
1. Ilocos Norte	Marcos	24. Cebu	Garcia
2. Ilocos Sur	Singson	25. Negros Occidental	Marañon
3. La union	Ortega	26. Leyte	Petilla
4. Pangasinan	Agbayani	27. Southern Leyte	Mercado
5. Isabela	Dy	28. Siquijor	Fua
6. Aurora	Angara-Castillo	29. Western Samar	Tan
7. Bataan	Roman, Garcia	30. Northern Samar	Daza, Ong
8. Tarlac	Yap, Cojuangco	31. Misamis Occidental	Ramiro
9. Zambales	Magsaysay	32. Biliran	Espina
10. Nueva Ecija	Joson, Umali	33. Bukidnon	Zubiri
11. Bulacan	Sy-Alvarado	34. Agusan del Norte	Amante
12. Cavite	Remulla, Revilla	35. Surigao del Norte	Ecleo, Barbers, Matugas
13. Laguna	San Luis	36. North Cotabato	Piñol
14. Batangas	Recto	37. Davao del Norte	Del Rosario
15. Quirino	Cua	38. Davao del Sur	Cagas
16. Camarines Norte	Padilla	39. Zamboanga del Sur	Cerilles
17. Quezon	Suarez, Enverga	40. Zamboanga del Norte	Amatong
18. Palawan	Mitra, Socrates	41. Sultan Kudarat	Mangudadatu
19. Masbate	Espinoa, Kho, Lanete	42. Lanao del Sur	Adiong
20. Marinduque	Reyes	43. Lanao del Norte	Dimaporo
21. Iloilo	Defensor, Tupas	44. Maguindanao	Ampatuan/Datumanong, Matalam
22. Antique	Javier	45. Basilan	Akbar
23. Guimaras	Nava	46. Sulu	Loong

Source: Rivera (2011), p. 68.

Due to impoverished living conditions and financial insecurity, most Filipinos are forced to care more for their personal fate than for the quality of democracy. They become clients of leaders that give them material benefits and protection. Accordingly, they vote for generous patrons and care less for their democratic values. In a recent survey from Social Weather Stations, a public opinion polling body, on local governance, 36 per cent of household heads regarded issues related to economy as the most important problem of the city/municipality, followed by 12 per cent for infrastructure, 11 per cent for social services, and 9 per cent for crime, while only 1 per cent saw the state of democracy as the main problem at the local level (Social Weather Stations 2011, p. 17).

Decentralization and Conflict Containment

The Muslim minority in the southern island of Mindanao is at the centre of the most critical internal conflict in the Philippines. Known as the Moro, they distinguish themselves as a unique people apart from the rest of the Filipino culture, comprising about 5 per cent of the population with approximately 4 million individuals. The conflict is deeply rooted in the colonial and post-colonial past of the Philippines. The Moro argue that their ancestral land has been taken away by Spanish and American colonial masters, only later to be given to Christian settlers, who today make up the majority of the population on the island of Mindanao. Additionally, there is widespread resentment among Muslims in Mindanao due to discrimination and treatment as second-class citizens (Rocamora 2004, p. 166). Grievances over economic, political and cultural marginalization led to often violent protests and a separatist movement against the central government in Manila in the decades after the independence of the Philippines in 1947.

When the Philippines returned to a democratic model in 1986, the drafters of the new democratic constitution were well aware that the violent conflict in the Muslim parts of Mindanao (*bangsamoro*) was not only a threat to the national integrity of the Philippines but to the deepening of democracy. Therefore, Article X, Section 1 of the 1987 Constitution provided a special autonomous province for the Muslim community in Mindanao. Consequently, the Autonomous Region of Muslim Mindanao (ARMM) was created on 1 August 1989 through Republic Act No. 6734. In 18 provinces, plebiscites were held in order to give their residents the choice of joining the ARMM or not.

However, hopes that the decentralization would contribute to peace, stability, and economic progress did not bear fruit. Separatist groups, among them most notably the Moro National Liberation Front (MNLF) and later the Moro Islamic Liberation Front (MILF), continued the fight against the national government and the Armed Forces of the Philippines (AFP). Several peace agreements worked only temporarily or quickly failed, and in August 2008 an attempt by the Philippine government's Peace Negotiating Panel to sign a Memorandum of Agreement on Ancestral Domain with the MILF was declared unconstitutional by the Philippine Supreme Court.

For a long time it seemed that the "contribution of the decentralization program on the Mindanao conflict has been minimal" (Hill, Balisacan, and Piza 2007, p. 44), but the question why is still discussed. I would argue that the combination of three factors — the inadequate financial autonomy of the ARMM, the political interference of Manila into local political affairs, and the persistent dominance of various undemocratic clans in the ARMM — contributed to the failure of decentralization.

In term of finances, the regional government of the ARMM has the official power to create its own sources of revenue and to levy taxes, fees, and charges. However, due to widespread poverty and missing opportunities for tax collection, the ARMM is *de facto* dependent on revenues allocated by the national government and Congress. Critical journalist and author on Muslim Mindanao, Glenda Gloria, asserts that "the ARMM still needs to go to the national departments to ask for money. This is no real autonomy."[40]

Mujiv Hataman party-list representative of Anak Mindanao (AMIN) in the House of Representatives, stated that

> the budget of the ARMM is mostly from subsidies of the national government. The ARMM is not independent. Different to Aceh, there is no fiscal autonomy for my region. The governor of the ARMM must have the support of the Philippine president. Some even say that ARMM means Autonomous Region of Muslim Malacañang.[41]

Beside the financial dependence on the national government, there is also a high interference from national politics in the affairs of the ARMM. Ongoing unrest leads to the permanent influence of the national government in questions of regional security, which also contributes to the deficit in legitimacy of the local government (Grigat 2009, p. 181). Furthermore, local elections still remain subject to irregularities and strong influence by the central government. Elections in the ARMM were postponed several times due to the influence of national parliamentarians and the government, such as by passing amendments (Grigat 2009, p. 179). In 2008, Zaldy Ampatuan was elected governor of the ARMM, but was expelled from his office in November 2009 after the previously mentioned massacre in Maguindanao. Then Vice-Governor Ansaruddin Adiong was appointed by the DILG as acting new governor. In early 2011, the Philippine president with the support of congress and the Supreme Court decided that the gubernatorial elections which were due to be held in August 2011, be postponed until May 2013. For the time being, President Noynoy Aquino appointed Mujiv Hataman as officer-in-charge governor of the ARMM in December 2011. The latter stated in an interview in 2007 that

> the ARMM is not controlled by the clans but by Malacañang. The problem of governance in the ARMM is that the local government is not only corrupt but a close ally of the national government. In order to democratize the ARMM the national government should drop their support for the clans, refuse to tolerate clanism, and disarm the private armies. The tolerance of clanism makes the peace process difficult to the extent that, in the long run, the relation to some clan leaders is not an asset but rather a liability for the national government.[42]

The previously described problems of family dominance, which is a common phenomenon in the Philippines, is aggravated in the ARMM by the widespread existence of private armies owned by clans and terrorist groups such as Abu Sayyaf. The former Special Advisor to the President on the Peace Process, Teresita "Ging" Quintos-Deles consequently stated that the government must "separate those who fight a legitimate fight for autonomy from those who are criminal gangs".[43]

However, recent developments give some hope for peace in the coming years. After several failed attempts from previous presidents, the Aquino administration reached a peace agreement with the MILF in October 2012. The parties agreed on the creation of a new autonomous political entity called Bangsamoro in place of the ARMM. In the Framework Agreement on the Bangsamoro, the government explicitly acknowledged the legitimate grievances of the Moro people and promised funding for the restructuring process. President Aquino expressed his wish for an agreement that "can finally seal genuine, lasting peace in Mindanao" (*Filipino Star* 2012). However, the three problems identified here of Muslim Mindanao (inadequate financial autonomy, political interference of the central government, dominance of undemocratic clans) were not major issues in the peace agreement. Thus, the framework agreement is only a possible starting point for political changes which could impact the quality of democracy in the whole country.

Interactions between Central and Local Levels of Government

The Philippines are centralized and decentralized at the same time. Some authors see the Philippines as ruled by a "pre-eminent central power" (de Dios 2007, p. 192). This is to some extent right, since many decisions on local politics are made in the capital Manila. Presidential prerogatives particularly on appointments influence local politics. The president has the power to appoint thousands of positions within the public service. The president also holds direct control over the police at all levels. Promotions or relocation of police officers are – at least in important cases – a presidential task. Additionally, as has been shown, Congress and the president share far-reaching powers to disburse general funds and to control additional special and discretionary funds. However, the "financial resources that are transferred from the central government via the IRA to the local level has helped to build local accountability and responsibility" (Hill, Balisacan, and Piza 2007, p. 42) at least to some degree. The decentralization in the Philippines is not a real devolution since only certain areas (mainly agriculture, school buildings, primary health, and social services) are devolved. In addition, national government agencies generally bypass local development plans formulated by LGUs (Brillantes and Sonco 2006, p. 372).

Nevertheless, decentralization has a big impact on national-local relations. Philippine politics is to a great extent characterized by interactions between local and national politics. Local politicians act

> primarily not as mobilizers of local initiative and local resources but as intermediaries and brokers with central powers. Political power and legitimacy will then derive not primarily from local leaders' ability to lead their constituents but rather from their network of vertical political and economic connections (de Dios 2007, p. 195).

On the other hand, national politicians, particularly members of the House of Representatives, transfer local issues to the national level.

Local interests are therefore an important node of power in national politics. It is not farfetched to say that local interests even dominate national politics. Joel Rocamora reiterates this notion: "the major weakness of the national government is that it is permeable for the influence of local clans."[44] From such a perspective, the Philippine president in a typically feudalistic fashion, acts as the ultimate patron of local families, who then act as the patrons for their respective areas. He or she relies on local political bosses and clans for the mobilization of electoral support and the implementation of government policies (Teehankee 2013, p. 191)

Local politicians continuously attempt to gain access to the national political decision-making process in order to access funds "that can be re-channeled to the locality as part of the political investment, as a source of corruption rents, or both" (de Dios 2007, p. 190). Most local politicians lobby relevant government agencies in order to get (financial) support for local projects. Local politicians throw their weight behind certain demands vis-à-vis the national departments, particularly in the process of drafting the national budget for the forthcoming year. A main source of revenue are funds from the Priority Development Assistance Fund (PDAF), to which all national congressmen (representing local interests) have access. This so-called "pork-barrel" fund gives the national legislators huge opportunities to spend national money for local projects on their own accord. The amount of funding from the "congressional initiative allocation" (usually described as "congressional insertions") is even larger, in which national legislators ask for financial support from certain departments during the budget negotiations with the national government.

Local political clans very often occupy both local and national government positions at the same time. The typical combination is to be a congressmen and provincial governor or city mayor at the same time (de Dios 2007, p. 191). Being in the legislative branch of government at the national level creates the necessary resources for political activities as an executive in the local government. The control of these two elective positions entitles the clans to have "easier access to national resources while at the same time facilitating control on the ground" (Rivera 2011, p. 68). The stakes consist of access to national resources. The Governor can count on institutionalized funding through the IRA, which can be utilized without detailed scrutiny from the national government. The Congressman receives institutionalized funding from the state through the pork barrel and other congressional insertions during budget negotiations. If the positions of mayor and House of Representatives member are not in the hands of the same clan, then the congressmen often tries to block resources going to the local level since that would possibly benefit their rivals.

Every three years, during election times, national-local relations become very important. Since all mayors, local councilors, governors, provincial councilors, national legislators, half of the senators, and the president are elected at the same time, national campaigns for the presidency and for the senate rely on agreements with local politicians and their clans. These groups thus combine votes for certain presidential or governor candidates with funds from their own local campaigns. Local elites bargain with national candidates for access to state resources in exchange for electoral support (Teehankee 2006, p. 244). On the widely disseminated sample ballot papers voters can clearly see the connections and who is aligned with whom. If local politicians bet on the right horse, there are great chances that they will be rewarded with additional funds for their constituencies and political influence in forthcoming decisions. In the absence of stable political parties, "such exchanges occur at a highly personal level – not least since they may comprehend both legal and illegal transactions" (de Dios 2007, p. 191). Local politicians are very pragmatic in choosing their running mates at the national level. Ideology, platform, or former affiliations, play a minor role compared to the chances for electoral victory.

As has been described, national-local relations do not take place in formal institutions. The Senate of the Philippines is – as described in chapter 3.3 – not composed of representatives of local interests. Neither do central-local relations go along party lines, since the affiliation to political parties plays only a minor role in national and local politics. Consequently, central-local relations are informal individual agreements between both levels of government.

Reforms

Decentralization was a major reform to stabilize the democratization process by empowering democracy at the local level. However, the described "structural weaknesses of Philippine democracy … delimit[ed] the democratizing potential of decentralization" (Ramos 2007, p. 114). Thus, the decentralization process in the Philippines is "neither a notable success nor a disappointing failure" (Hill, Balisacan, and Piza 2007, p. 42). In terms of vertical accountability, the local level can impact politics on the national level. However, the limited financial autonomy of LGUs leads to a dependence on central government and Congressional money. The national administration can use "the pork barrel and appointments as carrot to local governments. This diminishes local autonomy and forces local governments not to be critical with the national government."[45]

Except a few minor points, the Local Government Code of 1991 has not been updated since its enactment. All reform proposals from various senators and representatives, even on minor issues, have been stopped or indefinitely delayed. The biggest reform controversy arose around the proposed introduction of a federal political system as part of the Charter Change debate between 2000 and 2008. In the first draft version, the initiators sought to transform the Philippines into a federal state with a parliamentary system of government. The planned abolition of the Senate, however, met stiff resistance from the senators.

Therefore, a majority of the Senate put forth its own proposal (Joint Resolution 10/2008), in which a federal system with 75 elected senators (6 from each of the federal states plus 9 for overseas Filipinos) would replace the current system. Despite long political and academic debates (e.g. Abueva 2005) and policy initiatives, the federalization issue did not gain enough support from the political elite, who preferred to keep the established balance of power and modes of interaction between the central and local levels of government. Not least for these reasons, the Philippines witnessed stagnation in decentralization efforts. In contrast to Thailand and Indonesia, the percentage of local government expenditures from total government expenditures had not increased in the last decades.

Due to a lack of reforms, accountability between different levels of government is still determined mainly by patronage relations in the Philippines. Many local politicians "saw decentralization not as an alternative to patronage systems, but as [a] device to extend and renew those systems" (Manor 1999, p. 44). Some valuable reforms on local governance were initiated by Jesse Robredo, who was Secretary of the Department of Interior and Local Governance (DILG) from 2010 until his death after an airplane crash in August 2012. Robredo, former mayor of Naga in the Bicol region which is generally regarded as a model local government in the country, has given LGUs more capacities to manage their tasks. The introduction of the Local Governance Performance Management System (LGPMS) with a Seal of Good Housekeeping, resulted in new incentives for efficient working LGUs in 2011. Additionally, the introduced Full Disclosure Policy for local governments' financial documents and bidding procedures, as well as the programme Local Governance Watch, were promising reform measures to enhance transparency, citizens' participation and good governance at the local level.

Slowly, decentralization seems to impact the quality of democracy at the local level. In the last few years, many cities and villages witnessed a change of generations. Gradually, more and more of the 70-year-old *trapos* are retiring while a new generation of 30- to 40-year-old politicians with business and management skills are entering the scene. This does not automatically entail more democratic local politics, however, since power is still controlled by family clans, but it does at least signify better prospects for local governance and service delivery.

A survey from Social Weather Stations revealed that the people's net satisfaction (per cent satisfied minus per cent dissatisfied) with the performance of their city/town governments has risen in recent years (Social Weather Stations 2011, p. 10f.). In 2009, 54 per cent felt that "the government can be run without corruption", whereas 42 per cent felt that "corruption is part of the way government works"; this is close to a mere split opinion. In 2011, however, 65 per cent felt government can be run without corruption, or double the 33 per cent who feel otherwise; this is a significant improvement in public confidence (Social Weather Stations 2011, p. 48). It is not possible to give a comprehensive explanation for this rise. Probably, the anti-corruption rhetorics and policies of President Aquino had influence on public perception.

Notes

[1]   Interview with Naruemon Thabchumpon, Faculty of Political Science, Chulangalongkorn University, Bangkok, 14 August 2009.

[2]   Interview with Ong-art Klampaiboon, Minister to the Prime Minister's Office, Democrat Party, Bangkok, 14 October 2010.

[3]   Ibid.

[4]   Interview with Boonyad Sukthinthai, Democrat Party, Member of the House of Representatives, Bangkok, 14 October 2010.

[5]   Ibid.

[6]   Interview with Ong-art Klampaiboon, Minister to the Prime Minister's Office, Democrat Party, Bangkok, 14 October 2010.

[7]   Interview with Boonyad Sukthinthai, Democrat Party, Member of the House of Representatives, Bangkok, 14 October 2010.

[8]   Interview with Suthipon Thaveechaiyagarn, Secretary General of the Election Commission of Thailand, 17 August 2009.

[9]   Interview with Nataphol Teepsuwan, Director General of Democrat Party, Member of the House of Representatives, Bangkok, 11 October 2010.

[10] Interview with Ong-art Klampaiboon, Minister to the Prime Minister's Office, Democrat Party, Bangkok, 14 October 2010.

11 Interview with Boonyad Sukthinthai, Democrat Party, Member of the House of Representatives, Bangkok, 14 October 2010.

12 Interview with Nataphol Teepsuwan, Director General of Democrat Party, Member of the House of Representatives, Bangkok, 11 October 2010.

13 Interview with Kraisak Choonhavan, MP, Democrat Party, Bangkok, 17 August 2009.

14 Ibid.

15 Ibid.

16 Interview with Kraisak Choonhavan, MP, Democrat Party, Bangkok, 17 August 2009.

17 Interview with Ong-art Klampaiboon, Minister to the Prime Minister's Office, Bangkok, 14 October 2010.

18 Interview with Michael H. Nelson, Faculty of Political Science, Chulalongkorn University, Bangkok, 18 August 2009.

19 Interview with Heru Subiyantoro, Ministry of Finance, Directorate General of Fiscal Balance, Jakarta, 12 March 2008.

20 Interview with Heru Subiyantoro, Ministry of Finance, Directorate General of Fiscal Balance, Jakarta, 12 March 2008.

21 Interview with Roy Valiant Salomo, Head of Department, Faculty of Social and Political Science, University of Indonesia, Jakarta, 17 March 2008.

22 Pancasila is the state philosophy of Indonesia. It comprises five principles (belief in the one and only god, just civilized humanity, national unity, people's rule by deliberative consensus, and social justice).

23 SARA refers to *suku* (ethnicity), *agama* (religion), *ras* (race) and *antar-golongan* (inter-group relations).

24 Interview with Syamsul Arief Rivai, Directorate of Regional Development, Ministry of Home Affairs, Jakarta, 13 March 2008.

25 Interview with Suprayoga Hadi, Bappenas, Director for Special Area and Disadvantaged Region, Jakarta, 13 March 2008.

26 Interview with Eko Subowo (General Director, Direktur Administrasi dan Kewilayahan, Ministry of Home Affairs), Jakarta, 14 April 2008.

27 Interview with I Made Suwandi, Director of Regional Affairs, Ministry of Home Affairs, Jakarta, 17 March 2008.

28 Interview with Herwig Mayer, Program Manager, Decentralization Program of GTZ, Makati City, 2 September 2009.

29 Interview with Alma Salvador, Assistant Professor at the Department of Political Science, Ateneo University, Quezon City, 6 October 2010.

30 Ibid.

31 Interview with Joel Rocamora, Director, Secretary of the National Anti-Poverty Commission, Quezon City, 5 October 2010.

32 Ibid.

33 President Gloria Macapagal-Arroyo hosted a meeting with about 200 members of the Union of Local Authorities of the Philippines (ULAP) at the presidential

palace in October 2007. Several Congressmen and Governor Panlilio later reported that a palace staff personally gave them brown paper gift bags which comprised 500,000 Pesos (approximately 9,000 Euro) in cash as Christmas gifts (Philippine Daily Inquirer 2007).

34 Interview with Francisco Magno, Executive Director, Institute of Governance, De La Salle University, Manila, 1 September 2009.

35 Interview with Joel Rocamora, Secretary of the National Anti-Poverty Commission, Quezon City, 5 October 2010. Jueteng is a very popular, but illegal number game.

36 Recent US examples are the successful recall of California Governor Gray Davis in 2003 and the unsuccessful 2012 recall campaign against Governor Scott Walker in Wisconsin.

37 Interview with Francisco Magno, Executive Director, Institute of Governance, De La Salle University, Manila, 1 September 2009.

38 Ibid.

39 Ibid.

40 Interview with Glenda Gloria, Journalist, Chief Operating Officer ANC, Quezon City, 26 August 2009.

41 Interview with Mujiv Hataman, Member of the House of Representatives, party list A-MIN, Quezon City, 13 September 2007.

42 Ibid.

43 Interview with Teresita "Ging" Quintos-Deles, Former Special Advisor to the President on the Peace Process, Manila, 14 September 2007.

44 Interview with Joel Rocamora, Secretary of the National Anti-Poverty Commission, Quezon City, 5 October 2010.

45 Interview with Glenda Gloria, Journalist, Chief Operating Officer ANC, Quezon City, 26 August 2009.

5

THE HORIZONTAL ACCOUNTABILITY DIMENSION

In this chapter, I will analyse how institutional changes concerning mechanisms of horizontal accountability affected the quality of democracy in Thailand, Indonesia, and the Philippines. As described in chapter 2.6, horizontal accountability refers to a system of "checks and balances" between the different state institutions. This particularly applies to the accountability of the elected government *vis-à-vis* the other branches of government.

In the following I will analyse what kind of institutional reforms concerning the dimension of horizontal accountability took place in the three countries under research. Executive-legislative relations will be the first aspect, followed by the executive-judiciary relations. Finally I will analyse how independent watch-dog organizations, such as counter-corruption commissions, audit agencies, and election commissions were effective in exerting control over government actions. As in the previous chapters, I will start with Thailand and then continue with Indonesia and the Philippines.

5.1 THAILAND

Executive-Legislative Relations

The 1997 Constitution aimed to raise the institutional stability of the political system. A separation of powers, as described in chapter 2.6, is quite different in a parliamentary system, as the separation of powers between executive and legislative does not occur between government and parliament, but rather between the cabinet including its supporting parliamentary majority and the minority/opposition in parliament. In such a parliamentary system, the opposition in the parliament, a possible second chamber, an independent judiciary, and independent watch-dog organizations are possible institutions that might keep the government in check.

The drafters of the 1997 Constitution attempted to strengthen the executive power for stable governments and at the same time provide checks and balances to control governmental actions. The position of the prime minister was strengthened in comparison to previous constitutions in order to provide more political stability. The prime minister presided over the dominant coalition majority in the House of Representatives, was allowed to select the cabinet independently and without consent of any other institution, and had the right to dissolve the legislature.

Michael Nelson argued that

> the 100 party list seats introduced with the 1997 Constitution were notably not aimed at providing access to underrepresented political forces. Rather, the intention was ... to enable supposedly better qualified personnel to govern the country and strengthen the hand of the prime minister over them (Nelson 2007, p. 11).

The latter target was also reached by other electoral reforms in the 1997 Constitution. Ministers had to give up their parliamentary mandate if they decided to join the cabinet. Since they were not allowed to reclaim their parliamentary seat if they left the cabinet the prospects for breaking with the prime minister were significantly reduced. This reform intended to strengthen the cohesion of the cabinet and tried to end the long-lasting tradition of intra-party factionalism which led to frequent cabinet reshuffles.

Another regulation also strengthened the grip of the prime minister on his party MPs. Candidates running for elections had to be a member of the political parties under which they ran for at least 90 days. This rule was designed to end the traditional party-switching of legislators shortly before elections. Once the House was dissolved, elections had to be held within 45 or 60 days, a window of time not large enough for would-be party-switchers to make some last minute changes to their affiliations. Having the power to decide on a House dissolution, the prime minister gained considerably more clout, as he or she could now better control government party factions by preventing them from party-switching.

The influence of the legislature over the prime minister was limited in two ways. First, the number of cabinet members was limited to a maximum of 36 persons. This clause was intended to decrease the number of politicians without bureaucratic or administrative background in the executive, "thus facilitating policy implementation and reducing the number of politicos who seek to collect rent in the council of ministers" (Chambers 2002, p. 22). Second, legislative influence on the government was also limited by introducing an incompatibility clause for cabinet and parliament membership. MPs who were appointed to the cabinet had to give up their parliamentary mandate and had to be replaced by party fellows next on the party list. The prime minister thus had more control over his ministers since being sacked by the prime minister also entailed that one be out of the national institutions until the next election.

Furthermore, the stability of the prime minister was further enhanced by raising the necessary numbers for a vote of no confidence. Previously, any prime minister might have had to face a vote of no-confidence debate from the opposition, which could be easily initiated by just 20 per cent of the representatives. As a consequence "in order to be secure the prime minister not only had to maintain the support of his party factions and other coalition partners, he also had to successfully placate 81 percent of the members of the House" (Hicken 2007a, p. 51). This is indeed a difficult task which can often fail, as numerous cabinet dissolutions in the political history of Thailand attest.

Thus, in 1997, a high two-fifths vote was required in place of one-fifth for a censure motion. There would now have to be a very strong and united opposition to reach the 40 per cent of votes required to start a debate over the removal of the prime minister. This increased threshold was intended to stabilize Thai governments in order to prevent frequent votes of no confidence of opposition parties that had little chance of success. At the same time, raising the threshold to 40 per cent[1] meant that during the rule of Prime Minister Thaksin *de facto* no votes of no confidence was now possible. Complaints that the opposition was powerless under these circumstances and that the rights of parliamentary minorities had been curtailed[2] were, however, not due to the elevated ratio of votes of no confidence, but rather to the resulting composition of parliament, which was determined by the Thai voters.

Another argument that touches the field of horizontal accountability is the disregard of the Thaksin government towards the legislature. As one academic stated, "Thaksin had absolute power, since he had absolute power in parliament. The prime minister ruled without the parliament since the MPs were under his control."[3] However, it is a frequent feature of parliamentary systems in established majoritarian democracies that the ruling party and its leadership dominate parliament. Due to the fusion of power, which is typical for a parliamentary system, the government and the majority in parliament work closely together. In the British House of

Commons, for example, the prime minister and its government are not challenged in their daily work by all members of parliament, but only by those in opposition.

Another majoritarian feature which stabilized the government and weakened the parliamentary opposition was the provision of Section 185 of the 1997 Constitution. This provision stated that the opposition had to nominate the next suitable prime minister in case of a vote of no confidence, while the dissolution of the House of Representatives was not permitted. Such a regulation, usually termed "constructive vote of no confidence", makes it difficult for the opposition to topple a government. It might be easy to be united against a prime minister, but it is certainly more difficult to find a majority for a common opposition candidate.

To the contrary, however, the 1997 Constitution tried to balance government power with several institutional reforms. The drafters tried to keep the judiciary independent from the government and the Ministry of Justice. Rule of law as an essential part of democracy requires that the influence of politicians and bureaucrats over judicial review be abolished. Therefore, the 1997 Constitution tried to establish "a judicial review process independent of executive branch control, thereby enhancing both government accountability and the protection of civil liberties" (Klein 1998, p. 15). Additionally, several independent organizations were created in order to control executive power. Their role will be discussed later.

The constitutional system of checks and balances was soon challenged as Thaksin Shinawatra was elected as prime minister on 9 February 2001. Thaksin used the constitutional provisions that strengthened the position of the prime minister *vis-à-vis* parliament. Contributing to the enormous concentration of power in his hands was his huge and growing popularity, as reflected in the election results. As described in chapter 3.1, his Thai Rak Thai party obtained election results that no other party ever achieved in all of Thai history. After the merger with the New Aspiration Party of General Chavalit and a coalition with the Thai Nation Party of Banharn Silpa-Archa, the parliamentary majority for the government grew from 248 to 325 out of 500 seats. Additionally, TRT lured dozens of sitting MPs to join them in the forthcoming elections. These huge parliamentary majorities dramatically reduced the influence of the parliamentary opposition, particularly the Democrat Party. In the 2005 elections, Thaksin's TRT was able to win 376 of 500 seats. His leadership style was that of a CEO, based on directives instead of dialogue or debates. The opinion of parliament was ignored and sessions often failed to take place due to a missing quorum since

Thaksin's supporters in parliament did not show up (Phongpaichit and Baker 2009, p. 96).

While the dominance of TRT – and thus the limited possibilities of a parliamentary control – was the product of the voters' will, other intrusions concerning the constitutional system of checks and balances were not in accordance with the intentions of the 1997 Constitution. His neglect of parliament, his frequent criticism of judicial institutions, and his interference in the work of the Senate and independent organizations compromised democratic procedures guaranteeing horizontal accountability (Case 2010, p. 221).

Thaksin claimed that "he was the mechanism which translated the will of the people into action by the state, overriding democratic principles, judicial process, and the rule-of-law on grounds that these principles had never benefited the ordinary people" (Phongpaichit 2006, p. 2). Consequently, Thaksin used its powers widely. His appointment policy within the military and police, however, caused dissatisfaction among the ranks and files. Many previous colleagues from his police academy times were promoted (Ockey 2007, p. 136). When he unexpectedly appointed his cousin, Chaiyasit Shinawatra, to commander-in-chief of the Royal Thai Army Forces and his brother-in-law, Priewpan Damapong, to assistant national police chief, voices in the bureaucracy and the military grumbled.

After the 2005 elections, Thaksin and his TRT party controlled more than 75 per cent (377 out of 500) of the seats in parliament. The opposition was virtually powerless and could neither scrutinize nor curb the executive power effectively. With only 123 members, it was unable to start a vote of no confidence against the Prime Minister, which according to the 1997 Constitution needed 200 out of 500 members. Additionally, the opposition could not file a parliamentary impeachment against ministers because in the 1997 Constitution, 125 MPs were required to request the Senate to pass a resolution for their removal. Thai scholar Siripan Nogsuan concluded that the parliament, after the 2005 elections, "did not have an effective mechanism to check on the prime minister's decisions and the government's actions" (Nogsuan 2005, p. 59).

One of the major reform intentions of the 2007 Constitution was the attempt to prevent a prime minister from becoming as powerful as Thaksin again. Many academics argued that democracy under Thaksin was too majoritarian in the sense of Liphart's typology. A Thai professor of law said that, "Thaksin thinks in categories of a rule of a majority, but did not consider the protection of minorities",[4] in reference to the people who opposed his rule. He further argued that political rule should be in accordance with principles of consensus democracy and that the majority should not dictate to the others what course of action to take.[5]

However, the executive-legislative relations in Thailand under Prime Minister Thaksin were analogous to that in Western democracies within a parliamentary system of government which can be described as a stable government supported by a broad parliamentary majority. In Thailand, however, many people regarded the broad parliamentary majority as a danger for democracy and an abuse of power (Nelson 2011, p. 56). It was argued that the position of the government was too strong and the opposition too weak. It should be noted, however, that the composition of the parliament was determined by free elections and that only the typical distortion effects of the (mainly) plurality voting system were responsible for the huge majority of Thaksin supporters in parliament.

Parliamentary Powers after 2007

After the military coup, the coup-appointed Constitution Drafting Assembly (CDA) and Constitution Drafting Committee (CDC) were tasked with "drawing up a new charter that would prevent any political leaders and their parties from 'monopolizing power' again – a key accusation against Thaksin and his Thai Rak Thai Party" (Nelson 2011, p. 57).

The vote of no confidence, the most powerful weapon of the parliament's minority, was made easier to implement in Section 158 of the 2007 Constitution. Instead of 40 per cent of the total number of the members of the House, only 20 per cent (or one-fifth) was required to submit a motion for a general debate over passing a vote of no confidence in the Prime Minister. The power of the parliament *vis-à-vis* the government was enhanced. The right to interpellate a minister was given to every member of the House of Representatives or senator in Section 156. However, the minister had the right to refuse to answer if the Council of Ministers is of the opinion that the matter should not yet be disclosed on the ground of safety or vital interest of the State.

The PPP governments under Samak Sundaravej and Somchai Wongsawat were in a much weaker position than the Thaksin administration. Frequent and violent mass demonstrations organized by the PAD were responsible for a turbulent political atmosphere in which the government had to spend more time restoring order than pursuing policies. This is in accordance with the observation of a Democrat MP who stated that "the PPP government did not produce any laws during their time in government in 2007. There were few policy issues to debate about."[6] The unrest further escalated in June 2008 as demonstrators occupied the Government House and Thailand's international airports shortly after.

The opposition in the House of Representatives tried to bring Prime Minster Samak and his cabinet down by launching votes of no confidence in June 2008. The Democrat Party grilled several cabinet members' performances over three days in parliament and tried to damage the Samak government by trying to illustrate to the general public its alleged weaknesses. Members of the opposition Democrat Party accused Samak of being "immature" and "verbally and mentally dysfunctional" (Beech 2008). They described the Samak cabinet as a "puppet" of Thaksin and accused the government "of having focused most efforts in the last four months on restoring or protecting political interests of Thaksin and his allies" (An Lu 2008). During the heated debate, Prime Minister Samak showed his disdain by skillfully folding origami cranes and putting them on his table (Beech 2008). At the end of the day, Samak's six-party coalition, which controlled two-thirds of parliament, shot down the motion of no confidence by a vote of 280 to 162.

In December 2008, after the Constitutional Courts' disqualification of Samak and his successor Somchai Wongsawat, a new prime minister had to be elected. In this crucial election, not only did the smaller parties vote for the opposition's candidate from the Democrat Party, Abhisit Vejjajiva, but quite a number of members of the dissolved PPP as well. Most of the defectors came from a faction of the PPP controlled by Newin Chidchob, the so-called Friends of Newin.

From an academic perspective, the election of Abhisit was in accordance with democratic principles. In a parliamentary system with multiple parties, it is necessary to form coalitions to create parliamentary majority. The fact that smaller parties join another coalition every now and then is a common practice even in established democracies. This was also the view of the Democrat Party:

> The take-over of power in 2008 was completely in order. People elected the MPs and in a parliamentary system, the candidate with the most votes becomes prime minister. After Somchai was banned, there was a fair competition between all factions in the House of Representatives. Would Pheu Thai complain if their candidates had won? We had the numbers since the Chidchob block joined our camp.[7]

Moreover, the Director General of Democrat Party argued that the Democrats attracted the Friends of Newin only for pragmatic reasons: "You know, everywhere in the world, it is like this in politics. We had to deal with the Chidchob people in order to implement our policies. We can accept them and in a fragmented party system, it is necessary to find coalition partners."[8]

However, there were also critical voices, not only from the red-shirt camp but also from academics. They argued that the clear winner of the 2007 parliamentary elections was the PPP, and so the will of the Thai voters was not implemented. They also claimed that the Armed Forces under Commander General Anupong Paochinda were actively involved in convincing MPs to switch, a move what later has been titled an "Anupong-style *coup d'état*" (Farolan 2009). Chaturon Chaisang, former MP of Thai Rak Thai, declared: "Those who have the power made some persons switch sides with the backing of military. Some secretaries of small parties told me that the military approached them by phone and ordered them to vote for Abhisit."[9] The Abhisit government might have come to power in a legally and formally correct way, but doubts about its legitimacy continued to be repeatedly expressed in the following years. Democrat minister Ong-art Klampaiboon commented on the legitimacy issue: "We had enough legitimacy for this change, since most of the people supported us. The red-shirts claim that we forced the smaller parties to join our cabinet, but this is not true."[10] As written above, this statement remains controversial.

After the transition of power, the parliamentary opposition remained a critical opponent to the executive. Prime Minister Abhisit Vejjajiva had to survive votes of no confidence three times, in March 2009, May 2010, and shortly before the elections in March 2011. The opposition accused Abhisit of financial irregularities, malfeasance, and spending budgets inappropriately. All of these censure motions were unsuccessful, but that was not the main target. The opposition could present themselves as an alternative to a nationwide audience and publicly criticize government politics. Not least due to these reasons, one could conclude that "the parliamentary powers were quite strong in the 2007 Constitution. There were frequent votes of no-confidence against Prime Minister Abhisit and the opposition's arguments were broadcasted on all TV stations."[11]

The opposition Pheu Thai party also used other tactics to exert control on the government and – according to a Democrat MP – "blamed the government of always doing everything wrong", but described this as the usual parliamentary procedure: "We did this between 2000 and 2007 and now the Pheu Thai are taking our methods, for example checking the quorum for a decision of the House of Representatives. The opposition uses all parliamentary tactics."[12] The Yingluck government, which came into power after the 2011 elections, also had to face serious opposition in the House of Representatives. In the second half of 2012, Prime Minister Yingluck Shinawatra was grilled by the opposition legislators on the alleged irregularities in the rice-pledging scheme, flood-response budget, and failure to enforce anti-corruption laws (New Straits Times 2012). Votes of no confidence were held against the prime minister, Deputy Prime Minister Chalerm Yubamrung, Defence Minister Sukumpol Suwanatat and Deputy Interior Minister Chatt Kuldilok, but failed to get a parliamentary majority.

Second Chamber: Senate

One of the main functions of the Thai Senate is to supervise the government. As mentioned in chapter 3.1, the Senate consisted of appointed members, mainly from bureaucratic and military ranks, until 1997. In the Thai bicameral setting, the Senate had the informal function of a "conservative brake" (Lijphart 1999, p. 203) which prevents an elected government from taking too drastic steps which might endanger the vested interests of the bureaucratic and military elites.

After the 1997 Constitution came into force, the Senate was directly elected. According to the 1997 Constitution (Sections 303–07), the Thai Senate had a very strong position towards the executive as well as the judiciary branches. It had the right to remove all public officials, including the prime minister, members of the House of Representatives, senators, the president of the Supreme Court, the president of the Constitutional Court, and the president of the Supreme Administrative Court or prosecutor general for corruption, abuse of power or malfeasance in office (Constitution of the Kingdon of Thailand 1997, Section 303).

According to Section 304, at least 25 per cent of the members of the House of Representatives, 25 per cent of the senators, and a minimum of 50,000 Thai citizens were allowed to file a complaint to the Senate President to remove someone from the above mentioned positions. If the National Counter Corruption Commission agreed with the accusations (Section 305), the Senate had the right to decide on the resolution of the removal of the office-holder with a 60 per cent majority in a secret ballot (Section 307). If such a qualified majority was found, the person had to leave his or her position immediately and was automatically banned from holding any other public office for the next five years.

In this time, Thaksin and his Thai Rak Thai party tried to build a majority in what was supposed to be a politically-neutral senate. This step was taken not only to stabilize and broaden the political power of Prime Minister Thaksin, but also to ensure that the Senate would use its appointment powers to get Thaksin's political affiliates, relatives, business partners, and friends into various state agency positions (Mutebi 2008, p. 164).

After the military coup, the 2007 Constitution thus tried to restore the supposed neutrality of the Senate by installing a semi-appointed Senate, whose main purpose was as prior to 1997, "to serve as a conservative deadweight on the parliament" (Phongpaichit 2006, p. 3). The appointment of half of the senators was intended to strengthen the non-partisan aspect of the Senate. However, the supposed neutrality of the Senate is highly doubtful since it "became home to the wives, children and relatives of leading politicians, a development that effectively neutralized any checks and balances on the executive branch" (Dressel 2009, p. 298).

The 2007 Constitution provided the Senate with new rights related to the horizontal accountability dimension. The Senate was empowered to appoint members of independent state agencies, such as the National Election Commission. It was also entitled to introduce motions for general debate. The right to remove any person from public office was confirmed in the 2007 Constitution. However, the violation of ethical standards was introduced as a reason for a complaint and the required number of people filing such a complaint against a public official was reduced from 50,000 to 20,000.

The constitutional articles mentioned above give the Senate considerable opportunities for exercising influence and control over the government and the judiciary. With the right to remove any office-holder for power abuse or corruption with a 60 per cent majority of the total numbers of seats, the Senate would be a threat to any government. This becomes even more problematic in terms of democratic quality if one considers that since 2007 half of the Senate is appointed rather than democratically elected.

The Judiciary

Thailand saw major reforms concerning its judicial system in recent years. The 1997 Constitution tried to establish a neutral judiciary independent from politics. Previously, the Constitutional Court was "a political institution rather than part of the judiciary" (Klein 1998, p. 19). While some of its previous members were members of the Senate or the House of Representatives, the 1997 Constitution provided for 15 full-time judges appointed by the king under consultation of the Senate. No judges were allowed to be part of any political party or hold a political office (Constitution of the Kingdon of Thailand 1997, Article 256). To guarantee their independence, they were appointed for nine years and had to refrain from business activities (Constitution of the Kingdon of Thailand 1997, Article 258).

The first serious test of the newly established independence of the Constitutional Court was the asset declaration case against recently elected Prime Minister Thaksin Shinawatra in 2001. The National Counter Corruption Commission accused him of concealing assets and thus providing false asset declaration. The case seemed to be clear, since two of his domestic servants "figured among the top ten holders of shares on the stock exchange" (Phongpaichit and Baker 2009, p. 1). However, there was a conflict between those who argued that a person who won the elections with the highest margin ever, should not be prevented from governing due to "minor formal offences", while others argued that the constitutional and legal principles must be held by everybody, including the prime minister himself. In the end, after "huge influences on the Constitutional court",[13] the accusations against Thaksin were dropped by a narrow 8–7 majority of the judges, what in the eyes of many observers had irrevocably damaged the Constitutional Court's standing (Harding and Leyland 2011, p. 180).

In the following years, Prime Minister Thaksin tried to gain control over the Constitutional Court by appointing judges that sympathized with his policies. This was a difficult undertaking since the higher levels of the judiciary were traditionally conservative monarchists. In late 2005 and early 2006, as Thaksin faced increased public dissent, several court cases were decided against the government. A particular critical decision of the Constitutional Court during the Thaksin rule was the annulment of the snap elections in 2006, which the opposition rated as a clear sign of the independence of the Constitutional Court. A number of its judges made clear that their allegiance belonged to the king and not to the serving government. In accordance, some members of the Constitutional Court held anti-Thaksin press conferences (Norton 2012. p. 60).

After the military coup, the powers of the judiciary were enormously fortified. The intention by the majority of the drafters of the 2007 Constitution was to limit the influence of politicians and political parties and to increase the powers of the allegedly impartial bureaucracy and judiciary. Aurel Croissant wrote that the provisions of the 2007 Constitution on the judiciary represent the "most obvious example of military dominated constitutional engineering for the purpose of reducing the risk of ... the rise of future hegemonic party leaders who stand to challenge other key political institutions" (Croissant 2010, p. 573). The strengthening of the judiciary *vis-à-vis* other state institutions has led to a series of consequences. Hundreds of politicians were banned from politics, the Thai Rak Thai[14] and the PPP were dissolved, and Prime Ministers Samak Sundaravej and Somchai Wongsawat had to step down after the constitutional court found them guilty of having acted unconstitutionally.

The political influence of the judiciary became clearly visible in August 2008 when Prime Minister Samak Sundaravej was disqualified by the Constitutional Court for accepting 10,000 Baht (approximately 250 Euros) as honorarium for his weekly TV cooking show. Many political observers, among them Naruemon Thabchumphon, rate this disqualification "as ridiculous. The mentioned conflict of interests is a problem which nearly every public person has. Politicians should represent the society, so there cannot only be completely good persons with high moral standards."[15]

In contrast, a professor of law argued that "the courts always stayed independent. Samak deserved his conviction. The cooking show was an exercise of influence on the Prime Minister by private enterprises",[16] and a parliament member of the Democrat Party stated that "the removal of Samak was justified, since he was an employee of a private company. If for a cooking show or only a small salary does not play any role."[17]

Coup order no. 27 made it possible for political parties to be dissolved and the rights of party executives to be revoked for five years. This order was put into law in Section 68 and 237 of the 2007 Constitution. Consequently, the Constitutional Court used this right to dissolve the ruling PPP along with its coalition members of Thai Nation Party and Neutral Democratic Party (Phak Matchima), and banned their party executives from exercising their political rights for five years in "blitz" of court cases (Case 2010, p. 225). Thaksin and his wife were convicted on charges of tax evasion and went into exile soon afterwards, whereas the Democrat Party and its executives were acquitted.

The fact that nearly all the persons and parties which were dissolved or banned belonged to the Thaksin camp raised questions about the impartiality of the Constitutional Court. Whereas some of the interviewed persons, among them Professor Kittisak Prokati, stressed the neutrality and independence of the court,[18] the former member of parliament, Chaturon Chaisang, who received a ban for his political activities, stated that "the judicial system is terrible. The judges are one-sided and they intervene in politics too much."[19] Even the Secretary General of the Thai Election Commission stated:

> The drafters of the law had very good intentions with the law, but the outcome is flawed, resulting in a political crisis. It is easy to establish political parties, but it also too easy to dissolve them. Article 237 [of the 2007 Constitution dealing with the dissolution of political parties] is too strict.[20]

Most political observers concluded that the judgements of the courts after 2006 "have by and large been arbitrary and unfair" (Jha 2011, p. 334). Political scientist Naruemon Thabchumpon stated that the "Thai judiciary is the most conservative of all the state institutions. It is elitist and the judges do not have real-life experience. A judicialization of Thai politics does not help to promote democracy."[21] The question remains whether it is justified to "disqualify an elected Prime Minister and an entire political party [that won the elections] for relatively minor abuses" (Harding and Leyland 2011, p. 187).

Another questionable decision of the 2007 Constitution is the regulation that high-ranking members of the judiciary became permanent member of the selection commissions for all independent organizations and many state institutions. Whereas under the 1997 Constitution the judiciary had two out of seven seats in the selection committee, the number in the nomination process of members of independent watchdog organizations jumped to five under the 2007 Constitution.

Even more troublesome in terms of horizontal accountability is the selection nexus between the judiciary and the Senate. As mentioned above, four of the five members of the Senators Selection Committee, which has the right to appoint 73 senators, are from the judiciary. In turn, four of the nine constitutional court justices are selected by the Senate. The fact that the elected House of Representatives is completely excluded in the nomination of either constitutional court justices, appointed senate members, and members of independent government organizations is not favourable in terms of horizontal accountability since unelected officials mutually decide on the filling of important government positions, "at best muddying the lines of accountability, at worst raising the possibility of a *quid pro quo*" (Hicken 2009, p. 147).

Parinya Thewanarumitkul from Thammasat University, illustrated these contradictions using an example from sports: "It is like letting soccer referees choose which footballers get to play. The spectators will wonder if the referee will be able to perform his duty fairly because he has a stake in the selection of the players."[22]

The drafters of the 2007 Constitution used the judiciary to counter the formidable powers that had been given to the executive branch by the 1997 Constitution. Chaturon Chaisang argued in a similar way by stating that "the exaggerated power of the judiciary violates the principle of checks and balances".[23] Even a member of parliament of the Democrat Party agreed with that statement by stating that "the judiciary acted in an exaggerated manner in many cases. Now, the judiciary is too strong. The system of checks and balances was brought out of balance."[24] In this sense, the elected House of Representatives would no longer be the final arbiter for political decision-making and the election of government. This task would fall into the hands of the Constitutional Court, which could make decisions that transform the mandate of the people (Jha 2011, p. 338).

Independent Oversight Organizations

In order to improve horizontal accountability and to better guarantee a system of checks and balances, the Constitution of 1997 introduced several new independent government agencies. Among them were the National Counter Corruption Commission (NCCC), the National Human Rights Commission, the Anti-Money Laundering Office, the Consumer's Protection Organization, the Environmental Conservation Organization, and the office of the Ombudsman.

However, all of these fledgling independent institutions, which were mandated by the 1997 Constitution, "struggled to establish their authority and credibility" (Mutebi 2008, p. 156). The main tasks of the National Counter Corruption Commission (NCCC), which as an independent commission was appointed in April 1999, were to oversee mandatory annual disclosures of assets and liabilities of most politicians and senior bureaucrats. As stipulated by the Anti-corruption Law of 1999, it also had the mandate to inquire and decide whether public officials are unusually wealthy, demonstrate corruption, or make false and incomplete declarations. The authority of the NCCC was shortly afterward heavily undermined when its verdict on Thaksin Shinawatra for manipulation of his asset declaration was overturned by the Constitutional Court in 2001 (Eschborn 2001).

Thaksin supporters described the NCCC and other independent state agencies "as remnants of the old feudal-bureaucratic order, which 'stole power away from the people' by [trying to remove] ... their own chosen leader" (Phongpaichit and Baker 2009, p. 4f.). Consequently, Thaksin tried its best to reduce the checks on his governance. During the time of Thaksin's rule, "the so-called independent state agencies turned into government controlled agencies."[25] The military later used "interference in the work of independent agencies" as one of the reasons for their *coup d'état* in 2006.

However, the new power holders did not make the independent agencies more independent. After the military coup they were formally kept, but with a firmer grip on them by the judiciary and the senate. Their impartiality can be highly doubtful. Most of the chairmen and members were appointed under military rule for nine-year terms and will retain their positions until at least 2016 (Connors 2011, p. 105f.).

One organization was particularly strengthened by the 2007 Constitution: The National Election Commission (ECT), which replaced the Ministry of Interior (MoI) in overseeing local, provincial, and national elections. It can issue penalties to candidates who engage in electoral irregularities. First, there is the issuance of "red cards", which disqualify candidates from subsequent election rounds, forbids them from running in elections for one year, and forces them to pay for repeat elections. Secondly, there are "yellow cards", which quash the election results of candidates suspected of improprieties, but permit them to run in a second electoral round. After elections, the ECT receives complaints from the various constituencies and then either decides to endorse the elected candidates or to hand the cases over to the Constitutional Court, who then decides whether to disqualify anyone for the violation of election laws.

At least on paper, Thailand provides a framework for enforcing accountability of those in power. They have the constitutional rights to act as agencies of horizontal accountability. However, the independence of the so-called independent monitoring agencies should be questioned. The interference of governments in their affairs by appointments and political pressure led to a notable loss of legitimacy. Their change into a tool of those in power started during the rule of Prime Minister Thaksin, but was later aggravated with the military coup and the following 2007 Constitution.

5.2 INDONESIA

Executive-Legislative Relations

After decades of authoritarian rule by a president who was not effectively held in check by other state agencies, the constitutional amendments between 1999 and 2002 counteractively placed much emphasis on horizontal accountability. In the course of these institutional reforms, the "balance of power among the executive, legislative, and judicial branches was carefully designed and implemented so as to prevent the re-establishment of an authoritarian regime" (Kawamura 2010, p. 1).

In contrast to the presidential system of the United States, the Indonesian president has no direct veto power over legislation. Instead, Article 20, Section 2 determines that every bill must be discussed collectively by the national parliament, the DPR, and the president in order to reach joint approval (*persetujuan bersama*). Therefore, and again in contrast to many other presidential democracies, the Indonesian president and its ministers actively participate in deliberations on bills with the national parliament.

In place of veto power, the Indonesian president may intervene directly in the deliberation process by denying a bill before it is brought to a vote in parliament. This means that when a bill is voted on and passed by parliament, it also signifies the president's approval as well. In this way, the Indonesian president does not have a direct veto on parliamentary legislation, but rather an indirect one during the deliberations. Bills of which neither the president nor parliament approve are dropped.

This way of dealing with legislation among executive and legislative is consensus-oriented since it avoids a direct and public confrontation between government and parliament. Instead, an intensive search for compromise takes place behind closed doors in the negotiations between the two branches of government. Both sides can prevent legislation that they do not prefer, so that neither branch dominates the legislative process. Consequently, legislation is not a clear parliamentary prerogative since legislative outcomes have to be negotiated with government representatives. The government can thereby delay or even stall legislation that a parliamentary majority supports. The national budget also falls under the rubric of a bill and is thus subjected to a consensus-oriented procedure. The government prepares a draft of the state budget, which is then jointly discussed with parliament in the same way as other bills. Usually, the deliberation time for the yearly national budget is shorter than for other bills, but no less intensive. So far, the president and parliament have reached an agreement over the national budget at the end of every year, which marks a contrast to the Philippines (see chapter 5.3).

The joint approval of bills stipulated by the constitution is not the only reason why the Indonesian president is not able to control the legislative process. Political decision-making in Indonesia is generally based on *musyawarah* (deliberation) and *mufakat* (compromise), which are prescribed, for instance, in the DPR's Standing Orders. Debating until a compromise is reached that everybody can accept characterizes the Indonesian way of making decisions in parliament. In accordance with this third principle of Indonesia's state philosophy, *Pancasila*, majority votes are practically never held in the parliament's committees. The rule of consensus decision-making in a fragmented multi-part system results in long deliberations and manifold possibilities to amend or to delay bills.

Such a manner of decision-making is contrary to democratic accountability and makes it very difficult for the general public to identify and discern the political attitude of single legislators or factions. Reaching a consensus can often involve dubious back room dealings, horse-trading, and other non-transparent ways of decision-making prone to corruption. This process, which is "unique among democratic parliaments in the world, is probably the most important instrument for ... avoidance of transparency and public accountability" (Sherlock 2010, p. 168). However, it is also quite normal in other established democracies that crucial decisions and compromises are made behind back doors and not in the plenary session.

Due to the proportional election system of the national parliament (see chapter 3.2), the chances that the president's party has a majority within the DPR are very low. The party of President Susilo Bambang Yudhoyono, the Democrat Party, received only 7.5 per cent of votes and 57 out of 560 seats in the 2004 elections. In 2009, despite being the winning party, it received only 20.9 per cent of the votes and with 148 seats, just over one quarter of the total seats in parliament.

A president without a majority in parliament is according to scholarly literature on comparative politics and "conventional wisdom based on the experience of other legislatures internationally ... a formula for legislative deadlock and possible political instability" (Sherlock 2007, p. 16). These gridlock situations between the executive and legislative branches that are so characteristic of presidential systems in other countries became a possibility for Indonesian politics. In order to pursue his or her policies and avoid gridlock situations, every president thus has the task of establishing a stable political support base in parliament.

Therefore, SBY followed the example of his two predecessors, Abdurrahman Wahid, and Megawati Sukarnoputri, and formed multi-party coalition governments, so-called "rainbow coalitions". After both elections, in 2004 and 2009, President SBY was able to win the powerful Golkar faction for his camp. In 2004, Golkar, being the largest faction in the DPR, moved away from its initial opposition to SBY when his vice-president, Yusuf Kalla, was elected as new chairman of the party in December 2004. Golkar then left its oppositional role and became a faction in support of the Yudhoyono administration. Shortly before the presidential elections in 2009, Golkar left the coalition with the president and announced Yusuf Kalla as their own presidential candidate in competition to SBY. After the electoral defeat in the 2009 presidential elections, Golkar soon returned to the presidential camp, particularly after Aburizal Bakrie became the party's new chairman. Golkar's decision was awarded with various ministerial posts, and Bakrie became leader of the majority parliamentary coalition.

Without going into detail as to how President SBY was able to bring all the various parties into his coalition, it can be said that the incentives for being part of the presidential coalition weigh much more than formally being in opposition. From the perspective of the incumbent president,

> inviting major political parties into government provides a degree of political stability and support in parliament. Parties that choose to participate in cabinet in turn receive access not only to the levels of policy-making but also to the state resources and patronage that come with government office (Sukma 2010, p. 67).

Most ministers obtained their posts more on the grounds of their party's backing of the executive than of their actual competence or suitability (Braun 2008, p. 239), which is a global phenomenon of coalition governments. In contrast, it is not very attractive to remain in opposition. The only major party that opted for an oppositional role since 2004, the Indonesian Democratic Party – Struggle (PDI-P), did not gain additional voter support for its long time in opposition.

Given the overwhelming support for the incumbent presidents, the question is whether the principle of horizontal accountability between executive and legislative can still be upheld. Critics of the Indonesian "rainbow coalitions" argue that they are not supportive of the deepening of democracy in Indonesia since the DPR – due to the relatively low number of opposition members – cannot fulfill its regulatory function towards the government. In contrast to many other scholars (Slater 2009; Diamond 2009), I would argue that the Indonesian legislature still controls government actions effectively and is not subservient to the administration. In Indonesian democracy, there is "no guarantee that government parties in the DPR will consistently support the government" (Sukma 2010, p. 68). Indonesian presidents thus cannot expect unconditional support from their coalition partners in the DPR. The coalition parties, despite their leaders having ministerial posts, often opposed bills presented by the government and delayed them in negotiation rounds. Several bills sponsored by the administration have been deliberated for more than ten years now. Thus the majority of the presidents in the DPR and the "share of the ruling parties' seats in parliament turned out to be a merely nominal number" (Kawamura 2010, p. 44). The parliamentary factions of the pro-government parties felt little reluctance to criticize the government's actions even though they were part of the administration themselves (Sherlock 2010, p. 174). On various occasions President SBY underlined the necessity of mutual checks and balances as requirement for the working of horizontal accountability: *"Pandangan saya stabilitas politik dan kerukunan, langsung tidak langsung ditentukan apakah di negeri ini terjadi check and balancies"* [In my view, political stability and harmony depend directly or indirectly on whether in this country check and balances function, translation by the author] (Yudhoyono 2011).

An apposite example of this is the Bank Century Scandal in which the DPR held Finance Minister Sri Mulyani Indrawati and Central Bank President Boediono accountable for bailing out the financially stricken Bank Century in 2008 with several billion US dollars during the global financial crisis. Many legislators believed that the bank bailout was not to prevent financial contagion and bank runs, but rather to safeguard the personal interests of large deposit holders at the bank (Osman 2012). Every faction in the DPR, save the president's Democratic Party, vehemently criticized the administration. Since neither Boediono nor Sri Mulyani had any party affiliation, they were attacked by every faction.

Since Indonesian party politics are highly competitive (Tomsa 2010, p. 154), the various parties used this incidence to improve their support from the general public and initiated the creation of a parliamentary investigation committee. Boediono, at this time, was the vice-president and Sri Mulyani one of the closest associates of the president. The Golkar party in particular, whose chairman, Aburizal Bakrie, had a personal conflict with Finance Minister Sri Mulyani (von Luebke 2010, p. 85), tried its best to use the parliamentary investigation to remove the two non-partisan technocrats from government. Whereas Sri Mulyani soon resigned in May 2010, the inquiries into Boediono's role during the Bank Century bailout dragged on much longer.

In 2011, President SBY announced that he was willing to punish two of his coalition parties, Golkar and PKS, for their tendency to vote against the government in parliament, but eventually made only minor reshuffles within its cabinet (Mietzner 2012*b*, p. 121). The opposition to the administration is understandable. In a presidential system of government with a pluralistic party system such as that of Indonesia, "parties which aim to win in the coming presidential election have few incentives to maintain cooperation as coalition partners" (Kawamura 2010, p. 46). For this reason, the "rainbow coalitions" in Indonesia might be detrimental to horizontal accountability, but the high degree of electoral competition leads to a political reality in which the legislature exercises political control over government actions. Since his re-election in 2010, President Yudhoyono tried rather to stabilize his position, which was weakened not only by the Bank Century scandal but also by several corruption cases within his Democrat Party, than to push for reforms. Prominent members of his cabinet, as well as opposition figures and parties, "are already beginning to maneuver for the presidential elections to be held in 2014" (Kimura 2012, p. 194). For various reasons, the executive-legislative relations in Indonesia are balanced and presidential powers limited. The combination of a multi-party system resulting in coalition governments (as a result of the proportional election system for the DPR) and the legislative practice of *musyawarah/mufakat* work against the danger of gridlock and result in consensus-style decision-making.

Second Chamber: DPD

The re-organization of the state institutions also led to the formation of a second chamber of the national parliament, the DPD (*Dewan Perwakilan Daerah*), which underlined the broadening of power-sharing democracy in Indonesia. In the constitutional amendments of November 2001, the DPD was created as a directly elected parliamentary chamber based on territorial representation. Every single one of the 33 Indonesian provinces is represented by four elected representatives. This arrangement particularly favours the smaller and less populated provinces of the country, which are generally in the less developed eastern region. The strengthening of political representation of the smaller provinces must be seen as a counterbalance to the 60 per cent domination of Javanese constituents in the DPR, according to their share of the total population of Indonesia.

The first elections of the DPD took place in 2004. DPD candidates are not allowed to be members of political parties. The functions of the DPD are defined in Article 22D, which stipulates that the DPD may submit to the DPR bills dealing with regional autonomy, relations between the centre and the regions, the establishment and growth as well as the merger of regions, the management of natural and other economic resources, and matters related to the financial balance between the centre and the regions. It is also allowed to participate in debates on bills dealing with regional autonomy; relations between the centre and the regions; the establishment, growth and merger of regions; the management of natural and other economic resources; matters related to the financial balance between the centre and the regions; and, moreover, give recommendations to the DPR on bills dealing with the state budget and with taxation, education, and religion. Regarding the autonomy, establishment, merger and growth of regions, as well as the management of natural and other economic resources, state budget, taxation, education, and religion, the DPD may also supervise implementation and submit results to the DPR as input for follow-up considerations.

Although the DPD has only deliberative functions, it broadens the representation of otherwise excluded groups in the political decision-making process. The restricted powers of the DPD lead to an asymmetric power-sharing between the two chambers, however. In Indonesia, there is a weak bicameralism due to the relative powerlessness of the DPD in comparison to the DPR, as well as miniscule influence on the national government. Insofar the DPD's role for horizontal accountability is limited. It furthermore effectively fails to promote vertical accountability and is therefore not mentioned in chapter 4.2. The DPD leadership often demanded an upgrading of the DPD to a real second chamber, but the likelihood that this will happen within the coming years is dim.

The Judiciary

The judiciary generally has a bad reputation in Indonesia. The Supreme Court (*Mahkamah Agung*), the public prosecutor's office, and the lower courts have done little to improve the rule of law. Particularly the Supreme Court

> is universally condemned for its corruption, its lack of coordination and inefficient management, its factionalism, its malleability by the powers-that be, its poor training and educational standards, and its inability to influence the law-making process, especially for the country's lower courts (Davidson 2009, p. 300).

The most important judicial institution in terms of horizontal accountability, the Constitutional Court (*Mahkamah Konstitusi*), which was inaugurated in 2003, "has been trying to establish itself as a strong and respectable institution" (Hendrianto 2010, p. 172) and has delivered a much better performance. The authority to review the compatibility of laws with the constitution was the most crucial mandate given to the court. The Constitutional Court thus acts as the final interpreter of the constitution. Beside this important task, the Constitutional Court must, in accordance with Article 24c of the Indonesian Constitution, mediate disputes between state institutions, decide on the dissolution of political parties, and adjudicate disputes on general election results. The Constitutional Court additionally has the power to determine whether an impeachment of an incumbent president and/or vice president is warranted. The creation of a Constitutional Court was the most significant institutional reform in terms of horizontal accountability. The Law on the Constitutional Court (*undang-undang No. 24/2004 tentang Mahkamah Konstitusi*) gave this institution the power to annul any legislation enacted by the legislative and/or executive branches, if such legislation is deemed to have failed the test of constitutionality.

Since the inauguration of the Constitutional Court, legislative institutions were no longer able to formulate laws based on political strength alone, because despite having been passed democratically, the entire law or part of its substance can be annulled by the court if it deems its content or the method that engendered it to be in contradiction to the Constitution (Mahfud 2009, p. 33). In contrast to many other countries, the Indonesian Supreme Court has so far guarded its independence from the executive and issued many decisions which were not supported by the president and its administration. It has shown willingness to decide on politically unpopular causes, for example the previously mentioned scrapping of law articles that banned people accused of association with the Communist Party of Indonesia from participation in elections. The court also annulled Articles 154 and 155 of the criminal code that made defaming the government a criminal offense (Harvard Kennedy School Indonesia Program 2010, p. 79). In relation to this case, chief justice Mohammed Mahfud explained that

> the formulation of both articles may create a tendency toward abuse of power, since they can be easily interpreted according to the preference of the rulers. As a consequence, these articles hinder the freedom to express thoughts and attitudes as well as the freedom to convey opinions, and therefore, they are contradictory to … the 1945 Constitution (Mahfud 2009, p. 19f.).

As mentioned in chapters 3.2 and 3.3, the Constitutional Court dealt a potentially significant blow to the political establishment by permitting the participation of non-partisan candidates in elections for regional head positions (Braun 2008, p. 198).

The Constitutional Court thus acted as a major contender in the process of institutional engineering. However, by demonstrating its power, impartiality, and independence from the two other branches of government, the Constitutional Court has incurred the anger of many established political players (Braun 2008, p. 199). In June 2011, the Indonesian parliament reduced the powers of the Constitutional Court significantly. Beside the reduction in the term of service of court judges from three to two-and-a-half years, Law No. 8/2011 prohibits the court from creating new regulations by replacing provisions of a law that conflict with the constitution. Instead, formulating new legal provisions should be the sole task of the House of Representatives. Additionally, the court is no longer able to decide on matters on which it has not been asked to make decisions. Law Minister Patrialis Akbar lauded the bill on the Constitutional Court by stating that, "if [a law] gets cancelled, the Constitutional Court will not make its own rule. They should return [the matter] to the House" (Indrasafitri 2011).

Whereas representatives of the executive and legislative approved of limiting the powers of the court, several law experts voiced their concerns. The balance of power between executive, legislative, and judiciary has been moved to the advantage of the former two. The reduction of those powers of the Constitutional Court which have so far been an important check on executive and legislative decisions did not lead to an improvement in terms of horizontal accountability. However, if the Constitutional Court is serious in regaining its powers, it could declare Law No. 8/2011 as not in accordance with the constitution and annul it. To this proposition, Chief Justice Mahfud was quoted as saying: "if one day, someone challenges the law because he or she feels the law has seriously violated his or her constitutional rights, then I will seriously consider that" (Christanto 2011).

So far, the ultimate escalation of conflict between the state powers, the impeachment, has not occurred since 2004. Several members of the parliament threatened to impeach Vice-President Boediono due to his involvement in the previous Bank Century scandal between 2010 and 2012, but did not put their intentions to practice. As Article 7B of the Indonesian constitution prescribes, an impeachment proposal must be supported by a minimum of two-thirds of all DPR members. Then, the Constitutional Court must decide within 90 days if the allegations are judicially justified. Finally, the MPR (*Majelis Permusyawaratan Rakyat*, People's Consultative Assembly), which includes both chambers of the legislature, the DPR and the DPD, must hold a plenary assembly to decide whether or not to remove the president and/or vice president from office (Pangadaran and Parluhutan 2011, p. 128ff.).

Independent Oversight Organizations

The most notable independent accountability agencies in Indonesia since 2004 are the Corruption Eradication Commission (*Komisi Pemberantasan Korupsi*, KPK) and the Supreme Audit Agency (*Badan Pemeriksa Keuangan*, BPK).

The KPK has particularly been a major player in investigating power abuse and corruption of executives at the national and regional level. It has convicted more than a hundred prominent public officials (among them several national ministers and senior bureaucrats), over 20 national legislators, and more than 100 mayors, governors, or members of provincial and district parliaments. Most of them were removed from office, found guilty of graft, and jailed for several years (Fealy 2011, p. 337). Even the father of the daughter-in-law of President SBY, Aulia Pohan, a former top manager of the Central Bank of Indonesia, was investigated by KPK and, in 2009, finally found guilty of embezzling more than 100 billion Rupiah (approximately 8 million Euros) from a central bank foundation. He was sentenced to four years and six months in prison, which was later reduced to three years. Aulia Pohan was finally released on good conduct after serving just twenty months.

KPK thus served as an important element of horizontal accountability by holding those in power accountable. It enjoyed broad public support and "amid high expectations, ... has succeeded in maintaining the public trust" (Schütte 2009, p. 98). In all public opinion surveys, KPK has always been the most popular state institution, particularly in contrast to the national police, which is regarded as ineffective and corrupt. These two organizations have frequent clashes over competencies, and a well-known political image depicts the KPK as a small but smart gecko (*cicak*) fighting a big but ugly crocodile (*buaya*).

However, "KPK's success in uncovering corruption and bringing high-profile politicians and officials to justice has earned it the wrath of many in elite circles" (Fealy 2011, p. 338). KPK thus "faced not only a lack of resources, legal clarity and cooperation, but also counteraction from those who feel their interests are threatened" (Schütte 2009, p. 98). The national parliament, of whom many legislators have been convicted for graft, has in several cases attempted to reduce KPK's powers and independence. In 2009, the DPR proposed legislation that intended to strip KPK from its powers to wiretap and to prosecute (Case 2011, p. 29), but massive public protest from civil society groups and the media prevented the legislature from implementing their ideas. Additionally, the DPR, appointed "less credible or more compliant commissioners" (Fealy 2011, p. 338) to slow down KPK's investigations. Consequently, the national parliament "used its legislative powers ... to protect its patronage rather than to promote good governance and horizontal accountability" (Case 2011, p. 29). The ongoing trend to limit the powers of the KPK as the most important independent accountability agency is worrisome, since it prevents the discovery and conviction of power abuse and corruption of those in power.

The second most important independent monitoring organization is the Supreme Audit Agency (*Badan Pemeriksa Keuangan*, BPK). After several internal reforms, among them the adoption of standardized accounting methods, the BPK has emerged from a previously powerless and poorly functioning organization to a state institution which has helped to improve the accountability and performance of other state institutions. The public sector reforms received little attention from academics and the general public, but nevertheless contributed to a better oversight of public spending. Indonesia's remarkable reduction of public debts between 2002 and 2010 is not only due to responsible government behaviour but also to the improved audit capacities of BPK. In 2009, the International Organisation of Supreme Audit Institutions (INTOSAI) undertook a peer review of BPK and concluded: that since 2004, BPK "has laid strong foundations to function as a Supreme Audit Institution. .... Although the Peer Review team has made many recommendations (meant for further improvement) the overall conclusion is clearly very positive" (INTOSAI 2009, p. 2).

Law No. 15/2006 removed many previous legal inconsistencies on public auditing and determined BPK as the only external audit institution of Indonesia. Further internal reforms have strengthened the ability of BPK to act as an independent auditing institution. Table 5.1 depicts the reforms that have taken place since 2004.

In 2011, an evaluation of the Asian Development Bank concluded that BPK has

> achieved significant results in public expenditure management through strengthening the capacity of the public audit sector. However, various public finance related issues remain, such as the persistence of fraud and corrupt practices, weak financial management by the central and local governments, and lack of public participation in oversight of public expenditure management (Asian Development Bank 2011, p. 14).

Table 5.1
Institutional Reforms Concerning the Indonesian Supreme Audit Agency

No	Public Sector Auditing	Before Reform	After Reform
1.	External audit institution(s)	BPKP, BPK	Only BPK
	– The function of BPK	Limited auditing of central government	Auditing all state finances of central and local governments, SOEs and ROEs
	– The function of BPKP	Auditised central government, SOEs, and ROEs	Supporting internal auditing functions
	– Reporting to	The President and Parliament	Direct to Parliament and regional functions
	– Basic laws	ICW and IAR regulations	The third amendment of the 1945 Constitution, State Finances Package Laws (2003–04) and Law on BPK (2006)
	– Auditing standards	SAP (1995)	SPKN (2007)
	– Types of Audit	Financial and compliance audits	Financial, performance and specific purpose audits
	– Position of BPK	A high institution (a limited power of state institution)	A state institution (stronger position)
2.	Internal audit institution(s)	Bawasda, IG, SPI, Main Inspectorate	BPKP, Bawasda, IG, Main Inspectorate
	– The function	Post auditing	Pre-auditing for management of state finances
	– Basic laws	Colonial era of the Netherlands, IAR (1933)	Law on State Finances (2003), Law on Treasury, and Audit Law (GOI 2004)
	– Accounting standards	Not available	Based on Government Accounting standards (2005)

Source: Dwiputrianti (2011), p. 28.

As this study indicates, many problems remain and the strengthening of BPK by institutional reforms is only the start of improving horizontal accountability by a better public audit sector.

5.3 PHILIPPINES

The Philippines traditionally have a presidential system of government with a bicameral Congress and an independent Supreme Court. Like in the United States, a strict separation of powers is the main principle behind the Philippine Constitution of 1987. In terms of horizontal accountability, the power of the directly elected president should be controlled by the legislative and judicial branches as well as from several independent constitutional watchdog agencies. The formal system of checks and balances between government branches and agencies is well established in the Philippines (Dressel 2011, p. 534). However, as in the cases of Indonesia and Thailand, the political realities are somewhat different.

Executive-Legislative Relations

As regards most presidential systems, there is an ongoing academic debate whether the political system of the Philippines is executive-heavy or legislative-heavy. President GMA said in her 2007 State of the Nation Address that "from where I sit, I can tell you, a president is always as strong as she wants to be" (Romero and Sy 2007). Does the position of president in the Philippines hold too much power (as the quote from GMA seems to indicate)? To what degree is the president beholden to Congress, or dominant to it?

Like in the United States, the Philippine president has no right to directly initiate laws but must instead rely on his or her allies in the House of Representatives for bringing a proposal to the formal agenda of the law-making process. Once the process has started in the House of Representatives, the President has no direct influence on how fast or through what means a bill will be dealt with by the committees of Congress. Thus, the president depends in terms of legislative matters on the cooperation of Congress. At the same time, the Congressional powers of the law-making process are also limited. According to the Philippine Constitution (Article VI, Section 27 (1)), the President can veto any law passed by Congress. Both chambers then have to find a two-thirds majority to override a presidential veto. Such a situation rarely occurs. Indeed, since 1935 no presidential veto has been overridden by Congress (Bolongaita

2000, p. 71). This seems to be rather unusual for a presidential democracy, but, as will be later explained, is typical for executive-legislative relations in the Philippines.

A president also has informal ways of preventing unwanted legislation even without a veto. As a Philippine Congressman explained:

> If the president is against a bill, it will never make it on the agenda of the plenary session of the House of Representatives. If Malacañang doesn't want the law, then they will tell the House Speaker or the Majority leader to delay it indefinitely. This happened to the Compensation Bill for victims of the Marcos dictatorship, for example. The Speaker told us [the initiators] that he will first ask Malacañang's opinion on the proposal and then we never heard anything about it.[26]

The most crucial interactions between the executive and legislative branches are those concerning the national budget. The task of formulating and submitting the budget to the legislature rests with the executive. The budget is drafted by the national administration and then discussed as a General Appropriations Bill in Congress. A peculiarity of the Philippine system is that Congress cannot increase the expenditures proposed by the administration. After it is approved by the House of Representatives, the bill is sent to the Senate. The House is constitutionally empowered as the sole originator of all appropriation laws. The Senate can only concur and amend appropriation bills passed by House. This practice "makes the position of a district representative, potentially more powerful than a seat in the Senate" (Gutierrez 1998, p. 64). Both chambers then discuss their respective versions through a bicameral Committee and must agree to a final version, which is then delivered to the President for approval. Unlike other legislation, the Philippine president has not only a package veto but also a line-item veto, meaning that he or she can block single items from the budget bill. Legislative scope of action is restricted by the provision that the legislature may not increase the appropriations recommended by the President for the operation of the government as specified in the budget.

If a deadlock between both houses occurs, the preceding year's budget will be re-enacted. The same procedure is followed if the president refuses to sign the General Appropriations Bill. Practice in recent years shows that these provisions are not only theoretical. Particularly during the presidency of GMA (2001–10), conflicts between the President and Congress led to questionable practices by the executive. In just a few years of her presidency, an agreement was made between Congress and the President. In most cases, she vetoed the General Appropriations Bill on which Congress agreed and re-enacted the budget of the previous year.

The fact that GMA's budget proposals were three times not approved seemed to be negative for the president, since "it is important for any President to get his budget approved in order to conduct new operations."[27] However, the refusal of the budget can also give the Philippine president a greater leverage on spending public money. As Leonor Magtolis-Briones, former professor of Public Administration at the University of the Philippines, explained, a re-enacted budget would give greater elbow room to the president, since new projects proposed by Congress would have to be scrapped and the president can use "savings" from the reallocated funds for projects already completed last year to his or her own discretion (Benaning 2009).

The legislature occupies a strategic position in the budget process, since it can be used to control executive discretion as well as to impact the department's policies. Top officials of the national government have to "defend" their budget each year in front of the House Committee on Appropriations (HCA). Legislators not only monitor the spending of public funds, but also try to channel funds into their own projects and constituencies and to prevent rival legislators from doing so. Members of the HCA must have good connections and relations with the Department of Budget and Management (DBM). Only then can a smooth dealing with the national budget be guaranteed. The HCA is by far the biggest and most attractive committee in Congress and has a "strategic importance ... for the resource flows in the Philippine political system" (Rüland, Nelson, Jürgenmeyer, and Ziegenhain 2005, p. 206). Of the total 285 members of the House of Representatives in the 15th Congress (2010–13), 125 are members of the HCA. During budget negotiations, Congressmen pressure the departments and their secretaries to grant them their projects; otherwise, they threaten to cut the budget of the department (Calica 2010). Thus far, both can check on one another and the important details of the budget are known only to these two sides (Gutierrez 1998, p. 70).

Benjamin "Ben" Diokno, Secretary of the Department of Budget and Management (DBM) between 1998–2001, explained that

> the Congressmen always had long lists prepared with their wishes. In the first years of democracy since 1986, the needs of the legislators were simple, nowadays they ask for the moon. We had to wheel and deal, particularly in the Congressional bicameral committee where no minutes are taken and nothing will be known to the public.[28]

The budget negotiation process in the Philippines "has become an art, practiced by politicians skilled in the intricacies of budget decision-making and the mechanics of the political *areglo* (deal)" (Gutierrez 1998, p. 59) so that budget negotiations can be regarded as a kind of "institutional financial corruption".[29]

However, one can still argue that the Philippine president retains control over the budget since the administration which prepares the budget proposal as well as the legislators can only decrease and shift expenditures. Additionally, he or she can, as previously mentioned, use a line-item veto on the budget bill approved by Congress. The implementation of the national budget gives the president other scope of action for transferring budget items (Kawanaka 2010, p. 8). Thus, the "power of the purse" is not effectively in the hands of Congress, but in those of the president.

Pork Barrel

Another peculiarity of the Philippine executive-legislative relationship is the high amount of money which Filipino legislators receive from the national budget for the development of their constituencies. More than 200 million pesos (about 3.25 million Euros) for each senator and 70 million (about 1.14 million Euros) for each Congressman are spent in a programme called the Priority Development Assistance Fund (PDAF). These funds, generally called "pork barrel" in the Philippines, are of major importance for every legislator. In order to increase the chances of being re-elected, Congressmen are expected to channel national funds to their respective constituencies. In the Philippines, the pork barrel is also generally regarded as an instrument that politicians use for their own benefit. As explained in chapter 4.3, they can strengthen and expand their patronage network by giving projects to certain local allies. The Congressman can additionally allocate more money than the receiving company spends and get a kickback payment in return. Many reported cases have "reinforced the notion that legislators misuse large pools of public funds over which they have discretion" (Parreño 1998, p. 34). The pork barrel, the mentioned state resources over which an individual legislator exercises dispersal power, "is perhaps the most intriguing component of the national budget. It can be considered as the single greatest attraction to politicians to seats of power and has been the source of funding for many a politician's electoral base" (Gutierrez 1998, p. 59).

The release of the pork barrel can be used by the executive as a tool to apply pressure to force the support of politicians, particularly in the House of Representatives. The president might threaten to delay the disbursement of the funds to recalcitrant legislators. President GMA in particular broke with the tradition that every Congressman gets the same amount of pork-barrel money. Opposition legislators were excluded or disadvantaged from the state funds. She did not break a formal law by doing so, but rather a customary tradition. President Aquino, in contrast, reassured all 270 members of the House of Representatives and all senators that they would get their allocations (Porcalla 2010). In 2012, however, Navotas Representative Tobias Tiangco complained that the [Aquino] administration exerted pressure on him by delaying and withholding his pork barrel when he refused to support the impeachment initiatives against Merceditas Gutierrez and Renato Corona. Tiangco added that by doing so, "the President can make life miserable for you" (Esguerra 2012). In the same year, it became obvious that several members of the Makabayan coalition as well as the Arroyo-clan and its allies were excluded from the pork-barrel distribution (Cabacungan 2012). In turn, an ally of the president, Akbayan Representative Arlene "Kaka" Bag-ao was given the funds of another representative, who became a fugitive after being sentenced to a long prison term for graft (Cabacungan and Salaverria 2013). It seems that the practice of reward and punishment for legislators by government funds continues under the Aquino administration.

In general, the Philippine president nearly always has a majority in the House of Representatives. Due to the turncoatism phenomenon described in chapter 3.3, the fact that representatives "gravitate toward the party that the president belongs to is a normal occurrence in Philippine politics" (Holmes 2012, p. 89). After her election victory in 2004 and the following influx of supporters of the administration, President GMA controlled 191 of the 221 seats of the House of Representatives (Case 2011, p. 38). In the following years, she lost the support of various groups, but the majority of allies and supporters in the House was never endangered. The same can be said of President Noynoy Aquino, who, thanks to many legislators who decided to join his side after the May 2010 elections, can count on a large majority in the House. The 109 seats originally held by the pro-GMA camp dwindled to 25 by the end of 2011 (Baviera 2012, p. 246). However, as in the case of GMA, President Aquino should be aware that at the end of his non-extendable term, the support of the House legislators might decline since many of them will potentially move to the camp of the most promising candidate of the 2016 elections.

Presidential Appointments

The Philippine Constitution gives the president discretion over more than 10,000 government positions. Of particular note is the fact that the president can appoint members of the Supreme Court based on a list prepared by the Judicial and Bar Council. The approval of the Commission on Appointments is needed for other positions. This commission, described in Article VI, Section 18 of the Constitution, is a powerful congressional body whose main task is to scrutinize executive appointments. The president nevertheless has the sole right to propose ambassadors and promotions within the Armed Forces.

All presidents have made use of their appointment powers to create a strong network of supporters within the administration. Consequently, pre-democratic patronage structures have continued to dominate Philippine politics since the beginning of the democratization. All presidents controlled the administration by dismissing their opponents and hiring loyalists (Baum 2011, p. 104). Another way of appointing people was mentioned by the former Secretary of the Department of Budget and Management, Ben Diokno, who stated that then President Estrada

> appointed people whom he rarely knew. Take for example, the Secretary of the National Economic and Development Authority (NEDA), Felipe Medalla. When I met with Estrada one morning, he asked me who I could recommend as NEDA Secretary. When I mentioned Medalla, Estrada replied that he does not know this man, so I wrote down his name and address on a piece of paper. In the afternoon, I heard on TV that Estrada has announced Medalla as NEDA secretary.[30]

Estrada's successor, GMA, however, actively used her presidential appointment powers to consolidate her rule by building patronage networks within government structures. Most of the president's appointments were based on political loyalties and *quid pro quo* rather than suitability or principle (de Dios and Hutchcroft 2003, p. 67). A 2008 study by the Civil Service Commission revealed that she appointed 81 under-secretaries and assistant secretaries, and 53 presidential advisers and presidential assistants, in addition to several other consultants whose exact number was not mentioned in the study (Quimpo 2011, p. 4). That most of these appointed persons were not career bureaucrats from the departments – so-called Career Executive Service Officers (CESOs) – but persons without civil service eligibility proved problematic. GMA's "unqualified appointees bloated, politicized, and deprofessionalized the bureaucracy, and demoralized rank-and-file government workers" (Quimpo 2011, p. 4). A World Bank report concurred with this perception by stating that a large part of the administration consists of political appointees of the president. These people are replaced after every change of government. This practice "undermines promotion by merit or the development of any technocratic ethos. Even worse, it makes civil servants extremely vulnerable to pressure from politicians. The legal and institutional framework for managing civil service policy is thus inadequate and politicization is excessive" (World Bank 2005, p. 28). As former Secretary of Education Florencio "Butch" Abad reported, presidential patronage goes down to the local level, where uncooperative school heads can be removed by exerting influence on the department, or directly on the president. He quoted a joke within his former ministry: "Who does not comply will be sent to [the unruly island of] Basilan [in the ARMM]."[31]

Particularly disputed were the so-called "midnight appointments" that GMA ordered only a few days before her leave from office in 2010. Since the constitutional ban on presidential appointments to executive positions went into effect on 10 March 2010, GMA appointed from 1 to 9 March more than 250 people to positions in government agencies and government-owned and controlled corporations like the National Electrification Administration or the Philippine National Oil Company (Rufo 2010).[32] These midnight appointments, some of them lasting four or six years, were heavily criticized, not only by the general public, but by the following Aquino administration. Aquino's spokesman, Edwin Lacierda, said that GMA's late appointments were intended "to prevent the next administration from placing its own people in important posts in government. We find malice or bad faith in the midnight appointments. It intends to stifle the next administration" (Bautista 2010). Patricio Abinales, professor of Southeast Asian Studies, concluded that GMA's appointments in state agencies and government institutions "aimed to stymie her successor's ability to gain control over the huge state apparatus" (Abinales 2011, p. 165). Immediately after his election, Aquino issued Executive Order No. 2 and ordered the immediate removal of all "midnight appointees" in the executive branch. However, the Supreme Court invalidated his decision, which came as no surprise, since nearly all Supreme Court judges were appointed by GMA.

Executive-Legislative Cooperation

Much of the interaction between the executive and legislative branches takes place in the Legislative-Executive Development Advisory Council (LEDAC). Created by President Fidel Ramos in 1992, it is composed of seven members of the Cabinet designated by the president, four members of the House of Representatives, including the speaker, four members of the Senate, including the Senate President, and one representative from the Local Government Units (LGUs), from the Youth Sector, and from the private sector. The most important task of the LEDAC is to create a list of priority legislative measures.

Bernadino "Bernie" Sayo, undersecretary in the Presidential Legislative Liaison Office gave some insight into executive-legislative relations from the presidential perspective by stating that

> of course there is some presidential dominance over the House of Representatives, but we have to manage things smoothly. We have to be proactive and anticipate potential issues. We counteract against any opposition. We know the political origins, backgrounds, and affiliation of every single one of the over 200 Congressmen. We talk with their staff and their colleagues in order to get information. We also get their records from police and intelligence sources and have access to all departments and government agencies. Additionally, we have political officers in the field, who report to us what kind of statements they make in their districts. If a new set of legislators comes in after elections, we are very keen in knowing who they are. We approach them and ask how we can help each other. Generally, we have very collaborative working relationships with the legislators. Often, election candidates ask for support, and if they are not in the opposition, we help them to win their district.[33]

As former Undersecretary of Education Jose Luis "Chito" Gascon reported, presidential appointment powers are also used to interact with the Congressmen: "Every legislator has a relative or friend who needs a position in a state enterprise or a customs office. By making these appointments in favor of the personal interests of the legislator, the president tries to retain the support of the legislator."[34]

Bernadino "Bernie" Sayo added that

> we continue to court the opposition and try to understand their motives. Our success is to turn them to our camp. We try to be pre-emptive. If they are confrontational, we pit somebody against

> them in the plenary session or we try to turn the other actors in their
> sector or policy field against them. Of course, we cannot openly attack
> opposition legislators. We try to appease them or we make them happy
> and request an appropriate reaction. We don't want to lose legislators
> to the opposition. The motto is addition and not subtraction. But if a
> legislator still wants to be part of the opposition, we try to make sure
> that he will not win in the next elections.[35]

The latter attempt failed, since most opposition candidates were
re-elected in 2010, but the former mentioned approach of making as
many representatives as possible pleased and expecting their loyalty was
quite successful, since through the wily use of patronage and financial
support, GMA managed to maintain a huge pro-administration majority in
the House of Representatives until the end of her term in 2010. Therefore,
President Gloria Macapagal-Arroyo might rightfully "be called the great
compromiser, given her willingness to accommodate anyone able to help
her retain the presidency" (Quimpo 2009, p. 347).

The Philippine House of Representatives formally possesses more
powerful mechanisms to check the executive than those of Indonesia and
Thailand. More than 50 committees are each tasked with overseeing a
related department or agency. Four committees were explicitly created for
accountability functions: the Committee on Oversight, the Committee
on Good Government, the Committee on Ethics, and the Committee
on Justice, which are all empowered to subpoena executive officials
(Case 2011, p. 30f.). However, the House of Representatives has never made
effective use of these possibilities. In terms of horizontal accountability, the
continuing practice of voluntary subordination of the large majority of
the House of Representatives to the executive branch prevents an effective
control of government actions.

The Senate

The Senate plays a larger role in horizontal accountability than does the
other half of the Philippine Congress, the House of Representatives. Due
to the specific mode of election (see chapter 3.3), the Senate is dominated
by rich and powerful individuals. In an interview Senator Franklin Drilon
stated that, in contrast to House members, senators are not dependent on
funds from the president via the pork barrel or congressional insertions to
win re-election (quoted in Case 2011, p. 39), since their personal fortune
allows them to take an independent stance *vis-à-vis* the executive. Senator

Drilon is also quoted as saying that in terms of horizontal accountability, the Senate is urgently needed, since the House of Representatives "is, I don't want to say subservient, but supportive of the president" (quoted in Case 2011, p. 39).

Senator Aquilino "Nene" Pimentel stated that the

> Senate should neither be a partner nor an opponent of the government but rather an independent body that holds up the rights of the people. Even as opposition, I can often go along with the president. However, the Senate will not stop questioning the actions of the departments. This is needed in a corrupt political system, such as that of the Philippines. President GMA does not like it if the Senate is too critical. Very often she said that the Senate should be a partner of the president and promoted unity among state institutions.[36]

Many senators envisage themselves as presidents. Accordingly, a critical distance to the incumbent president allows them to gain popular support. When President GMA lost popularity and legitimacy after the "Hello Garci" scandal (see chapter 3.3) in 2005, many senators who previously supported the administration turned into political opponents. By around the end of 2005, a stable anti-GMA coalition had the majority in Senate and blocked all legislation initiated by the GMA administration. This classic gridlock situation became even worse after the mid-term elections in 2007 when opposition candidates clearly won the majority of the 12 senatorial positions. After the 2010 elections, the gridlock ended, and since then there is a clear majority of pro-Aquino senators.

Formally, horizontal accountability is exercised by the Blue Ribbon Committee of the Senate, whose official name is Committee on Accountability of Public Officers and Investigation. It is tasked with investigating alleged or real government irregularities. However, the intention of such investigations is to create publicity by painting a positive picture of the senators rather than produce tangible results. Congressional investigations are often not meant to correct or to improve legislation but rather serve as an occasion for the legislators to be in the media.[37] It is also commonly known that senators "use such probes as leverage for persuading government agencies and bureaucrats to strike deals with them" (Rüland, Nelson, Jürgenmeyer, and Ziegenhain 2005, p. 243). Senatorial negotiation powers are more effective in terms of horizontal accountability than these investigations, however.

The Judiciary

The Philippine Supreme Court is vital in terms of horizontal accountability, since it has the explicit task of supervising the government. According to Article VIII, Section 1: "Judicial power includes the duty of the courts of justice ... to determine whether or not there has been a grave abuse of discretion amounting to lack or excess of jurisdiction on the part of any branch or instrumentality of the government" (Constitution of the Philippines). The Supreme Court is composed of 15 justices appointed by the president without consultation with Congress.

Despite the fact that justices cannot be dismissed until they reach the mandatory retirement age of 70 years, the independence of the Supreme Court justices is questionable. Although the president has to choose from a list of three nominees drawn up by the Judicial and Bar Council (JBC), the president has considerable clout in the nomination process since he or she can appoint several members of that council. In the late presidency of GMA, she had appointed four of the JBC's eight members and the fifth member was her justice secretary (Quimpo 2011, p. 10). Not surprisingly, the appointed justices are seen by the general public as "generally close to the interests of the President, where packing the Court is a regular practice" (Escresa and Garoupa 2012, p. 17).

The question remains whether or not the appointed Supreme Court judges decide in favour of those who appointed them. To answer this question, Laarni Escresa and Nuno Garoupa examined 1,592 decisions made by the Supreme Court between 1986 and 2010. They found that "if a Justice is an incumbent administration appointee, the chances of voting for the administration increase around 66%" (Escresa and Garoupa 2012, p. 20). A close examination by Ronja Zimmermann of the voting behaviour of individual Supreme Court judges after the 2010 elections re-enforces these findings (Zimmermann 2012b). It is thus obvious that the nomination practice leads to a significant loss of independence in favour of the executive.

This becomes particularly crucial if a president stays longer in office than the constitutionally prescribed six years. After nine years as president, all 14 Supreme Court judges were appointed by GMA. She also personally appointed three different presiding members (called Chief Justices) of the Supreme Court, deliberately ignoring the unwritten tradition of appointing the most senior judge to the position of Chief Justice in all three cases.

This was also the case in the appointment of Renato Corona to the position of Chief Justice on 12 May 2010, two days after the presidential elections in which she was no longer able to run. This most pivotal of GMA's above mentioned midnight appointments caused public outcry since Article VII, Section 15 of the Philippine Constitution clearly states that

> two months immediately before the next presidential elections and up to the end of his term, a President or Acting President shall not make appointments, except temporary appointments to executive positions when continued vacancies therein will prejudice public service or endanger public safety (Constitution of the Philippines).

Despite, the Supreme Court, now headed by Corona, upheld GMA's right as incumbent president to appoint the Chief Justice.

To show his protest against this appointment, newly elected President Aquino refused to be sworn in by Corona and instead took his oath of office in front of Associate Justice Conchita Carpio-Morales, who also opposed the midnight appointment of Corona. The confrontation between President Noynoy Aquino and the Supreme Court further escalated when the Supreme Court stopped the creation of a truth commission, which was intended to "seek and find the truth on ... graft and corruption ... committed by public officers ... during the previous administration" (Government of the Philippines 2010).

In various other cases between 2010 and 2011 – among them a travel ban for GMA issued by the Department of Justice – the Supreme Court vehemently decided against initiatives of the Aquino administration. The Supreme Court also personally "attacked" President Aquino with a decision in November 2011 that the lands of the Hacienda Luisita owned by the Aquino family should be distributed to landless farmers in accordance with the Comprehensive Agrarian Reform Program from 1988, which, in practice, had been rarely implemented since then.

On the one hand, the decisions of the Supreme Court show that the separation of powers, and consequently horizontal accountability mechanisms, between executive and judiciary were working. On the other hand, impartiality, independence, and objectivity must be the guiding principles for a judiciary which has the task of keeping government actions in check. Alongside the Aquino administration, as a "victim" of the Supreme Court, neutral and international observers also had the impression that the Supreme Court did not meet the above mentioned pre-conditions. President Noynoy Aquino argued in a similar way by publicly stating in December 2011:

> Iginagalang po natin ang pagkakapantay sa kapangyarihan ng hudikatura at ng ehekutibong sangay ng gobyerno. Wala po tayong balak na tapakan ang karapatan nila, o bastusin ang kredibilidad ng sinuman. Pero kailangan nating balikan ang mga batayang prinsipyo ng ating demokrasya. Kami pong mga nanumpa sa tungkulin ay iisa lamang ang pinagkakautangan ng loob: kayong mga Boss namin, ang sambayanang Pilipino. Narito kami para maglingkod sa ating bansa; at para may manilbihan nang buong katapatan at sigasig sa mga Pilipino. Ngayon, kung may isang lingkod-bayan na tumatanaw ng utang ng loob, hindi sa taumbayan na siyang dapat na bukal ng aming kapangyarihan, kundi sa isang padron na isiniksik siya sa puwesto, maaasahan po kaya natin siyang intindihin ang interes ng Pilipino? [We remain respectful of the separation of powers between the judiciary and the executive branches. We have no intention of encroaching on their duties, disregarding their rights, or tarnishing anyone's reputation. But we need to remind ourselves of the bedrock principles of our democracy. We in public service owe it all to our Boss, the Filipino people. We are here only to serve the people, and to serve our fellow Filipinos with utmost industry and integrity. Now, if there is one public servant who thinks he does not owe his countrymen - who, after all, is the wellspring of our power - but a patron who had snuck him into position, can we reasonably expect him to look after the interests of our people?] (Government of the Philippines 2011).

Though Corona and GMA are not explicitly named, the last sentence makes clear who was meant by the "public official" and the "patron". In the end, the Aquino administration saw the initiation of an impeachment process to be the only possible solution to hold the judiciary accountable and end the confrontation between the executive and Supreme Court. In line with constitutional regulations, the House of Representatives initiated with an overwhelming majority the impeachment process in December 2011 and delegated the case to the Senate for trial. The main accusation was that Corona had

> betrayed the public trust through his track record marked by partiality and subservience in cases involving the Arroyo administration from the time of his appointment as Supreme Court justice which continued to his dubious appointment as a midnight chief justice and up to the present (House of Representatives 2011, p. 11).

A further accusation was that Corona had accumulated large sums of ill-gotten wealth.

With regards to the system of checks and balances, an impeachment against a Supreme Court judge, whose decisions are approved by the government, is highly questionable and damages the entire democratic system (Zimmermann 2012a, p. 114). Not without reason, Corona characterized the impeachment process as one that "will destroy democracy" and appealed to "fight against any and all who dare to destroy the Court and the independence of the Judiciary. We do not want to see a constitutional crisis befall our democracy, but ... we are challenged to defend [the] independence [of the Supreme Court]" (Corona 2011, p. 2f.]. Roan Libarios, president of the Integrated Bar of the Philippines, commented: "[The impeachment against the Chief Justice] is sending a chilling effect. This sends a signal to judges that if the president does not like your ruling, they can make life difficult for you, or worse [you may] be impeached and removed" (quoted in Baviera 2012, p. 244). Indeed, a presidential initiative for an impeachment against the highest representative of the judiciary undermines horizontal accountability. However, the specific circumstances, including the doubtful legitimacy of Corona, make this interference more understandable.

After a rather hectic and not extensively deliberative process, Corona was impeached by the Senate in May 2012 with 20–3 votes. The Senate as an impeachment court found it very difficult to prove Corona's impartiality, so its members instead concentrated on Corona's wealth declaration. In the end, the Senate found Corona guilty of having not disclosed to the public a bank account with US$2.4 million and another with PHP80 million (approximately US$2 million) in his statement of assets, liabilities, and net worth (SALN), which every senior public official in the Philippines is required to file each year. The impeachment thus was legally appropriate. However, a bitter taste remained since making wrong particulars is a common practice and regarded as a *peccadillo* in Philippine politics. Tellingly, none of the senators and representatives "volunteered to make their SALN public as proof that their hands are cleaner than the chief justice they have convicted" (Holmes 2012, p. 86).

President Noynoy Aquino continued the politicized appointment tradition of GMA by making his ally, Maria Lourdes Sereno, the successor of Corona as chief justice. Aquino broke as well with the tradition of appointing the most senior judge. He appointed Sereno, born in 1960, a relatively inexperienced Supreme Court judge, who may be in power until 2030. That the other Supreme Court judges did not all approve of the president's decision became evident when, at the inauguration of Sereno, during a flag-raising ceremony, only six justices appeared, while seven others, led by Antonio Carpio, who by tradition was next in line as chief justice under the previously respected seniority rule, were absent (Avendaño and Ramos 2012).

The Supreme Court, which has been rather positive in terms of horizontal accountability until the early 2000s, has increasingly lost its independence in the last decade. Consequently, the Philippines, to which scholars once accredited "a well-functioning separation of powers and effective horizontal accountability" (Croissant 2003, p. 90), have now turned towards a strong presidential influence on judicial affairs and decisions that in turn undermine horizontal accountability. In a similar direction goes the analysis of Philippine scholar Ronald "Ronnie" Holmes who commented that the surroundings of the Corona impeachment highlighted the difficulties of implementing horizontal accountability and that the system of checks is constrained largely by a powerful executive (Holmes 2012, p. 88).

Independent Watchdog Organizations

The Philippine Constitution provided for a large variety of independent watchdog organizations to supervise the actions of the government. Among the most important are the Commission on Elections (COMELEC), the Commission on Audit (COA), the Civil Service Commission (CSC), the Sandiganbayan (a special appellate collegial court for corruption cases), the National Human Rights Commission, the Ombudsman Office, and, from 2001 until 2010, the Presidential Anti-Graft Commission (PAGC).

That all of these organizations are highly influenced by the administration in office is problematic. A good example is the PAGC, which was founded by President GMA in 2001 to probe and hear administrative cases and complaints against presidential appointees. However, the PAGC was not able to detect the rampant abuse of power and the arbitrary appointment policy of the president, so that Noynoy Aquino was conscious enough to abolish this "wasteful and inefficient" organization (Sisante 2010).

Other organizations, such as the COMELEC, which is responsible for the administration of democratic elections, have a serious credibility problem. Beside enormous management shortcomings in the past elections (e.g. inaccurate voter lists), scandals like the "Hello Garci" affair (mentioned in chapter 3.3) and the affair concerning the deal of a nationwide broadband network with the Chinese company ZTE (Zhongxing Telecommunication Equipment) which had implicated and forced the resignation of the

COMELEC chairman (Quimpo 2011, p. 3), further deteriorated the image of COMELEC. A political analyst consequently commented: "The COMELEC rank-and-file are very good and honest persons, but the politicized top is very bad."[38]

Other institutions are simply overridden by more powerful forces. The Sandiganbayan, a special court for graft and corrupt practices, convicted former President Joseph "Erap" Estrada of plunder after long lasting thorough investigations and sentenced him to forty years in prison. However, then President GMA gave the convicted a presidential pardon, freeing him so as to once again re-enter politics and finish second in the presidential elections of 2010. The dismal record of the Sandiganbayan to vindicate public accountability attests not only to its institutional weaknesses, but also to the lack of political and normative commitment to stop corruption in the Philippines (Pangalangan 2010, p. 299).

Notes

[1] In other parliamentary systems of government, there are usually lower numbers required. In Germany, for example, a quarter of the MPs must support a vote of no confidence.

[2] Interview with Boonyad Sukthinthai, Democrat Party, Member of the House of Representatives, Bangkok, 14 October 2010.

[3] Interview with Prinya Thaewanarumitkul, Vice Rector for Student Affairs, Thammasat University, Bangkok, 18 August 2009.

[4] Interview with Kittisak Prokati, Faculty of Law, Thammasat University, Bangkok, 13 August 2009.

[5] Ibid.

[6] Interview with Boonyad Sukthinthai, Democrat Party, Member of the House of Representatives, Bangkok, 14 October 2010.

[7] Interview with Nataphol Teepsuwan, Director General of Democrat Party, Member of the House of Representatives, Bangkok, 11 October 2010.

[8] Ibid.

[9] Interview with Chaturon Chaisang, Former MP, Thai Rak Thai, Bangkok, 17 August 2009.

[10] Interview with Ong-art Klampaiboon, Minister to the Prime Minister's Office, Bangkok, 14 October 2010.

[11] Interview with Kittisak Prokati, Faculty of Law, Thammasat University, Bangkok, 13 August 2009.

[12] Interview with Nataphol Teepsuwan, Director General of Democrat Party, Member of the House of Representatives, Bangkok, 11 October 2010.

[13] Interview with Naruemon Thabchumpon, Chulangalongkorn University, Faculty of Political Science, Bangkok, 14 August 2009.

14   The TRT was not dissolved by the Constitutional Court under the 2007 Constitution but by an interim constitutional tribunal.

15   Interview with Naruemon Thabchumpon, Chulangalongkorn University, Faculty of Political Science, Bangkok, 14 August 2009.

16   Interview with Kittisak Prokati, Faculty of Law, Thammasat University, Bangkok, 13 August 2009.

17   Interview with Boonyad Sukthinthai, Democrat Party, Member of the House of Representatives, Bangkok, 14 October 2010.

18   Interview with Kittisak Prokati, Faculty of Law, Thammasat University, Bangkok, 13 August 2009.

19   Interview with Chaturon Chaisang, Former MP, Thai Rak Thai, Bangkok, 17 August 2009.

20   Interview with Suthipon Thaveechaiyagarn, Secretary General of the Election Commission of Thailand, 17 August 2009.

21   Interview with Naruemon Thabchumpon, Chulangalongkorn University, Faculty of Political Science, Bangkok, 14 August 2009.

22   Interview with Parinya Thewanarumitkul, Deputy Rector of Thammasat University, quoted in: "The Cost of the 2006 Coup", *Bangkok Post*, 19 October 2010.

23   Interview with Chaturon Chaisang, Former MP, Thai Rak Thai, Bangkok, 17 August 2009.

24   Interview with Kraisak Choonhavan, MP, Democrat Party, Bangkok, 17 August 2009.

25   Interview with Nataphol Teepsuwan, Director General of Democrat Party, Member of the House of Representatives, Bangkok, 11 October 2010.

26   Interview with Mujiv Hataman, Member of the House of Representatives, party list A-MIN, Quezon City, 13 September 2007.

27   Interview with Benjamin "Ben" Diokno, Former Secretary of the Department of Budget and Management (1998–2001), Quezon City, 14 September 2007.

28   Ibid.

29   Interview with Risa Hontiveros, Party-List Representative from Akbayan, Quezon City, 29 August 2007.

30   Interview with Benjamin "Ben" Diokno, Former Secretary of the Department of Budget and Management (1998–2001), Quezon City, 14 September 2007.

31   Interview with Florencio "Butch" Abad, Former Secretary of Education, Manila, 12 September 2007.

32   A full list of all appointments with exact date and term is available at: "Summary of Key Midnight Appointments in GOCCs", no author, no date, available at <http://de.scribd.com/doc/32885733/GMA-Midnight-Appointments> (accessed 5 March 2013).

33   Interview with Bernadino "Bernie" Sayo, Presidential Legislative Liaison Office (PLLO), Quezon City, 13 September 2007.

34 Interview with Jose Luis "Chito" Gascon, former Undersecretary of Education, Quezon City, 10 September 2007.
35 Interview with Bernadino "Bernie" Sayo, Presidential Legislative Liaison Office (PLLO), Quezon City, 13 September 2007.
36 Interview with Senator Aquilino "Nene" Pimentel, Manila, 4 September 2007.
37 Interview with Carolina Hernandez, Emeritus Professor of Political Science, University of the Philippines, Quezon City, 24 August 2007.
38 Interview with Glenda Gloria, Journalist, Chief Operating Officer of ABS-CBN News Channel, Quezon City, 26 August 2009.

6

THE CONSEQUENCES OF INSTITUTIONAL ENGINEERING

In the previous chapters I analysed institutional reforms in regards to the three dimensions of accountability in the three countries under research. In this chapter I will give a comparative analysis of the impact these institutional reforms have had on the quality of democracy.

Reforms on Electoral Accountability and their Impact on Democratization: A Comparative Perspective

There were few institutional reforms concerning the presidential elections in the two presidential systems of the Philippines and Indonesia. In the Philippines, the electoral system has not been altered since it was inaugurated in the 1987 Constitution. It has retained problematic features, such as the non-requirement of an absolute majority in a single round and the missing possibility for re-election of an incumbent president. In contrast, the Indonesian president enjoys much higher legitimacy than his Philippine counterpart due to an electoral process that is in accordance with an amended constitution, which contributes to the stabilization of the democratization process. The absolute majority of the votes, which is required in Indonesia and made possible by run-off elections, guarantees that at least half of the voters supported the winning candidate. The possibility for a single re-election in Indonesia holds the president under the judgement of the general public for his or her first term. If the president performs well in the eyes of the electorate he or she can hope for another five-year term. This scenario, which occurred with President SBY in 2009, is generally not possible in the Philippines. In terms of electoral accountability, Philippine presidential elections are thus a prospective rather than retrospective measure. Here, the president is a "lame duck", beholden to all the negative consequences from the first day in office. The re-election of an incumbent president in 2004 was an unusual exception to the rule, and in terms of constitutionality very controversial.

The nomination process for presidential candidates is another remarkable difference between the two countries. In the Philippines, every natural-born citizen who is literate and at least forty years of age (Constitution of the Philippines, Article VII, Section 2) can run for the presidency. In Indonesia, access is more restricted. There, candidates for the presidency can only be nominated by political parties represented in the House of Representatives (DPR). The only major institutional reform that changed the mode of presidential elections concerned the required percentage of votes and seats for a presidential nomination. Whereas in 2004 only 5 per cent of the votes and 3 per cent of the seats were necessary for political parties or coalitions in the DPR, this number was increased to 25 and 20 per cent respectively in 2009. This institutional change must be seen ambiguously in terms of the quality of democracy. It is a drastic limitation of choices for the people who must choose between the few candidates offered to them by the bigger parties in the DPR. The system favours senior party politicians who are able to forge coalitions over independent people's candidates. Big parties were institutional winners to the detriment of the small ones. However, it must also be considered that the mentioned institutional reform may stabilize democracy when people with little parliamentary support are excluded from the presidential race in order to avoid gridlock between the executive and legislative branches.

The Indonesian provisions on the vice-presidency, introduced after the constitutional amendments in 2004, are also better for the stability of a democratic government. Since the president and vice-president are elected as a package in Indonesia, the presidential candidates usually run with top politicians from other parties in order to increase their chances. Coalitions must be built between several political parties before every election round. In the Philippines, on the contrary, the segmented elections for the president and the vice-president result in higher competition because coalition-building is not required and often leads to a divided government.

The electoral accountability for the parliamentary elections varies among the three countries under research. Whereas Indonesia still uses a fully proportional election system, Thailand and the Philippines both introduced proportional elements in their previous plurality election systems. Between a quarter to a fifth of the seats in their Houses of Representatives are now distributed with a proportional election mode in segmented elections. In general, the move towards mixed election systems can be rated as positive since the advantages and disadvantages of the two election types balance each other. However, these institutional reforms were made due to different intentions in both countries. Thailand aimed to strengthen the bigger parties which had already won in the plurality elections while also giving smaller parties a few seats. The effects of this alteration fulfilled these expectations. However, after the electoral victories of TRT and its successor parties, many doubted the positive contribution to democracy of the inherent majoritarian tendency of the segmented proportional seats added to the district seats. Democracy was strengthened in another way, however: rural voters now had to care about national politics, as represented by the major parties, instead of regarding only their local patrons, whom they had elected for generations in the pure plurality system. Consequently, the traditional individual patronage networks were partly replaced by patronage provided by political parties and their leaders (Nogsuan 2005, p. 68).

The Philippines, in contrast, introduced the so-called party-list seats in accordance with a constitutional provision that intended to represent under-privileged groups of society. This idea would be beneficial for the quality of democracy because it widens the possibilities for electoral representation and political participation. In practice, however, the implementation of the party-list system is fraught with irregularities and distortions. As shown in chapter 3.3, the representation of marginalized groups occurs only to some extent while the power of the party-list groups is artificially restricted by a seat cap of three.

A straight proportional election, which among the three countries under research is only adopted in Indonesia, is responsible for a more inclusive parliament and strengthens the role of political parties therein. The composition of the Indonesian parliament is in comparison with the other two countries less dominated by wealthy local elites. Particularly in the Philippines, but also to some extent in Thailand, members of the House of Representatives care much more for the transfer of state money to their constituencies than for national political affairs. Though there were also some tendencies in this direction in Indonesia, the work of the parliamentarians is generally more policy-oriented and focused on committee work.

The dependence of individual legislators on parties instead of voters comes as a disadvantage to proportional election systems. In Indonesia, this disadvantage was counterbalanced by the introduction of open candidate lists for the national parliamentary elections. The 2009 elections marked the first time voters could effectively vote for their specific candidate of choice instead of those designated by a closed party list. Another effective institutional reform was the introduction of an effective parliamentary threshold of 2.5 per cent. Through this combination of reforms, Indonesia tried to mitigate the less desirable results of the proportional elections system, namely the lack of electoral accountability of candidates and the extreme fragmentation of parliament. These institutional reforms contributed positively to the deepening of democracy.

With the exception of the above mentioned seat caps for party-list groups, no threshold exists in the plurality election system of the Philippines. In Thailand, a 5 per cent threshold for the 100 proportional seats was introduced in the 1997 Constitution, but abolished in the 2007 Constitution after the military coup. Whereas the introduction of the threshold in 1997 aimed at making the elections more majoritarian by eliminating small parties, the conservative forces after the coup used the "constitutional reform as a tool to try to return to an era where despite regular elections, parties were weak, [and] governments were large and unstable" (Hicken 2008, p. 220).

The electoral mode for the second chambers in the three political systems under research varies to a great extent. In the Philippines (Senate) and Indonesia (DPD) no institutional reforms concerning this issue were enacted between 1987 and 2004 respectively. In Thailand, the mode for access was for decades decided upon by bureaucratic appointment instead of by the will of voters. The 1997 Constitution changed this by demanding a direct election of all senators. This move established electoral accountability for the Senate and deepened the quality of democracy to a great extent. This improvement was partly revised after the military coup when the coup-makers decided that half of the Senate be appointed while the other half be popularly elected. Though this decision did not completely devolve the country into something akin to the pre-democratic era, it is a setback for the democratization process in Thailand.

Vote-buying and other forms of electoral manipulation are widespread in all three countries in question. Additionally, election-related violence and intimidation still constitute a major problem for free and fair elections. Corruption and money politics are still rampant in all three countries, though electoral politics in Indonesia are relatively less dominated by criminal networks and mafia structures compared to Thailand and the Philippines. Voter intimidation and vote-buying are more common features during elections in Thailand and the Philippines than in Indonesia. Here, the institutionalization of the "democratic electoral system and processes has undermined the effectiveness of political gangsterism as a means of contesting, winning and maintaining political power" (Wilson 2010, p. 216). Furthermore, cases of electoral violence are much lower in Indonesia than in Thailand and particularly, the Philippines (Tomsa 2010, p. 155).

The Indonesian Constitutional Court removed electoral restrictions on former communists in 2004. However, Indonesia's voting rights are still compromised by the ban on voting for members of the military and police force, which constitutes a major social group. Similarly, the right to run as a candidate in Thailand was limited by the constitutional requirement of a formal higher education.

Weak electoral administration with missing or wrong registration lists can impact election results in all three countries under research. While the worst technical problems occur in Indonesia, rural areas in the Philippines are not much better off. In Indonesia, at least, the national election commission seems to be non-partisan, in which cannot be said of the 2005 Philippine elections ("Hello Garci" scandal).

Several institutional reforms in all three countries were made in an attempt to reduce electoral irregularities. In Thailand, the 1997 Constitution introduced yellow and red cards, which the election commission can issue for candidates cheating and vote-buying during elections. If properly applied, this mechanism could contribute positively in combating electoral fraud and hence towards an increased quality of democracy. In the Philippines, the 2010 elections brought the introduction of ballot papers with pre-printed candidate names and automated counting machines. Both measures improved the speed and clarity of vote counting while reducing possibilities for manipulation.

The situation in which elected representatives change their party affiliation or camp after elections poses many problems for young democracies, for the stability of their political systems and in terms of electoral accountability. In the Philippines, where party-switching and joining the presidential bandwagon is a common phenomenon (Kasuya 2009), no institutional reforms have yet been decided upon. In Thailand, both the 1997 and 2007 Constitutions sanctioned turncoatism.

However, these provisions could not prevent the Friends of Newin from switching from the government camp to the opposition, which in turn was able to take over the government in December 2008. This case was a clear violation of electoral accountability since the renegades were elected to the red camp in 2007 only to join the yellow camp a year later. Australian scholar Kevin Hewison commented: "Denigrating voters and their decisions are unlikely to enhance democratic development" (Hewison 2010, p. 126). Compared to the other two countries, party-switching is not such a common phenomenon in Indonesia. This has more to do with the proportional election system creating a dependence of individual legislators on parties than the possibility of the recall mechanism which has been rarely applied in recent years.

The political parties in the countries under research generally show several features which do not contribute positively to electoral accountability. Most of them are leader-centric parties with weak subnational level organizations, low policy capacity, and vague if not altogether lacking ideologies. Consequently, they are poor at articulating and aggregating the interests of citizens. They often fail to develop close, regular ties to their constituencies. In general, political parties in all three countries concentrate on their own financial and power interests, which are usually closely connected to those of their leaders. Even those few parties that have managed to develop substantial roots in several constituencies are often more built on patronage ties than on interest representation (Carothers 2006, p. 11).

The importance of political parties for electoral accountability is dependent on the institutional context. In the Philippines, with its presidential system and plurality election system, individual candidates rule over political parties, whereas in Indonesia these parties are much more decisive. Despite having a presidential system, the above mentioned nomination right for the presidency, and the proportional election system (even with the newly introduced open party list), political parties remain key players of the political process in Indonesia.

In Thailand, political parties in parliament determine who becomes prime minister and is able to form a government. The parliamentary system has since 2000 turned into a nearly perfect two-party system, in which the TRT (and its successor parties) as well as the Democrat Party compete for power in a plurality election system. These features, which are classic components of a majoritarian democracy, should increase electoral accountability because there is always a clear electoral winner. All the elections under this system have so far been won by TRT (and its successor parties). Voters clearly assigned the responsibility to govern to the respective governments led by Thaksin Shinawatra and his successors.

That these governments were not voted out of office in popular elections constitutes a major problem in terms of electoral accountability. Instead, they were removed by a military coup in 2006, a party ban on the election winning PPP and Prime Minister Samak, and the turnaround of the Friends of Newin in December 2008. The major institutional reform concerning political parties in Thailand — the introduction of the right of the Constitutional Court to dissolve political parties for alleged cheating in the elections — thus had serious side effects for electoral accountability.

In Indonesia, the changes and reinterpretation of the electoral laws illustrate that even small changes to electoral procedures can have enormous political ramifications and sometimes do not work as intended. The law-makers in the House of Representatives tried to reduce the number of parties competing in elections by the introduction of electoral thresholds and high requirements for registration. However, the Constitutional Court stopped these thresholds and interpreted the open party list in such a way that voters could change the order of the candidates in the party list.

While this decision strengthened electoral accountability, the party system became more fragmented. The introduction of the open-list system weakened the links between candidates and their party and thus further weakened the organizational and ideological coherence of the political parties. This could result in a situation in which "the only glue between a candidate and his/her party will become 'money politics'. For the individual candidate on the campaign trail, the incentives to resort to a personal campaign of vote-buying and 'pork barreling' are made even more compelling" (Sherlock 2009, p. 38f). Pork barrels would, of course, have negative consequences for electoral accountability. The power of Indonesia's major political parties, which are not as short-lived as in Thailand nor as corrupt and superficial as in the Philippines (Tomsa 2010, p. 157), suffer from the Constitutional Court's decisions in favour of the open-list system and the ban on an electoral threshold.

Compared to Indonesia, the youngest democracy of the three, the lack of an institutionalized party system is "more worrying for Thailand and the Philippines, both of which have enjoyed sustained periods of generally free and fair elections. Ironically, along some dimensions, Indonesia actually looks more institutionalized than either of its neighbors" (Hicken 2006a, p. 42). The (not pure) plurality systems in

Thailand and the Philippines weaken political parties and give advantage to individuals over parties. An increase of the proportional elements in both countries could help balance the entrenched oligarchic power of clans and dominant political families in their respective Houses of Representatives. More proportional representation could "be an incentive for the programmatic parties representing broader interests as they can win more seats proportional to their actual strength while discouraging those identified with the narrowest interests and constituencies" (Rivera 2011, p. 79). However, this proposal does not seem very realistic, as one Philippine expert clearly states: "There is no way that Congress will pass a law which supports a proportional election system."[1]

Political parties hold a difficult position in all three countries. Due to their institutional deficiencies and self-interested policies, they are often seen as a major hindrance for further democratization. Various attempts of party engineering have been undertaken in Thailand and Indonesia, but, despite an ongoing public debate, not in the Philippines (Tomsa 2013, p. 23ff.). Both decision-makers in Thailand and Indonesia initially tried to reduce the number of parties through electoral reforms. However, recent developments have seen a reversal. Whereas the shift from multi-member to single member districts was annulled in the 2007 Constitution of Thailand, the Constitutional Court of Indonesia skipped all efforts to introduce effective electoral thresholds.

Since nearly all parties in the three Southeast Asian countries are hybrids between traditional clientelistic, electoralist catch-all and personalistic parties (Tomsa 2013, p. 36), political parties will not be the main drivers of democratic deepening in the region. Political decision-makers in all three countries often play the anti-party card in a populist manner since they can match a widespread popular resentment against them (Tan 2013, p. 95).

The reduction of powers for political parties in favour of allegedly independent organizations, such as the Constitutional Courts in Indonesia and Thailand, is dangerous, particularly in terms of electoral accountability. Even if

> parties are nothing more than a necessary evil, international experience strongly indicates that they are an integral part of a well-functioning democracy. If the presence of parties on the political scene is an unavoidable fact, it would be wiser to improve the quality of their structural role rather than trying to squeeze them to the margins (Sherlock 2009, p. 39).

Reforms on Vertical Accountability and their Impact on Democratization: A Comparative Perspective

The vertical dimension of accountability, as understood in this study, deals with the quality of democracy at the local level and the contribution of central-local relations for the deepening of democracy. Local governments need to have a certain level of autonomy in order to influence national politics. It is remarkable that the provincial governments are directly elected only in the Philippines and Indonesia, whereas in Thailand governors are appointed from the national Ministry of Interior. Indonesia is unique insofar as the second tier of administration, districts and cities, enjoy a higher degree of autonomy than the provinces, while in the other two countries hierarchical order is maintained.

Budgetary independence is a major precondition for the ability of local governments to impact national politics. To meet this precondition, local administrations in Thailand and the Philippines witnessed an increase in their spending of up to 25 per cent of the national GDP until around 2005 when it began to stagnate. As has been described in chapters 4.1 and 4.3, local governments in both countries are financially dependent on transfers from the national government. These transfers are often subject to disputes between both levels of government in which the centre uses its power of disbursement to exert pressure on local administrators and politicians. The politicized nature of inter-governmental money transfers or problematic allocation formulas in revenue sharing results in conflicts between central and local government units (Rocamora 2007, p. 194). In Indonesia, by contrast, local governments have a much larger budgetary scope and are less dependent on financial transfers from Jakarta. Districts with natural resources and industrial structures in particular profit from the taxes remaining at their level, whereas less developed and remote districts with limited resources still depend on state support via the DAU.

Local legislation is far-reaching in Indonesia and covers many aspects of daily life. In the Philippines such legislative competencies exist to a much lower extent, whereas in Thailand regulations from local governments are less common. Considering all the mentioned criteria to determine the level of autonomy, Indonesia is by far the most decentralized or better devolved country under research, followed by the Philippines. Thailand is in many regards a country not so much devolved as deconcentrated.

A high level of autonomy, however, does not automatically result in better democratic practices at the local level. In all three countries, local politics are often dominated by powerful clans or families, particularly in Thailand and the Philippines. In both countries, the formal institutional changes could "not be equated with substantive change in local politicians' behavior and practices" (Choi 2011, p. 13). There is no guarantee that decentralization encourages elected local officials to be more responsive and accountable to their citizens. The great variety of local government performance makes it difficult to formulate general judgements. While in some local administrations, credible and honest governors/mayors are accountable to the citizens and their needs, others perform poorly, are corrupt, and manipulate local elections to their favour.

Out of all three countries, Indonesia is the only one which had made substantial institutional reforms in order to improve the quality of democracy at the local level. The reform of the election mode for district leaders and mayors, from an indirect election by local parliaments to a direct election by the people (*pilkada*), was of particular importance. This reform has significantly increased the accountability of local leaders. The decision of the Constitutional Court to allow independent candidates to run is another notable step in the right direction. Previously they had to be nominated by (corrupt) local political parties. Both changes have increased the quality of democracy at the local level.

These Indonesian-style reforms, however, were not necessary in the Philippines, as these regulations were already part of the Local Government Act of 1991. Nevertheless, local leaders in the Philippines can (with some notable exceptions) be characterized as members of persistent family/clan networks that have controlled a multitude of the constituencies for decades. Though the introduction of direct local elections improved the local quality of democracy in Indonesia, the same cannot be said of the Philippines. Local democracy in Thailand is more akin to that of the Philippines than Indonesia. With some exceptions, particularly in more urbanized areas, Thailand's local level politics are dominated by local dynasties. Local elections are generally more competitive in Indonesia and produce more political talents than those of Thailand and the Philippines, which directly impacts the overall state of democracy.

In terms of the containment of regional and ethnic conflicts, the effects of decentralization reforms in the three countries under research led to significantly different results. In Indonesia, the worrisome situation in the first years of democracy could have been successfully contained, not only by the creation of rights of special autonomy as that for the province of Aceh, but also by giving the local administrative units access to power and resources. The grievances of minorities are now directed to their new local elites, who are involved in power struggles with their peers, instead of challenging the national government. These positive repercussions of decentralization did not resolve the long-lasting conflicts surrounding the Muslim minorities in the South of Thailand and the Philippines, however. In the latter, the creation of the ARMM was a failure. The prospects for the newly created *Bangsamoro* political entity, which replaced the ARMM after the peace agreement in October 2012, are also bleak. The half-hearted decentralization process in Thailand did not lead to a significant reduction in the violence of the Southern provinces. In contrast to Indonesia, the decentralization processes in the Philippines and Thailand did not contribute substantially to the containment of ethnic conflicts and thereby the stabilization and deepening of the fragile democratic conditions in the respective countries. From a comparative perspective, the most devolved country, Indonesia, was most successful in conflict management.

Devolution can be effective only if the central political elites accept the transfer of decision-making power to the lower levels of government. In this regard, resistance against further decentralization is by far strongest in Thailand. As shown in chapter 4.2, mistrust of local autonomy is very characteristic of Thai politics. As can be seen by the CEO governors during the rule of Prime Minister Thaksin and the continuing appointment policy of governor positions, regional and local governments are seen as deconcentrated instruments of the national government. Additionally, Thailand lacked a window of opportunity enjoyed by Indonesia around 1999, when central elites were in a relatively weak position to oppose the far-ranging decentralization process initiated by the Habibie government. The initial "big bang" regulations created a dynamic situation in which the autonomy of local governments could not be taken back later without enormous political and economic costs.

In the Philippines, the situation is different. The central government never had the power nor the intervention opportunities of its Thai and Indonesian counterparts. Instead, since colonial times, the centre has been captured by powerful local elites. It comes as no surprise that even today central-local relations are dominated by local clans and dynasties which exploit central powers and resources to their own ends. The interactions between local and central elites, such as members of the House of Representatives, are focused on resource-fetching. In the Philippines, the notorious pork barrel serves as a case in point. In Thailand, similar forms of interaction prevail. Vertical accountability, in the sense that local governments can influence national politics, is limited in all the three countries under research. In the absence of effective second chambers representing regional interests, central-local relations are informally structured. Personal relations among individuals involved in the exchanges between the two levels count much more than formal and administrative methods of cooperation. These informal networks are a key factor in central-local power struggles, particularly in these three Southeast Asian countries where personalized state-society relations dominate politics (Choi 2011, p. 13).

Due to the "reinforcing dynamics between political dominance in the province and bargaining power in the national sphere" (Ardanaz, Leiras, and Tommasi 2010, p. 22f.), province governors (and district heads/ mayors in Indonesia) are important intermediaries between central and local levels in all three countries. In the first-past-the-post election systems of Thailand and the Philippines, parliamentarians act as mediators of local interests at the national level as well. While this transfer mechanism could strengthen democratic practices, the reality is often less promising. Many House members represent more the personal and power interests of their clans than those of ordinary citizens.

The decentralization processes in Thailand and the Philippines progressed to a certain extent in the early 2000s, but have stagnated since then. Further substantial reforms, such as the long-discussed Charter Change in the Philippines, which would transform the country into a federal state, are unlikely. The Philippines were the first of the three to initiate major reforms concerning vertical accountability. However, the Local Government Code provision, which requires a review and revision of the code every five years, has never been conducted, "not even once ... since the passage of the law" (Rocamora 2007, p. 203) in 1991.

A closer look at the reforms undertaken in the decentralization processes of the three countries reveals significant differences. In Thailand, decentralization certainly did not progress, but has rather declined in the last ten years. In the Philippines, no major reforms have given the ongoing process a further push, resulting in a problematic and stagnant state. In Indonesia, however, decentralization was among the top priorities of the SBY administration, and has continued to be a supportive factor for the deepening of democracy in Indonesia.

Reforms on Horizontal Accountability and their Impact on Democratization: A Comparative Perspective

Executive-legislative relations are a crucial part of horizontal accountability. In this regard, the three countries under research act under different contexts. In the parliamentary system of Thailand, the majority of the House of Representatives must support the government. Here, the control of the government is exerted by the parliamentary minority, i.e. the opposition. In the presidential systems of Indonesia and the Philippines, the DPR and the Congress are – due to the separation of powers – more independent towards the executive. However, the supervisory function of the Philippine House of Representatives is limited in practice. As has been demonstrated in chapter 5.3, Philippine presidents can always convince a parliamentary majority in their camp with the carrot and stick method. The carrot is the pork barrel and better access to resources, whereas the stick is the exclusion from both. In Indonesia, most parties represented in the DPR also prefer to be in the government's camp. However, the prevailing rainbow coalitions are somewhat fragile because critical legislators scrutinize government activities more thoroughly than their counterparts in the Philippines.

In Thailand the contrast between government and opposition is the most distinct among the three countries. The rights of the minority in parliament were restricted in the 1997 Constitution, which lead to the impression among opposition politicians that Thaksin was able to rule without any major parliamentary oversight. After the military coup, the drafters of the 2007 Constitution lowered the percentage for the initiation of a vote of no confidence from 40 to 20 per cent of the House members with the aim to put the government under better control of the House of Representatives.

In all the three political systems, parliaments do not give the impression that they are the key movers in politics. However, they do fulfill a significant role, not only in terms of horizontal accountability, but also in performing vertical and electoral accountability (Stapenhurst and O'Brien 2008, p. 2). Formally, the parliaments of Thailand, Indonesia, and the Philippines have enough constitutional and legal rights to strictly monitor government activities and to sanction misconduct. In practice, however, it is less the force of their constitutional rights than the preferences of their individual members that are pivotal (Case 2011, p. 2). Do the legislators really want to confront the government by exposing government failures, or do they prefer to be a more or less uncritical supporter of the government? Most members of the Philippine House of Representatives and the Indonesian DPR have chosen the latter option. They prioritized individual profits from government access over horizontal accountability. In the Thai House of Representatives, the smaller parties had also chosen the easy way of jumping on the bandwagon by joining the majority party in order to participate in government. In contrast, the two big camps, the Democrats and the TRT/PPP/Pheu Thai, take their oppositional roles very seriously and try to undermine the other party in power by all parliamentary means.

Horizontal accountability is sometimes even exerted by legislators who formally support the government, but nevertheless pose critical questions or demand amendments, for example in budget negotiations. In these cases, it matters whether they act for policy reasons or for personal gain. In the three countries under research, the critical pro-government legislators often impose accountability only to wring additional patronage and resources from the executive (Case 2011, p. 61).

This feature also fits to some extent the second chambers in the three countries. However, the powers of the second chambers vary to a great degree. Whereas the DPD in Indonesia is *de facto* powerless, the Thai Senate can obstruct government activities and exert some horizontal accountability. The role of this senate in the executive-legislative relations was engineered with two different meanings in the 1997 and the 2007 Constitutions. The Senate, under the 1997 Constitution, was intended as a political control instrument and was popularly elected. After the *coup d'etat*, the role of the Senate, with its half-appointed composition, was a return to previous times in which senior bureaucrats and military officers tried to prevent the government and its majority in the House of Representatives from passing anti-establishment legislation.

The most powerful second chamber for horizontal accountability is the Philippine Senate. Due to its controversial election mode, its 24 members are all extremely wealthy individuals with considerable popularity. Due to their financial and often political independence, the president has a hard time luring them into his camp. Their intentions to become president themselves one day converts them into harsh government critics. This specific context makes the Philippine Senate the most effective institution for horizontal accountability in the three countries under research.

Of at least equal importance for horizontal accountability are the major institutions of the judiciary. The Supreme Court of the Philippines and the Constitutional Courts in Indonesia and Thailand are powerful veto-players to their respective governments and have been responsible for major institutional reforms. Particularly in Thailand, the Supreme Court became so powerful that it is justified to speak of a judicialization of politics. By dismissing two prime ministers and dissolving parties that had just won the elections for alleged corruption and vote-buying, the Constitutional Court has greatly influenced Thai politics over the last decade. The required impartiality of the judges is doubted by many scholars, politicians and the general public. This can also be said of the Supreme Court of the Philippines, which, however, according to a political expert "is not as one-sided as that in Thailand".[1] Nevertheless, the Philippine Supreme Court judges, which were appointed by President GMA, stubbornly blocked initiatives from the Aquino government to check on the power abuses of the previous administration. The gridlock between the executive and the Supreme Court led to a constitutional crisis that culminated in the successful impeachment trial against Chief Justice Renato Corona. In contrast to its counterparts in Thailand and the Philippines, the Indonesian Constitutional Court guarded a critical distance from the government and reformed several laws passed by the president and parliament.

A lack in necessary critical distance towards those in power is also problematic for the allegedly independent government watchdog organizations of all three countries, particularly in Thailand and the Philippines. As has been described in the chapters 5.1 and 5.3, the anti-corruption agencies, as well as the national election commissions, were often subservient tools of the respective governments in both countries. The Indonesian anti-corruption commission, KPK, in contrast, took its job more seriously, convicting several high-ranking state officials and parliamentarians. However, recent developments seem to indicate that the KPK might become an example of what Ackerman called a "life cycle" for independent agencies. According to him, government watchdog organizations

> often start out relatively weak and dependent on their creators. Then the successful ones break out of their shells and start to have a significant impact on governance. In response, politicians, government officials and other affected parties try to cut back on the independence or the powers of the agency (Ackerman 2009, p. 12).

All three countries have remarkable and powerful mechanisms of horizontal accountability to prevent power abuse of the government. In recent years, however, the effects were different in each of the three countries: whereas the system of checks and balances worked relatively well in Indonesia, the mechanisms of horizontal accountability led to long lasting gridlocks in the Philippines. Between 2005 and 2010, the executive and the Senate could not cooperate and blocked common political decision-making, while between 2010 and 2012, the conflict between the president and the Supreme Court led to significant political standstill. In Thailand, the checks on the government have been significantly strengthened after the military coup. Appointed bureaucrats and military members in the Senate and a very powerful judiciary strongly limit the scope of action for the elected government.

Does More Accountability Automatically Result in a Higher Quality of Democracy?

All three countries witnessed gradual change over time. The institutional reforms did not completely overhaul the existing political orders. The most dramatic change was the 2007 Constitution in Thailand after the military coup. However, as has been shown before, this constitution adopted several features of its predecessor from 1997 and its inherent institutional reforms were thus not revolutionary.

Among the three countries under research, Indonesia was the most capable in deepening democracy after the inauguration. Despite very problematic conditions at the start of democratization in 1998, "successive governments were able to initiate and oversee significant reform of the major political institutions during the next decade" (Crouch 2010, p. 349). However, all three countries endured serious setbacks in establishing mechanisms of accountability that deterred those in power from exploiting public office for private gains.

Indonesia enjoys more democratic stability due to its features of a consensus democracy. In regard to the electoral accountability dimension the proportional election system effectively reduces distortions in favour of the bigger political parties and allows smaller parties to have a say in national politics. The implemented decentralization disperses power away from the national capital to the hundreds of districts and cities. In terms of horizontal accountability, an impartial and powerful constitutional court controlled decisions on which the president has agreed with the parliament.

Whereas in Thailand, particularly under the Thaksin government, and in the Philippines, particularly under the GMA administration, government leaders tried to maximize their power by curtailing parliamentary and judicial competencies and excluding political opponents from co-decision-making, all Indonesian presidents built grand coalitions and included many of their political opponents by giving them ministerial posts. This consensual style of political leadership in Indonesia marks a decisive difference to that of Thailand and the Philippines. In the latter two countries, the pungent polarization between rival individuals and political parties has led to the collapse of democracy in Thailand in 2006, to a permanent gridlock in the Philippines in the second half of the GMA administration, and a troublesome confrontation between the government and opposition after the election of "Noynoy" Aquino in 2010.

Compared to the political leaders in Thailand and the Philippines, Indonesian President Susilo Bambang Yudhoyono "stands out as a conciliatory and unifying figure, one willing to share power, to compromise and to build broad coalitions. These are very worthy attributes in a democracy – but they can go too far" (Diamond 2009, p. 337). Larry Diamond argues that grand coalitions do not contribute to democratic deepening because they undermine the vigour of democracy by depriving it of a powerful opposition that has the incentive to check the ruling party or coalition and hold it accountable. Consensual decision-making "reduces accountability by rendering policy making less transparent and deprives voters of their right to choose between political alternatives" (Braun 2008, p. 243). Additionally, according to Diamond, they dilute and erode governmental decision-making powers because with many involved players little can be agreed upon and they lead to increased patronage and corruption (Diamond 2009, p. 338).

Many scholars writing about Indonesia (Aspinall 2010; Slater 2009; Buehler 2011, p. 81f.) question the practice of all-party coalitions. They claim that voters cannot punish any particular party since no party has to fear that it will not be part of the government (Slater 2004, p. 72). This would result in a collusive democracy in which a party cartel (Katz and Mair 1995) from established parties dominates politics. I would argue that grand coalitions make the president and the elected legislators less accountable, but this is not necessarily bad for democracy. In the current institutional context, a broad cabinet is not a sign of a cartel, but rather an attempt to avoid being vetoed by the parliamentary majority. Colluding after competing in elections is not undemocratic but rather a feature of a consensus democracy with all its advantages and disadvantages. If political leaders or their parties fail to win the presidency or other executive positions in Indonesia, they can still exercise significant influence in national and local legislatures, provincial and district administrations, and independent state agencies (Dressel and Mietzner 2012, p. 407). In Thailand and the Philippines, electoral losers are excluded from power access and either switch sides – what dilutes electoral accountability –

or, as in Thailand, resort to mass mobilization, which has particularly destabilized Thai democracy since 2005.

This debate leads to the crucial question whether a higher degree of accountability automatically leads to a higher quality of democracy. In other words, does democracy really derive its vigour from personal and partisan competition and a fierce battle between government and opposition? Does governmental decisiveness count more than inclusive but slow decision-making, which is supported by more actors but with all the disadvantages of broad compromises?

A general answer is difficult, but the case studies of Indonesia, Thailand, and the Philippines indicate that the deepening of democracy went hand in hand with a more consensus-style oriented form of decision-making including power dispersion at the national and subnational level. The stability of the democratic order was rather supported by working inter-elite consensus (as in Indonesia) whereas heavy inter-elite competition (as in Thailand and in the Philippines under GMA) did not contribute to a deepening of democracy.

In Indonesia, the *reformasi* period brought about a "broadening but not a replacement of the political elite" (Crouch 2010, p. 6). While in the *Orde Baru* access to power was strictly limited to a small group of people around President Soeharto, the democratization process opened up space for many new political forces. However, these newcomers had to arrange themselves with the many remnants of the authoritarian past, who continued their careers. Those who came into politics after 1998 were the driving forces of the institutional reforms. Due to the Indonesian *musyawarah-mufakat* practice, the opponents of reforms were forced into compromises that did not radically change the political system, but rather incrementally transformed Indonesia into a more democratic order. In Indonesia, "democracy calls for decision makers to be ready for long-dwindling process, to utilize negotiations skills, and to accept a compromise with other stake-holders" (Kumorotomo 2009, p. 1f.).

In Thailand, Thaksin Shinawatra represented an agent of change. He wanted "to usher Thailand into a new era, into the 21st century, ending its anachronistic neo-feudal hierarchy" (Pongsudhirak 2008, p. 1). Thaksin himself once stated "I'm very, very revolutionary. I want to reform. I reformed so many things. I reformed ministries that have been there for 100 years. I was about to reform the whole legal system to make it modern" (Times Online 2009, p. 18). However, established forces, such as the bureaucracy, the judiciary, and the military, proved to be more powerful in blocking reform than the country's institutional reformers had anticipated. The Constitution of 2007 was a step back insofar as it strengthened these political actors, who are not directly accountable to the people. Thailand, under the 2007 Constitution is a "custodial democracy" rather than a liberal democratic order, which the 1997 charter attempted to forge but fell short of in the face of Thaksin's ambitions of power (Pongsudhirak 2008, p. 3).

Only a few institutional reforms have been implemented since the enactment of the 1987 Constitution in the Philippines. A major reason was resistance from the dominant clans and dynasties which were able to prevent institutional reforms that would reduce their powers. As one political analyst put it: "In the Philippines, constitutional engineering is impossible. You can't expect politicians to change. They are working on their own favors."[3] If the people who are able to initiate reforms (the political elite) are the very ones who are allergic to reform, no major institutional change can be expected (Quiros 2012).

Limits of Institutional Engineering

The main obstacle to institutional development in the three countries under research is the limited acceptance of formal rules and accountability among the political elites. Instead, informal patterns of influence dominate all three Southeast Asian countries. It would require a change of the political culture towards one in which the "interests of all parties to adhere to universally accepted rules rather than attempt to manage intra-elite competition informally through payoffs and threats" (Harvard Kennedy School Indonesia Program 2010, p. 81) would be the standard. A striking example of the consequences of not playing to the unwritten rules of the political establishment is Thaksin Shinawatra. His failed efforts "to adequately observe the traditional hierarchies of the Thai power structure earned him multiple enemies and identified him as a danger to the old oligarchy" (Hewison 2010, p. 128).

However, a change in political culture and tradition is much more difficult to achieve than merely through institutional reforms. The political practice shows the limits of institutional engineering. Power structures, in which political elites (family clans in the Philippines, a bureaucratic-military elite in Thailand) exert informal power irrespective of formal rules in a society which is still largely kept in feudal social structures, do not change if a new constitution or law is passed. Among these elites, informal political dealings that take place behind the scenes are more important than formal accountability relationships. Indonesia, Thailand,

and the Philippines illustrate "how formal democratic institutions are dominated by informal power structures but also how the legitimacy of democracy can come increasingly in question" (Dressel 2011, p. 530). The deepening of democracy is thus closely connected to reforms in which informal power structures are transferred into transparent accountability relations.

A culture of deeply entrenched corruption and patronage presents a profound problem in all three countries. Since "corruption equals monopoly plus discretion minus accountability" (Klitgaard 1988, p. 75), the deepening of democracy is significantly imperiled. The corruption that stems from the discretion of individual leaders in all three countries cannot yet be reduced by institutional engineering in terms of horizontal, electoral, and vertical accountability. However, such reform measures are a *conditio sine qua non* for the deepening of democracy. Formal accountability mechanisms make political decision-making transparent and comprehensible to the sovereign of a democracy, the people. In order to increase accountability, institutions must be equipped with adequate rights and sanctioning abilities. Yet, a strengthening of the often weak democratic institutions is not sufficient, since in all three countries there are indications that the democratic institutions have already been warped or subverted by vested interests. The challenge is therefore "more to dismantle predatory and clientelist institutions and build democratic ones, or to transform the former into the latter" (Quimpo 2009, p. 351). The three cases in this study show that in all constitutions, several accountability institutions exist, but for various reasons do not perform as they should. The transformation of these institutions is a difficult task because they are either too dependent on the executive branch or in other cases dominated by selfish rent-seeking elites. In other words, those who ought to do the checking contribute to the problem rather than the solution.

While it might be far-fetched to say that the stability of Indonesia's political system "has so far been guaranteed primarily through institutional engineering" (Tomsa 2010, p. 158), the institutional reforms nevertheless contributed to an incremental increase in the quality of democracy. Particularly in comparison to Thailand and the Philippines, Indonesian reform processes concerning accountability changed the political landscape after 2004. The reform activities of the constitution strengthened horizontal accountability, the electoral reforms (open list, threshold) improved electoral accountability, and the reforms on local democracy and decentralization (*pilkada*) benefited vertical accountability. In contrast, the political elites of the Philippines were able to prevent major institutional change that might have endangered their vested interests. In Thailand, the institutional changes after the military coup in 2006 led to a decline rather than a deepening of democracy.

The different paths of development of the three democratization processes had various reasons. In this study, I showed that institutional engineering was a decisive variable for the different outcomes, though not the only one. Many structural, cultural, and historic factors are as important as actor constellations and leader personalities. However, the fact that the quality of democracy is generally regarded as higher in Indonesia than the other two countries can be explained by the successful implementation of institutional reforms concerning the three accountability dimensions. In contrast, the stagnation or regression of democracy in Thailand and the Philippines has been due to under-developed accountability mechanisms and a lack of institutional reforms which mitigate these deficiencies.

Notes

[1]   Interview with Joel Rocamora, Director, Secretary of the National Anti-Poverty Commission, Quezon City, 5 October 2010.

[2]   Interview with Ronald Holmes, Department of Political Science, De La Salle University, Manila, 24 August 2009.

[3]   Interview with Prospero "Popoy" de Vera, Professor at the National College of Public Administration and Governance, University of the Philippines, Quezon City, 13 September 2007.

7

CONCLUSION

In this study, I analysed in what ways institutional reforms concerning the three dimensions of accountability (electoral, vertical, and horizontal) reshaped the quality of democracy in Thailand, Indonesia, and the Philippines. In other words, I addressed to what degree institutional engineering concerning these three dimensions of accountability contributed to a deepening, stagnation, or regression of the democratization processes in the three countries.

To this end, I first analysed what kind of institutional reforms have been undertaken by political decision-makers who intended to transform political accountability in each of the three cases. Then I connected these findings with their impact on the respective democratization processes. From a comparative perspective, this study found that electoral accountability is strongly determined by the respective type of government and election systems. In Thailand and Indonesia, major electoral reforms contributed to changes in how voters can hold their representatives accountable, whereas in the Philippines, only technical modifications took place. In Thailand, electoral reforms introduced by the 2007 Constitution reduced the accountability of legislators and the government, and thus democratic quality. In Indonesia, the modified rules for the election of the president and the parliament can be interpreted as a power struggle between political parties who want to retain their power as intermediaries between citizens and political institutions. In this case the institutional reforms stabilized democracy.

In terms of vertical accountability, defined as the impact of subnational institutions on the overall quality of democracy, the three countries varied to a great extent. Due to a lack of power, Thai subnational administrative structures are less capable of acting in accountability relations with the national level. This is different in Indonesia and the Philippines. In Indonesia, the far-reaching autonomy and successful transfer of democratic procedures to the local level has brought a new dynamic and generally positive impact on the quality of democracy at the national level. In the Philippines, local authorities enjoy sufficient autonomy and impact national politics to a great extent. However, local democracy is, in most cases, limited by the dominance of wealthy and powerful clans, which translates into the capture of political institutions at the national level. Because of this vertical accountability relations do not support the deepening of democracy in the Philippines.

Reforms on horizontal accountability were manifold in all three countries. Particularly the mushrooming of independent government watchdog organizations was remarkable. However, with the exception of the KPK in Indonesia, these organizations failed to contribute positively to the democratization processes. In contrast to public perception, the parliaments in all three countries served as important checks on the respective governments. The strengthening of the judiciary, particularly in Thailand, was a common trend. While theoretically increased sanction potentials for judicial institutions can be positive for horizontal accountability, the lack of judicial impartiality and independence in the cases of Thailand and the Philippines show the limits of this practice.

Prospects for the future of democracy depend on the ability of the political actors to promote institutional reforms for better adapting their systems of government to political, social, and economic challenges in the years to come. These reforms are only possible if powerful political and business actors come to accept (or are driven to accept) that the rules of the game must be redefined. If these elites stubbornly resist political change, an improvement of democratic quality is unlikely.

In this regard, Indonesia and its consensus-style democracy seem to offer more opportunities for institutional reforms aiming at the strengthening of democracy than does Thailand and the Philippines. In these two countries, oligarchic powers prevent the true meaning of democracy: government of the people, not of elites.

However, Indonesia's democracy is far from being full-fledged. Despite the mentioned institutional reforms and a steady support from its population, the quality of democracy has — according to all democracy indices and country experts — stagnated or even regressed slightly in recent years (Mietzner 2012a, p. 210f.). Yet, in comparison with Thailand and the Philippines, Indonesia's state of democracy — measured by the three dimensions of political accountability — is still in a better condition.

Thai democracy is particularly fragile since there is disagreement over the principal rules of the political game (Norton 2012, p. 60). The present Yingluck government and its supporters see the Constitution of 2007 as illegitimate, since it was drafted under military rule in the wake of the 2006 coup. Institutional engineering has already started with constitutional reform proposals being debated in the national parliament. In the Philippines, in contrast, the long overdue constitutional reforms have not yet taken place, despite an abundance of reform initiatives launched by civil society groups and several politicians. Indonesia will also most likely witness significant institutional change in the coming years. Consequently, this study on institutional engineering and political accountability is inevitably a work in progress.

My working hypothesis that the democratization processes in the countries under research went in different directions because of significant variations in the reforms to build and establish electoral, horizontal and vertical accountability can be verified rather than falsified. From a comparative perspective, it became obvious that various factors – prominently among them institutional engineering – led to different courses of the respective democratization processes. Despite structural constraints and a much higher level of difficulty, Indonesia was relatively successful in reforming its political system by institutional engineering. Compared to the structurally advanced countries of Thailand and the Philippines, with their longer democratic track records, Indonesian decision-makers managed to break the resistance of powerful vested interests by including them in decision-making processes. Indonesia is a good example for the assumption that procedural consensus is more probable, if "the participants in the democratic process do not expect to lose all the time and think that no dire consequences will follow when they lose" (Valenzuela 1992, p. 83). As has been described in the empirical parts of this study, accountability mechanisms are also flawed to some extent in Indonesia, but less so than in the other two countries under research.

Several conclusions for the general study of democratization processes can be drawn from this study. The improvement of accountability mechanisms is not the only path towards democratic advancement. Institutional reforms do not automatically lead to improvements, but can also cause unintended "institutional consequences that diverge from the goals sought by the agents who originally established or altered the institution" (Cortell and Peterson 2004, p. 771).

The founding of more accountability institutions is not always beneficial for democracy. Increasing the degree of accountability with regard to the vertical and horizontal dimensions by strengthening subnational governments and government watchdogs at the national level leads to more veto-players and a consensus-style democracy. Consequently, a system with a high degree of inter-institutional accountability can in practice lead to opaque backroom dealings by a political elite who is not accountable to its citizens.

The creation of independent agencies to increase horizontal accountability is also only a viable improvement if their independence is guaranteed and their rights to intervene into the affairs of other state institutions are *de facto* significant. The same refers to judicial institutions which are often idealistically seen as impartial and pro-democratic. As has been illustrated in this study, this cannot be assumed automatically.

As has been explained in chapter 2.4, first-past-the-post election systems offer better chances for voters to exert electoral accountability. However, as the examples of Thailand and the Philippines show, the side effect is that wealthy and powerful local oligarchies dominate in their constituencies, that political parties are weak, and that platforms consist of a few populist slogans.

The creation of political accountability, which is a necessary and important part of "quality democracy" (Diamond and Morlino 2004, p. 22), is not an easy task. Particularly, if one includes – as in this study – the working of local democracy and central-local relations as criteria for the measurement of accountability, the transformation of a political system is a long-term process, as institutional reforms do not necessarily change actor behaviour and the political culture. In other words, institutional engineering after the inauguration of democracy is a necessary but not sufficient condition for the improvement of the quality of democracy. The effects of institutional reforms are particularly limited if clientelism is deeply ingrained and the political elite remains the same (Rüland 2003, p. 477). A political culture rooted in feudalism and elitism compromises electoral accountability and working systems of checks and balances. The result will hardly be compatible with a "quality democracy".

Many of the accountability deficiencies are procedural, meaning that the reform of the institutional framework might be a solution. However, this study has shown that the belief of institutionalists that political change towards democratic deepening is manageable by merely transforming the institutional setting (Sartori 1994) is questionable. An accountable political system without major weaknesses can hardly be constructed through institutional engineering alone: this illustrates the limits of institutional engineering.

Particularly in Southeast Asia, with its idiosyncratic political cultures and traditions, one-size-fits-all solutions and conventional Western recipes for success are not applicable without serious drawbacks. Pragmatic flexibility and a case-sensitive approach are thus required in order to improve institutional deficiencies and the overall quality of democracy.

BIBLIOGRAPHY

Aarts, Kees and Jacques Thomassen. "Satisfaction with Democracy: Do Institutions Matter?". *Electoral Studies*, vol. 27, no. 1 (2008): 5–18.

Abinales, Patricio N. "The Philippines: Weak State, Resilient President". In *Southeast Asian Affairs 2008*, edited by Daljit Singh and Tin Maung Maung Than. Singapore: Institute of Southeast Asian Studies, 2008.

————. "The Philippines in 2010". *Asian Survey*, vol. 51, no. 1 (2011): 163–72.

Abramowitz, Alan I., Brad Alexander, and Matthew Gunning. "Incumbency, Redistricting, and the Decline of Competition in U.S. House Elections". *The Journal of Politics*, vol. 68, no. 1 (2006): 75–88.

ABS-CBN News. "Panlilio sees Malacañang's Hand in Recall Petition", 7 October 2008. Available at <http://rp3.abs-cbnnews.com/nation/regions/10/17/08/panlilio-sees-malaca%C3%B1angs-hand-recall-petition> (accessed 5 March 2013).

Abueva, José V. "Some Advantages of Federalism and Parliamentary Government", 2005. Available at <www.pcij.org/blog/wp-docs/abueva-federalism.pdf> or <www.muslimmindanao.ph/conflict/abueva-federalism.pdf> (accessed 5 March 2013).

Ackerman, John M. "Independent Accountability Agencies & Democracy: A New Separation of Powers?". Paper presented at a Workshop on Comparative Administrative Law, Yale University, 8–9 May 2009. Available at <http://www.law.yale.edu/documents/pdf/CompAdminLaw/John_Ackerman_CompAdLaw_paper.pdf> (accessed 23 October 2012).

————. "Understanding Independent Accountability Agencies". In *Comparative Administrative Law*, edited by Susan Rose-Ackerman and Peter L. Lindseth. Cheltenham/Northampton: Edward Elgar, 2010.

Afrida, Nani. "Pork-Barrel Politics Lure Poor Farmers". *The Jakarta Post Online*, 26 July 2011. Available at <http://www.thejakartapost.com/news/2011/07/26/pork-barrel-politics-lure-poor-farmers.html> (accessed 4 August 2011).

Ager, Maila. "Brillantes Prefers Rich People Barred from Joining Party-List Elections". *Philippine Daily Inquirer Online*, 8 November 2012. Available at <http://newsinfo.inquirer.net/304020/brillantes-prefers-rich-people-barred-from-joining-party-list-elections> (accessed 28 February 2013).

Aguilar, Filomeno V. "Betting on Democracy: Electoral Ritual in the Philippine Presidential Campaign". In *Elections as Popular Culture in Asia*, edited by Chua Beng Huat. New York: Routledge, 2007.

Alicias, Denden and Djorina Velasco. "Decentralization and Deepening Democracy". In *Decentralization Interrupted: Studies from Cambodia, Indonesia, Philippines and Thailand*, edited by Denden Alicias et al. Quezon City: Institute for Popular Democracy, 2007.

Amornvivat, Sutapa. "Fiscal Decentralization: The Case of Thailand". Paper presented at the International Symposium on Fiscal Decentralization in Asia Revisited, Tokyo, February 2004. Available at <http://www.econ.hit-u.ac.jp/~kokyo/APPPsympo04/FiscDect%20_Thailand.pdf> (accessed 10 August 2011).

An Lu. "Thai PM, Seven Ministers Survive No-confidence Vote". *Xinhua English News*, 27 June 2008. Available at <http://news.xinhuanet.com/english/2008-06/27/content_8449237.htm> (accessed 14 September 2011).

Antlöv, Hans. "Not Enough Politics! Power, Participation and the New Democratic Polity in Indonesia". In *Local Power and Politics*, edited by Edward Aspinall and Greg Fealy. Singapore: Institute of Southeast Asian Studies, 2003.

Ardanaz, Martín, Marcelo Leiras, and Mariano Tommasi. "The Politics of Federalism in Argentina and Its Effect on Governance and Accountability", 2010. Available at <http://faculty.udesa.edu.ar/tommasi/papers/wp/Ardanaz%20Leiras%20Tommasi.pdf> (accessed 23 October 2013).

Arghiros, Daniel. *Democracy, Development and Decentralization in Provincial Thailand*. Richmond: Curzon Press, 2001.

Aritonang, Margareth S. "More Political Parties Look to Contest Polls". *The Jakarta Post Online*, 31 August 2012. Available at <http://www.thejakartapost.com/news/2012/08/31/more-political-parties-look-contest-polls.html> (accessed 13 May 2013).

Asian Development Bank. "Indonesia: State Audit Reform Sector Development Program", 2011. Available at <http://www.adb.org/sites/default/files/PVR-232.pdf> (accessed 10 February 2013).

Askew, Marc. *Performing Political Identity: The Democrat Party in Southern Thailand*. Chiang Mai: Silkworm Books, 2008.

Aspinall, Edward. "Indonesia: The Irony of Success". *Journal of Democracy*, vol. 21, no. 2 (2010): 20–34.

Aspinall, Edward and Greg Fealy, eds. *Local Power and Politics*. Singapore: Institute of Southeast Asian Studies, 2003.

Assegaf, Rifqi S. "Judicial Reform in Indonesia, 1998–2006". In *Reforming Laws and Institutions in Indonesia: An Assessment*, edited by Naoyuki Sakumoto and Hikmahanto Juwana. Chiba: Institute of Developing Economies/Japan External Trade Organization, 2007.

Avendaño, Christine O. and Marlon Ramos. "7 SC Justices 'Snub' Sereno - Chief Justice: My Appointment is God's Will". *Philippine Daily Inquirer*, 4 September

2012. Available at <http://newsinfo.inquirer.net/263508/7-sc-justices-snub-sereno> (accessed 28 February 2013).

Baker, Chris. "Pluto-Populism: Thaksin and Popular Politics". In *Thailand beyond the Crisis*, edited by Peter Warr. London/New York: Routledge, 2005.

Balisacan, Arsenio M., Hal Hill, and Sharon Faye A. Piza. "Regional Development Dynamics and Decentralization in the Philippines: Ten Lessons from a 'Fast Starter'". *ASEAN Economic Bulletin*, vol. 25, no. 3 (2006): 293–315.

Bangkok Post Online. "Governors Pay Penalty For Not Halting Protests: Political Axe Wielded in Provincial Reshuffle". *Bangkok Post Online*, 29 September 2010. Available at <http://www.bangkokpost.com/news/politics/198665/governors-pay-penalty-for-not-halting-protests> (accessed 24 August 2011).

――――. "Yingluck Pressed on Zone Vow: Muslims Tell Govt to Fulfil South Pledge". *Bangkok Post Online*, 17 July 2011*a*. Available at <http://www.bangkokpost.com/news/politics/247391/yingluck-pressed-on-zone-vow> (accessed 24 August 2011).

――――. "Special Administrative Zone Plan Premature, Says Prayuth". *Bangkok Post Online*, 22 July 2011*b*. Available at <http://www.bangkokpost.com/news/local/248188/special-administrative-zone-plan-premature-says-prayuth> (accessed 24 August 2011).

Bappenas. *Studi Evaluasi Dampak Pemekaran Daerah*. Jakarta: UNDP, 2008.

Bardhan, Pranab and Dilip Mookherjee. "Capture and Governance at Local and National Levels". *American Economic Review*, vol. 90, no. 2 (2000): 135–39.

Baum, Jeeyang Rhee. *Responsive Democracy: Increasing State Accountability in East Asia*. Ann Arbor: The University of Michigan Press, 2011.

Bautista, Maricar. "Midnight appointments stifle next admin". abs-cbnNEWS.com, 5 June 2010. Available at <http://www.abs-cbnnews.com/ nation/06/05/10/midnight-appointments-stifle-next-admin> (accessed 5 September 2011).

Baviera, Aileen. "Aquino: Pushing the Envelope, Single-mindedly". In *Southeast Asian Affairs 2012*, edited by Daljit Singh and Pushpa Thambipillai. Singapore: Institute of Southeast Asian Studies, 2012.

Beech, Hannah. "Thai PM Fights for His Political Life". *Time Magazine Online*, 27 June 2008. Available at <http://www.time.com/time/world/article/0,8599,1818419,00.html> (accessed 14 September 2011).

Behn, Robert D. *Rethinking Democratic Accountability*. Washington, D.C.: Brookings Institution Press, 2001.

Benaning, Marvyn N. "Solons Warned on Evils of Reenacted Budget". *Manila Bulletin*, 25 November 2009. Available at <http://www.mb.com.ph/articles/231173/solons-warned-evils-reenacted-budget> (accessed 30 August 2011).

Biela, Jan and Yannis Papadopoulos. "Strategies for Assessing and Measuring Agency Accountability". Paper presented at the 32nd EGPA Annual Conference 2010, 7–10 September 2010, Toulouse. Available at <http://soc.kuleuven.be/io/egpa/org/2010Toul/Papers/Jan_Biela_EGPA%202010.pdf> (accessed 23 October 2012).

Bjarnegård, Elin. "Who's the Perfect Politician? Clientelism as a Determining Feature of Thai Politics". In *Party Politics in Southeast Asia: Clientelism and Electoral Competition in Indonesia, Thailand, and the Philippines*, edited by Dirk Tomsa and Andreas Ufen. London/New York: Routledge, 2013.

Bolongaita, Emil. "The Philippines in 1999: Balancing Restive Democracy and Recovering Economy". *Asian Survey*, vol. 40, no. 1 (2000): 67–77.

Bordadora, Norman. "Senate Passed Antipolitical Dynasty Bill in 1987". *The Philippine Daily Inquirer*, 9 November 2012. Available at <http://newsinfo. inquirer.net/304298/senate-passed-antipolitical-dynasty-bill-in-1987 > (accessed 4 March 2013).

Bovens, Mark. "Analysing and Assessing Accountability: A Conceptual Framework". *European Law Journal*, vol. 13, no. 4 (2007): 447–68.

―――. "Two Concepts of Accountability: Accountability as a Virtue and as a Mechanism". *West European Politics*, vol. 33, no. 5 (2010): 946–67.

Bowornwathana, Bidhya. "Autonomization of the Thai State: Some Observations". *Public Administration and Development*, vol. 26, no. 1 (2006): 27–34.

Brandsma, Gijs Jan and Thomas Schillemans. "The Accountability Cube: Measuring Accountability". *Journal of Public Administration Research and Theory Advance Access*, published 18 September 2012. Available at <http://jpart. oxfordjournals.org/content/early/2012/09/13/jopart.mus034.full.pdf+html?sid= c883b0a0-1400-4d48-baab-a19b71f9f042> (accessed 13 May 2013).

Brata, Aloysius G. "Creating New Regions: Improving Regional Welfare Equality?". MPRA Paper no. 12540 (2008). Available at <http://mpra.ub.uni-muenchen. de/12540> (accessed 13 May 2013).

Bratton, Michael. "Second Elections in Africa". *Journal of Democracy*, vol. 9, no. 3 (1998): 51–66.

Braun, Sebastian Kwame. "Indonesia's Presidential Democracy: A Factor of Stability or Instability?". Ph.D. thesis, Department of Political Science, Humboldt University Berlin, 2008.

Brillantes, Alex B. *Innovations and Excellence: Understanding Local Governments in the Philippines*. The Philippines: NCPAG, University of the Philippines, 2003.

Brilliantes, Alex and Jose Tiu Sonco II. "Decentralization and Local Governance in the Philippines". In *Public Administration in Southeast Asia: Thailand, Philippines, Malaysia, Hong Kong, and Macao*, edited by Evan M. Berman. Boca Raton/London/New York: CRC Press, 2006.

Buehler, Michael. "Countries at the Crossroads: Indonesia". Washington, D.C.: Freedom House, 2010*a*. Available at <http://www.freedomhouse.org/report/ countries-crossroads/2012/indonesia> (accessed 17 February 2013).

―――. "Decentralisation and Local Democracy in Indonesia: The Marginalisation of the Public Sphere". In *Problems of Democratization in Indonesia: Elections, Institutions and Society*, edited by Marcus Mietzner and Edward Aspinall. Singapore: Institute of Southeast Asian Studies, 2010*b*.

————. "Indonesia's Law on Public Services: Changing State-Society Relations or Continuing Politics as Usual?". *Bulletin of Indonesian Economic Studies*, vol. 47, no. 1 (2011): 65–86.

Bünte, Marco. "Indonesia's Protracted Decentralization: Contested Reforms and Their Unintended Consequences". In *Democratization in Post-Suharto Indonesia*, edited by Marco Bünte and Andreas Ufen. London/New York: Routledge, 2009.

Bünte, Marco and Andreas Ufen. *Democratization in Post-Suharto Indonesia*. London/New York, 2009.

Cabacungan, Gil. "Militant Party-lists not getting their pork". *Philippine Daily Inquirer*, 10 December 2012. Available at <http://newsinfo.inquirer.net/321463/militant-party-lists-not-getting-their-pork> (accessed 5 March 2013).

Cabacungan, Gil and Leila B. Salaverria. "Akbayan Lawmaker Defends Role as Caretaker of Dinagat Pork". *Philippine Daily Inquirer*, 3 January 2013. Available at <http://newsinfo.inquirer.net/334089/akbayan-lawmaker-defends-role-as-caretaker-of-dinagat-pork> (accessed 5 March 2013).

Calica, Aurea. "No Congressional Insertions in 2010 Budget – Abad". *The Philippine Star*, 28 July 2010. Available at <http://www.philstar.com/Article.aspx?articleId=597414&publicationSubCategoryId=63> (accessed 30 August 2011).

Calonzo, Andreo. "House OKs Bill Punishing 'Political Butterflies'". *GMA News*, 10 October 2012. Available at <http://www.gmanetwork.com/news/story/277695/news/nation/house-oks-bill-punishing-political-butterflies> (accessed 5 March 2013).

Capuno, Joseph J. "The Quality of Local Governance and Development under Decentralization". In *The Dynamics of Regional Development: The Philippines in East Asia*, edited by Arsenio M. Balisacan and Hal Hill. Quezon City: Ateneo de Manila University Press, 2007.

Carey, John M. "Presidentialism and Representative Institutions". In *Constructing Democratic Governance in Latin America*, edited by Jorge Domínguez and Michael Shifter. Baltimore: Johns Hopkins University Press, 2003.

Cariño, Ledivina V. "Devolution and Democracy: A Fragile Connection". In *East Asia's New Democracies: Deepening, Reversal, Non-Liberal Alternatives*, edited by Yin-wah Chu and Siu-lun Wong. London/New York: Routledge, 2010.

Carnegie, Paul J. *The Road from Authoritarianism to Democratization in Indonesia*. New York: Palgrave McMillan, 2010.

Carothers, Thomas. "The End of the Transition Paradigm". *Journal of Democracy*, vol. 13, no. 1 (2002): 5–21.

————. *Confronting the Weakest Link: Aiding Political Parties in New Democracies*. Washington, D.C.: Carnegie Endowment for International Peace, 2006.

Case, William. "Democracy's Quality and Breakdown: New Lessons from Thailand". Working Paper Series, no. 83. Southeast Asia Research Centre, City University of Hong Kong, 2007.

————. "Democracy, Governance, and Regime Cycling in Thailand". In *Public Governance in Asia and the Limits of Electoral Democracy*, edited by Brian Bridges and Lok Sang Ho. Cheltenham/Northampton: Edward Elgar Publishing, 2010.

————. *Executive Accountability in Southeast Asia: The Role of Legislatures in New Democracies and under Electoral Authoritarianism*. Honolulu: East West Center, 2011.

Castro, Renato Cruz De. "The Philippines in 2011: Muddling through a Year of Learning and Adjustment". *Asian Survey*, vol. 52, no. 1 (2012): 210–19.

Chambers, Paul. "Good Governance, Political Stability and Constitutionalism in Thailand". Occasional Paper. King Prajadhipok's Institute, 2002.

————. "Superfluous, Mischievous or Emancipating? Thailand's Evolving Senate Today". *Journal of Current Southeast Asian Affairs*, vol. 28, no. 3 (2009): 3–38.

Chambers, Paul W. and Aurel Croissant. "Monopolizing, Mutualizing, or Muddling Through: Factions and Party Management in Contemporary Thailand". *Journal of Current Southeast Asian Affairs*, vol. 29, no. 3 (2010): 3–33.

Chantornvong, Sombat. "The 1997 Constitution and the Politics of Electoral Reform". In *Reforming Thai Politics*, edited by Duncan McCargo. Copenhagen: Nordic Institute of Asian Studies, 2002.

Chardchawarn, Supasawad. *Local Governance in Thailand: The Politics of Decentralization and the Roles of Bureaucrats, Politicians, and the People*. Chiba: Institute of Developing Economies, Japan External Trade Organization, 2010.

Choi, Nankyung. *Local Politics in Indonesia: Pathways to Power*. London/New York: Routledge, 2011.

Christanto, Dicky. "House Passes Amendments to Constitutional Court Law". *Jakarta Post Online*, 22 June 2011. Available at <http://www.thejakartapost.com/news/2011/06/22/house-passes-amendments-constitutional-court-law.html> (accessed 10 February 2013).

————. "With Great Power Comes a Great Chance to Steal". *Jakarta Post Online*, 27 August 2012. Available at <http://www.thejakartapost.com/news/2012/08/27/reportage-with-great-power-comes-a-great-chance-steal.html> (accessed 15 May 2013).

Co, Edna E.A., Jorge V. Tigno, Maria Elissa Jayme Lao, and Margeita A. Sayo. *Philippine Democracy Assessments: Free and Fair Elections and the Democratic Role of Political Parties*. Quezon City: Ateneo de Manila University Press, 2005.

Connors, Michael Kelly. "Ambivalent Human Rights: Thai Democracy". In *Human Rights in Asia*, edited by Thomas W.D. Davis and Brian Galligan. Cheltenham: Elgar, 2011.

Constitution of the Kingdom of Thailand 1997. "Constitution of the Kingdom of Thailand, B.E. 2540 (1997)", 1997. Available at <http://thailaws.com/law/t_laws/claw0010.pdf> (accessed 13 March 2013).

Constitution of the Kingdom of Thailand 2007. "Constitution of the Kingdom of Thailand, B.E. 2550 (2007)", 2007. Available at <http://www.wipo.int/int/edocs/lexdocs/laws/en/th/th021en.pdf> (accessed 13 March 2013).

Constitution of the Philippines. "The 1987 Constitution of the Republic of the Philippines", 1987. Available at <http://www.gov.ph/the-philippine-constitutions/the-1987-constitution-of-the-republic-of-the-philippines/> (accessed 13 March 2013).

Corona, Renato C. "We stand together". Speech delivered before Supreme Court Justices and Court Officials, 12 December 2011. Available at <http://sc.judiciary.gov.ph/pio/speeches/12-12-11-speech.pdf> (accessed 13 March 2013).

Coronel, Sheila S. "The Philippines in 2006: Democracy and Its Discontents". *Asian Survey*, vol. 47, no. 1 (2007*a*): 175–82.

———. "Houses of Privilege". In *The Rulemakers: How the Wealthy and Well-Born Dominate Congress*, edited by Sheila S. Coronel, Yvonne T. Chua, Luz Rimban, and Booma B. Cruz. Pasig City: Anvil, 2007*b*.

Cortell, Andrew P. and Susan Peterson. "Limiting the Unintended Consequences of Institutional Change". *Comparative Political Studies*, vol. 35, no. 4 (2004): 768–99.

Croissant, Aurel. "Legislative Powers, Veto Players, and the Emergence of Delegative Democracy: A Comparison of Presidentialism in the Philippines and South Korea". *Democratization*, vol. 10, no. 3 (2003): 68–99.

———. "Provisions, Practices and Performances of Constitutional Review in Democratizing East Asia". *The Pacific Review*, vol. 23, no. 5 (2010): 549–78.

Crook, Richard C. and James Manor. *Democracy and Decentralization in South Asia and West Africa: Participation, Accountability and Performance*. Cambridge: Cambridge University Press, 1998.

Crouch, Harold. *Political Reform in Indonesia after Suharto*. Singapore: Institute of Southeast Asian Studies, 2010.

Dahl, Robert A. *Polyarchy: Participation and Opposition*. New Haven/London: Yale University Press, 1971.

———. "Democracy and Human Rights under Different Conditions of Development". In *Human Rights in Perspective: A Global Assessment*, edited by A. Eide and B. Hagtvet. Oxford: Blackwell, 1992.

Daslani, Pitan. "Indonesia 'Too Fragile' for Police, Military Vote: Defense Ministry". *Jakarta Globe Online*, 12 August 2012*a*. Available at <http://www.thejakartaglobe.com/archive/indonesia-too-fragile-for-police-military-vote-defense-ministry> (accessed 13 May 2013).

———. "Indonesia's Election Threshold Levels Called Unconstitutional". *Jakarta Globe Online*, 30 September 2012*b*. Available at <http://www.thejakartaglobe.com/archive/indonesias-election-threshold-levels-called-unconstitutional> (accessed 13 May 2013).

Davidson, Jamie S. "Dilemmas of Democratic Consolidation in Indonesia". *The Pacific Review*, vol. 22, no. 3 (2009): 293–310.

de Dios, Emmanuel S. "Local Politics and Local Economy". In *The Dynamics of Regional Development: The Philippines in East Asia*, edited by Arsenio M. Balisacan and Hal Hill. Quezon City: Ateneo de Manila University Press, 2007.

de Dios, Emmanuel S. and Paul D. Hutchcroft. "Political Economy". In *The Philippine Economy: Development, Politics, and Challenges*, edited by Arsenio M. Balisacan and Hal Hill. New York: Oxford University Press, 2003.

Desierto, Diane A. "Universalist Constitutionalism in the Philippines: Restricting Executive Particularism in the Form of Executive Privilege". *Verfassung und Recht in Übersee*, vol. 42, no. 1 (2009): 80–105.

Diamond, Larry. *Developing Democracy toward Consolidation*. Baltimore: Johns Hopkins University Press, 1999.

———. "Is a 'Rainbow Coalition' a Good Way to Govern?". *Bulletin of Indonesian Economic Studies*, vol. 45, no. 3 (2009): 337–40.

Diamond, Larry and Leonardo Morlino. "The Quality of Democracy: An Overview". *Journal of Democracy*, vol. 15, no. 4 (2004): 20–31.

———, eds. *Assessing the Quality of Democracy*. Baltimore: Johns Hopkins University Press, 2005.

Diamond, Larry, Marc F. Plattner, and Andreas Schedler. "Introduction". In *The Self-Restraining State: Power and Accountability in New Democracies*, edited by Andreas Schedler, Larry Diamond, and Marc F. Plattner. Boulder/London: Lynne Rienner Publishers, 1999.

Diokno, Benjamin E. "Decentralization in the Philippines After Ten Years: What Have We Learned?". In *Decentralization Policies in Asian Development*, edited by Shinuchi Ichimura and Roy Bahl. Singapore: World Scientific Publishing, 2009.

Dix, Robert. "Democratization and the Institutionalization of Latin American Political Parties". *Comparative Political Studies*, vol. 24, no. 4 (1992): 488–511.

Dodson, Michael and Donald W. Jackson. "Horizontal Accountability and the Rule of Law". In *Democratic Accountability in Latin America*, edited by Scott Mainwaring and Christopher Welna. New York: Oxford University Press, 2003.

Dressel, Björn. "Thailand's Elusive Quest for a Workable Constitution, 1997–2007". *Contemporary Southeast Asia*, vol. 31, no. 2 (2009): 296–325.

———. "The Philippines: How Much Real Democracy?". *International Political Science Review*, vol. 32, no. 5 (2011): 529–45.

Dressel, Björn and Marcus Mietzner. "A Tale of Two Courts: The Judicialization of Electoral Politics in Asia". *Governance: An International Journal of Policy, Administration, and Institutions*, vol. 25, no. 3 (2012): 391–414.

Dwiputrianti, Septiana. "Role of the Indonesian Supreme Audit Institution (BPK) in Financial Transparency and Performance Accountability". Paper presented in the Innaugural International Workshop for Young Scholars in Public Policy and Administration Research, Xiamen University, China, 31 May–3 June 2011. Available at <http://www.academia.edu/607358/Role_of_the_Indonesian_Supreme_Audit_Institution_BPK_in_Financial_Transparency_and_Performance_Accountability> (accessed 10 February 2013).

Ebrahim, Alnoor. "Placing the Normative Logics of Accountability in 'Thick' Perspective". *American Behavorial Scientist*, vol. 52, no. 6 (2009): 885–904.

Eckardt, Sebastian. *Accountability and Decentralized Service Delivery: Explaining Performance Variation Across Local Governments in Indonesia*. Baden-Baden: Nomos, 2006.

————. "Political Accountability, Fiscal Conditions, and Local Government Performance: Cross Sectional Evidence from Indonesia". Working Paper 02/2007. Institute of Local Public Finance, 2007. Available at <http://www.ilpf.de/en/download/wp-02-2007.pdf > (accessed 31 October 2012).

Election Commission of Thailand. "Information, Statistics and the Result of the House of Representative Elections", 2011. Available at <http://www.ect.go.th/newweb/th/election> (accessed 12 November 2011).

Elklit, Jørgen. "Electoral Institutional Change and Democratization: Election Administration Quality and the Legitimacy of 'Third World' Elections". In *Democracy and Political Change in the 'Third World'*, edited by Jeff Haynes. London/New York: Routledge, 2001.

Elster, Jon. "Introduction". In *Constitutionalism and Democracy*, edited by Jon Elster and Rune Slagstad. Cambridge: Cambridge University Press, 1988.

Eschborn, Norbert. "Thaksin gewinnt, der Rechtsstaat verliert: Thailands politische Reform am Scheideweg?". St. Augustin: Konrad Adenauer Foundation, 2001. Available at <www.kas.de/wf/doc/kas_4187-544-1-30.pdf> (accessed 5 April 2013).

Escresa, Laarni and Nuno Garoupa. "Judicial Politics in Unstable Democracies: The Case of the Philippine Supreme Court. An Empirical Analysis 1986–2010". *Asian Journal of Law and Economics*, vol. 3, no. 1 (2012): article 2.

Esguerra, Christian Y. "Look Who's Talking: Senator Santiago Wants to Ban 'Turncoatism'". *The Philippine Daily Inquirer Online*, 24 June 2011. Available at <http://newsinfo.inquirer.net/17623/look-who%E2%80%99s-talking-senator-santiago-wants-to-ban-%E2%80%98turncoatism%E2%80%99> (accessed 19 July 2011).

————. "Tiangco Defies House, Testifies for Corona". *The Philippine Daily Inquirer Online*, 13 March 2012. Available at <http://newsinfo.inquirer.net/160439/tiangco-defies-house-testifies-for-corona> (accessed 28 February 2013).

Esmaquel, Paterno. "Comelec Approves 79 Party-List Groups". *Rappler*, 29 November 2012. Available at <http://www.rappler.com/nation/16978-comelec-approves-79-party-list-groups> (accessed 28 February 2013).

Farolan, Ramon. "Thailand Revisited". *The Philippine Daily Inquirer Online*, 22 February 2009. Available at <http://business.inquirer.net/money/topstories/view/ 20090222-190435/Thailand_revisited> (accessed 14 September 2011).

Farrelly, Nicholas. "Thailand: Thaksin Survives Yet Disquiet Floods the Kingdom". In *Southeast Asian Affairs 2012*, edited by Daljit Singh and Pushpa Thambipillai. Singapore: Institute of Southeast Asian Studies, 2012.

Fealy, Greg. "Indonesian Politics in 2011: Democratic Regression and Yudhoyono's Regal Incumbency". *Bulletin of Indonesian Economic Studies*, vol. 47, no. 3 (2011): 333–53.

Fearon, James D. "Electoral Accountability and the Control of Politicians: Selecting Good Types versus Sanctioning Poor Performance". In *Democracy, Accountability, and Representation*, edited by Adam Przeworski, Susan C. Stokes, and Bernhard Manin. Cambridge/New York: Cambridge University Press, 1999.

Fesler, James W. "Approaches to the Understanding of Decentralization". *The Journal of Politics*, vol. 27, no. 3 (1965): 536–66.

Filipino Star. "There's Hope for a Peaceful Mindanao". *Filipino Star*, 3 November 2012. Available at <http://www.filipinostarnews.net/editorial/theres-hope-for-a-peaceful-mindanao.html > (accessed 5 March 2013).

Flores, Helen. "Disqualification Case Filed vs El Shaddai's Buhay Party-list". *The Philippine Star Online*, 20 May 2010. Available at <http://www.philstar.com/Article.aspx?articleId=576762&publicationSubCategoryId=63> (accessed 19 July 2011).

Fox, Jonathan. *Accountability Politics: Power and Voice in Rural Mexico*. New York: Oxford University Press, 2007.

Gatmaytan, Dante B. and Cielo Magno. "Averting Diversity: A Review of Nominations and Appointments to the Philippine Supreme Court (1988–2008)". *Asian Journal of Comparative Law*, vol. 6, no. 1 (2011): article 3.

Geddes, Barbara. "Initiation of New Democratic Institutions in Eastern Europe and Latin America". In *Institutional Design in New Democracies, Eastern Europe and Latin America*, edited by Arend Lijphart and Carlos H. Waisman. Boulder/Oxford: Westview Press, 1996.

Geertz, Clifford. "Thick Description: Toward an Interpretive Theory of Culture". In *The Interpretation of Cultures: Selected Essays*. New York: Basic Books, 1973.

George, Alexander L. and Andrew Bennett. *Case Studies and Theory Development in the Social Sciences*. Cambridge (Mass.): MIT Press, 2005.

Gershman, John. "Indonesia: Islands of Conflict". *Asia Times Online*, 26 October 2002. Available at <http://www.atimes.com/atimes/Southeast_Asia/ DJ26Ae05.html> (accessed 28 July 2011).

GMA News. "Palawan Gov Faces Petition for Recall Election", 16 September 2011. Available at <http://www.gmanetwork.com/news/story/232534/ news/regions/palawan-gov-faces-petition-for-recall-election> (accessed 5 March 2013).

Government of the Philippines. "Executive Order No. 1: Creating the Philippine Truth Commission of 2010". Available at <http://www.gov.ph/2010/07/30/ executive-order-no-1> (accessed 13 March 2013).

———. President Aquino's speech at the 1st National Criminal Justice Summit, 5 December 2011. Available at <http://www.gov.ph/2011/12/05/president-aquinos-speech-at-the-1st-national-criminal- justice-summit-december-5-2011> (accessed 13 March 2013).

Grigat, Sonja. "Problems of Territorial Conflict Regulation in the Philippines: The Future of the ARMM". In *Conflict in Moro Land: Prospects for Peace?*, edited by Arndt Graf, Peter Kreuzer, and Rainer Werning. Pulau Pinang: Universiti Sains Malaysia, 2009.

Grindle, Merilee S. and John W. Thomas. *Public Choices and Policy Change: The Political Economy of Reform in Developing Countries*. Baltimore/London: The Johns Hopkins University Press, 1991.

Gross, Jeremy. "Behind the Jamboree". *Inside Indonesia*, no. 90 (2007). Available at <http://www.insideindonesia.org/weekly-articles/behind-the-jamboree> (accessed 26 March 2013).

Gunawan, Iwan. "'Pork barrel' is Undemocratic, Corrupt-minded". *The Jakarta Post Online*, 26 June 2010. Available at <http://www.thejakartapost.com/news/2010/06/23/%E2%80%98pork-barrel%E2%80%99-undemocratic-corruptminded.html> (accessed 28 July 2011).

Gutierrez, Eric. "The Public Purse". In *Pork and Other Perks: Corruption and Governance in the Philippines*, edited by Sheila Coronel. Quezon City: Philippine Center for Investigative Journalism, 1998.

Habibie, Bacharuddin Jusuf. *Decisive Moments: Indonesia's Long Road to Democracy*. Jakarta: Ilthabi Rekatama, 2006.

Hadar, Leon T. *Averting a 'New Kosovo' in Indonesia: Opportunities and Pitfalls for the United States*. Washington, D.C.: Cato Institute, 2000.

Hadiwinata, Bob S. "The 2004 Parliamentary and Presidential Elections in Indonesia". In *Between Consolidation and Crisis. Elections and Democracy in Five Nations in Southeast Asia*, edited by Aurel Croissant and Beate Martin. Munster: LIT, 2006.

Hadiz, Vedi R. *Localising Power in Post-Authoritarian Indonesia*. Stanford: Stanford University Press, 2010.

Hall, Peter A. "Historical Institutionalism in Rationalist and Sociological Perspective". In *Explaining Institutional Change: Ambiguity, Agency, and Power*, edited by James Mahoney and Kathleen Thelen. New York: Cambridge University Press, 2010.

Haque, M. Shamsul. "Decentralizing Local Governance in Thailand: Contemporary Trends and Challenges". *International Journal of Public Administration*, vol. 33, nos. 12–13 (2010): 673–88.

Harding, Andrew and Peter Leyland. *The Constitutional System of Thailand: A Contextual Analysis*. Oxford: Hart Publishing, 2011.

Harvard Kennedy School Indonesia Program. *From Reformasi to Institutional Transformation: A Strategic Assessment of Indonesia's Prospects for Growth, Equity and Democratic Governance, 2010*. Available at <http://unpan1.un.org/intradoc/groups/public/documents/UN-DPADM/UNPAN042322.pdf> (accessed 10 February 2013).

Heiduk, Felix. "Two Sides of the Same Coin? Separatism and Democratization in Post-Suharto Indonesia". In *Democratization in Post-Suharto Indonesia*, edited by Marco Bünte and Andreas Ufen. London/New York: Routledge, 2009.

Heilmann, Sebastian and Patrick Ziegenhain. "Editorial". *ASIEN*, no. 109 (2008): 7f.

Hendrianto. "Institutional Choice and the New Indonesian Constitutional Court". In *New Courts in Asia*, edited by Andrew Harding and Penelope Nicholson. New York: Routledge, 2010.

Hewison, Kevin. "Thaksin Shinawatra and the Reshaping of Thai Politics". *Contemporary Politics*, vol. 16, no. 2 (2010): 119–33.

Hicken, Allen. "Combating Corruption through Electoral Reform". In *New International IDEA Handbook*, edited by International IDEA. Stockholm: International Institute for Democracy and Electoral Assistance, 2005.

———. "Stuck in the Mud: Parties and Party Systems in Democratic Southeast Asia". *Taiwan Journal of Democracy*, vol. 2, no. 2 (2006*a*): 23–46.

———. "Party Fabrication: Constitutional Reform and the Rise of Thai Rak Thai". *Journal of East Asian Studies*, vol. 6, no. 3 (2006*b*): 381–407.

———. "How Do Rules and Institutions Encourage Vote Buying". In *Elections for Sale: The Causes and Consequences of Vote Buying*, edited by Frederic Charles Schaffer. Boulder/London: Lynne Rienner Publishers, 2007*a*.

———. "The 2007 Draft Constitution: A Return to Politics Past". *Crossroads*, vol. 19, no. 1 (2007*b*): 128–60.

———. "Politics of Economic Recovery in Thailand and the Philippines". In *Crisis as Catalyst: Asia's Dynamic Political Economy*, edited by Andrew McIntyre, T.J. Pempel, and John Ravenhill. Ithaca and London: Cornell University Press, 2008.

———. *Building Party Systems in Developing Democracies*. New York: Cambridge University Press, 2009.

Hill, Hal. "Regional Development: Analytical and Policy Issues". In *The Dynamics of Regional Development: The Philippines in East Asia*, edited by Arsenio M. Balisacan and Hal Hill. Quezon City: Ateneo de Manila University Press, 2007.

Hill, Hal, Arsenio M. Balisacan, and Sharon Faye A. Piza. "The Philippines and Regional Development". In *The Dynamics of Regional Development: The Philippines in East Asia*, edited by Balisacan Arsenio M. and Hal Hill. Quezon City: Ateneo de Manila University Press, 2007.

Hiskey, Jonathan T. "Principals, Agents, and Decentralized Democratic Development: A Conceptual Framework for Democratic Local Governance". Washington, D.C.: USAID and the Urban Institute, 2006. Available at <http://www.fiscalreform.net/library/pdfs/intergovernmental-decentralization/UI%20Concept%20Paper%20Hiskey_Final2%2010%2027.pdf> (accessed 6 November 2012).

Hobolt, Sara B., James Tilley, and Susan Banducci. "Electoral Accountability in Context: How Political Institutions Condition Performance Voting", 2010. Available at <http://ssrn.com/abstract=1670741> (accessed 13 May 2013).

Holmes, Ronald D. "The Philippines in 2011". *Philippine Political Science Journal*, vol. 33, no. 1 (2012): 81–97.

House of Representatives, Republic of the Philippines. "Impeachment of Renato C. Corona as Chief Justice of the Supreme Court of the Philippines", 2011. Available at <http://www.gov.ph/downloads/2011/12dec/20111212-Articles-of-Impeachment.pdf> (accessed 13 March 2013).

Human Rights Watch. "You Can Die Any Time", 7 April 2009. Available at <http://www.hrw.org/node/82034/section/2> (accessed 11 March 2013).

Huntington, Samuel P. *The Third Wave: Democratization in the Late 20th Century*. Oklahoma: University of Oklahoma Press, 1991.

————. "Democracy for the Long Haul". *Journal of Democracy*, vol. 7, no. 2 (1996): 3–14.

Hutchcroft, Paul D. "Centralization and Decentralization in Administration and Politics: Assessing Territorial Dimensions of Authority and Power". *Governance*, vol. 14, no. 1 (2001): 23–53.

————. "The Arroyo Imbroglio in the Philippines". *Journal of Democracy*, vol. 19, no. 1 (2008): 141–55.

IDEA. "Voter turnout data for Indonesia", 2011. Available at <http://www.idea.int/vt/countryview.cfm?id=101> (accessed 19 March 2013).

Indrasafitri, Dina. "Minister Lauds New Constitutional Court Bill". *The Jakarta Post Online*, 2011. Available at <http://www.thejakartapost.com/news/2011/06/14/minister-lauds-new-constitutional-court-bill.html> (accessed 10 February 2013).

InterAksyon.com. "Too Many Partylist Groups with 'A' Names, Comelec to Stop Using Alphabetically Arranged Ballots", 4 January 2013. Available at <http://www.interaksyon.com/article/51939/too-many-partylist-groups-with-a-names-comelec-to-stop-using-alphabetically-arranged-ballots> (accessed 28 February 2013).

International Crisis Group. "Thailand: The Evolving Conflict in the South". *Asia Report*, no. 241 (2012). Available at <http://www.crisisgroup.org/~/media/Files/asia/south-east-asia/thailand/241-thailand-the-evolving-conflict-in-the-south.pdf> (accessed 4 April 2013).

INTOSAI. "Peer Review of the Audit Board of the Republic of Indonesia", 2009. Available at <http://www.bpk.go.id/web/files/2009/01/peer-review-report.pdf> (accessed 10 February 2013).

Jacobson, Gary C. *The Politics of Congressional Elections*. Menlo Park: Longman, 1997.

Jha, Ganganath. "Thai Politics in the Post-Thaksin Period". *India Quarterly*, vol. 67, no. 4 (2011): 325–39.

Kasuya, Yuko. "Weak Institutions and Strong Movements: The Case of President Estrada's Impeachment and Removal in the Philippines". In *Checking Executive Power: Presidential Impeachment in Comparative Perspective*, edited by Jody Baumgartner and Naoko Kada. Westport: Praeger, 2003.

————. *Presidential Bandwaggon: Parties and Party Systems in the Philippines*. Pasig City: Anvil, 2009.

Katz, Richard S. and Peter Mair. "Changing Models of Party Organization and Party Democracy: The Emergence of the Cartel Party". *Party Politics*, vol. 1, no. 1 (1995): 5–27.

Kawamura, Koichi. "Is the Indonesian President Strong or Weak?". IDE Discussion Paper no. 235. Institute of Developing Economies/Japan External Trade Organization, 2010.

————. "Consensus and Democracy in Indonesia: Musyawarah-Mufakat Revisited". IDE Discussion Paper no. 308. Institute of Developing Economies/Japan External Trade Organization, 2011.

Kawanaka, Takeshi. "Interaction of Powers in the Philippine Presidential System". IDE Discussion Paper no. 233 (2010). Available at <http://www.ide.go.jp/ English/Publish/Download/Dp/pdf/233.pdf> (accessed 28 February 2013).

Key, Valdimer Orlando. *The Responsible Electorate: Rationality in Presidential Voting, 1936–1960*. New York: Vintage Books, 1966.

Kimura, Ehito. "Marginality and Opportunity in the Periphery: The Emergence of Gorontalo Province in Indonesia". *Indonesia*, vol. 84 (2007): 71–95.

————. "Indonesia in 2010". *Asian Survey*, vol. 51, no. 1 (2011): 186–95.

————. "Indonesia in 2011". *Asian Survey*, vol. 52, no. 1 (2012): 186–94.

King, Dwight Y. *Half-Hearted Reform: Electoral Institutions and the Struggle for Democracy in Indonesia*. Westport: Praeger Publishers, 2003.

Klein, James R. "The Constitution of the Kingdom of Thailand, 1997: A Blueprint for Participatory Democracy". The Asia Foundation Working Paper no. 8. San Francisco, 1998.

Klitgaard, Robert. *Controlling Corruption*. Berkeley: University of California Press, 1988.

Kokpol, Orathai. "Electoral Politics in Thailand". In *Electoral Politics in Southeast and East Asia*, edited by Aurel Croissant, Gabriele Bruns, and Marei John. Singapore: Friedrich Ebert Foundation, 2002.

Kreuzer, Peter. "Philippine Governance: Merging Politics and Crime". PRIF Reports no. 93. Frankfurt: Peace Research Institute, 2009.

Kumorotomo, Wahyudi. "Serving the Political Parties: Issues of Fragmented Public Policy and Accountability in Decentralized Indonesia". Paper presented at the Fourth International Conference on Public Policy and Management (CPPM), Bangalore, 9–12 August 2009. Available at <http://www.kumoro.staff.ugm. ac.id/file_artikel/Full%20paper-Serving%20the%20Political%20Parties.pdf> (accessed 10 February 2013).

Laguatan, Ted. "Arroyo's Kiss of Death on Teodoro and Villar". *Inquirer Global Nation*, 18 April 2010. Available at <http://globalnation.inquirer.net/viewpoints/ viewpoints/view/20100418-264952/Arroyos-kiss-of-death-on-Teodoro-and-Villar> (accessed 28 February 2013).

Lauth, Hans-Joachim. "'Horizontal Accountability'. Aktuelle Aspekte der Gewaltenteilung: Ein Vorschlag zur Systematisierung der Kontrollfunktion der Gewaltenteilung". In *Gewaltenteilung und Demokratie. Konzepte und Probleme der 'horizontal accountability' im interregionalen Vergleich*, edited by Sabine Kropp and Hans-Joachim Lauth. Baden-Baden: Nomos, 2007.

Lavides, Myrna N. "The Congressional Committee and Philippine Policymaking: The Case of the Anti-Rape Law". *Philippine Journal of Public Administration*, vol. 43, nos. 3–4 (1999): 226–44.

Legaspi, Amita. "Sarmiento: Comelec Post a Liability, not an Asset, due to 'Garci'". *GMA News*, 24 July 2007. Available at <http://wwt.gmanews.tv/story/52543/sarmiento-comelec-post-a-liability-not-an-asset-due-to-garci> (accessed 28 February 2013).

Legowo, T.A. and M. Djadijono. "Decentralization in Indonesia: How Far Can It Go?". In *Decentralization Interrupted: Studies from Cambodia, Indonesia, Philippines and Thailand*, edited by Denden Alicias et al. Quezon City: Institute for Popular Democracy, 2007.

Lijphart, Arend. *Electoral Systems and Party Systems: A Study of Twenty-Seven Democracies, 1945–1990*. Oxford: Oxford University Press, 1994.

———. *Patterns of Democracy: Government Forms and Performance in Thirty-Six Countries*. New Heaven: Yale University Press, 1999.

Linz, Juan. *The Breakdown of Democratic Regimes*. Baltimore/London: Johns Hopkins University Press, 1978.

"The Local Government Code of the Philippines", 1991. Available at <http://ppp.gov.ph/wp-content/uploads/2010/11/The-Local-Government-of-the-Philippines.pdf> (accessed 5 March 2013).

Lord, Christopher and Johannes Pollak. "Representation and Accountability: Communicating Tubes?". *West European Politics*, vol. 33, no. 5 (2010): 968–88.

Lustermann, Henning. "Indonesia: On the Way to a Federal State?". *Mimbar Hukum*, vol. 10, no. 2 (2002). Available at <www.efa-schriften.de/pdfs/Lustermann.pdf> (accessed 18 February 2013).

Machiavelli, Niccolò. "The Prince". In *Princeton Readings on Political Thought*, edited by Mitchell Cohen and Nicole Fermon. Princeton: Princeton University Press, 1514.

Madison, James. "The Federalist No. 57". In *The Federalist Papers*, edited by Clinton Rossiter. New York: The New American Library, 1788*a* (1961).

———. "The Federalist No. 51". In *The Federalist Papers*, edited by Clinton Rossiter. New York: The New American Library, 1788*b* (1961).

———. "The Federalist No. 48". In *The Federalist Papers*, edited by Clinton Rossiter. New York: The New American Library, 1788*c* (1961).

Maggetti, Martino. "Legitimacy and Accountability of Independent Regulatory Agencies: A Critical Review". *Living Reviews in Democracy*, vol. 2, no. 1 (2010): 1–9.

Maharani, Sian. "KPU: Hanya 10 Parpol yang Penuhi Syarat untuk Pemilu 2014". *Kompas Online*, 8 January 2013. Available at <http://nasional.kompas.com/read/2013/01/08/02572488/KPU.Hanya.10.Parpol.yang.Penuhi.Syarat.untuk.Pemilu.2014> (accessed 10 January 2013).

Mahfud, Mohammad. "The Role of the Constitutional Court in the Development of Democracy in Indonesia". Paper presented at the World Conference on Constitutional Justice, Cape Town, 23–24 January 2009. Available at <http://www.venice.coe.int/WCCJ/Papers/INA_Mahfud_E2.pdf> (accessed 10 February 2013).

Mahoney, James and Kathleen Thelen. "A Theory of Gradual Institutional Change". In *Explaining Institutional Change: Ambiguity, Agency, and Power*, edited by James Mahoney and Kathleen Thelen. Cambridge/New York: Cambridge University Press, 2010.

Mainwaring, Scott. "Introduction: Democracratic Accountability in Latin America". In *Democratic Accountability in Latin America*, edited by Scott Mainwaring and Christopher Welna. New York: Oxford University Press, 2003.

Malixi, Charisma. "Review and Assessment of Decentralization in the Philippines Focusing on Local Resource Mobilization". Ph.D. thesis, Department of Political Science, University of Freiburg, 2008. Available at <http://www.freidok.uni-freiburg.de/volltexte/4589/pdf/diss.pdf> (accessed 13 May 2013).

Manasan, Rosario G. "Local Public Finance in the Philippines: Lessons in Autonomy and Accountability". *Philippine Journal of Development*, vol. 32, no. 2 (2005): 31–102.

Mang, Anne-Hélène. "Wahlsystemdefizite auf den Philippinen". Master Thesis, Department of Political Science, University of Trier, 2011.

Manin, Bernhard, Adam Przeworski, and Susan C. Stokes. "Introduction". In *Democracy, Accountability, and Representation*, edited by Adam Przeworski, Susan C. Stokes, and Bernhard Manin. Cambridge/New York: Cambridge University Press, 1999*a*.

———. "Elections and Representation". In *Democracy, Accountability, and Representation*, edited by Adam Przeworski, Susan C. Stokes, and Bernhard Manin. Cambridge/New York: Cambridge University Press, 1999*b*.

Manor, James. *The Political Economy of Decentralization*. Washington, D.C.: The World Bank, 1999.

Mansrisuk, Chiwatt. "Decentralisation in Thailand and the Limits of the Functionalist Perspective of Institutional Reform". *European Journal of East Asian Studies*, vol. 11, no. 1 (2012): 71–97.

Maravall, José Maria. "Accountability and Manipulation". In *Democracy, Accountability, and Representation*, edited by Adam Przeworski, Susan C. Stokes, and Bernhard Manin. Cambridge/New York: Cambridge University Press, 1999.

———. "Accountability and the Survival of Governments". In *The Oxford Handbook of Comparative Politics*, edited by Susan C. Stokes and Carles Boix. Oxford: Oxford University Press, 2009.

March, James G. and Johan P. Olsen. "The New-Institutionalism: Organizational Factors in Political Life". *American Political Science Review*, vol. 78, no. 3 (1984): 734–49.

Mashaw, Jerry L. "Accountability and Institutional Design: Some Thoughts on the Grammar of Governance". In *Public Accountability: Designs, Dilemmas and Experiences*, edited by Michael W. Dowdle. Cambridge/New York: Cambridge University Press, 2006.

Maulia, Erwida. "President blasts Golkar as 'immature' in fund rift", 19 June 2010. Available at <http://www.thejakartapost.com/news/2010/06/19/president-blasts-golkar-%E2%80%98immature%E2%80%99-fund-rift.html> (accessed 28 July 2011).

McCargo, Duncan. "Alternative Meanings of Political Reform in Contemporary Thailand". *The Copenhagen Journal of Asian Studies*, vol. 13 (1998): 5–30.

———. "Network Monarchy and Legitimacy Crises in Thailand". *The Pacific Review*, vol. 18, no. 4 (2005): 499–519.

McCargo, Duncan and Ukrist Pathmanand. The *Thaksinization of Thailand*. Copenhagen: Nordic Institute of Asian Studies, 2005.

McLeod, Ross. "The Struggle to Regain Effective Government under Democracy in Indonesia". *Bulletin of Indonesian Economic Studies*, vol. 41, no. 3 (2005): 367–86.

McWilliam. "Marginal Governance in the Time of Pemekaran: Case Studies from Sulawesi and West Papua". *Asian Journal of Social Science*, vol. 39, no. 2 (2011): 150–70.

Meisburger, Tim. "Will Automated Elections in the Philippines Increase Public Confidence?". *The Asia Foundation: In Asia. Weekly Insight and Features in Asia*, 5 May 2010. Available at <http://asiafoundation.org/in-asia/2010/05/05/will-automated-elections-in-the-philippines-increase-public-confidence> (accessed 28 February 2013).

Merkel, Wolfgang, Hans-Jürgen Puhle, and Aurel Croissant, eds. *Defekte Demokratien 1*. Opladen: Leske + Budrich, 2003.

———. "Embedded and Defective Democracies". *Democratization*, vol. 11, no. 5 (2004): 35–58.

Mezey, Michael L. *Comparative Legislatures*. Durham: Duke University Press, 1979.

Mezey, Michael L. and David M. Olson. *Legislatures in the Policy Process: The Dilemma of Economic Policy*. Cambridge/New York: Cambridge University Press, 1991.

Mietzner, Marcus. "Indonesia's Democratic Stagnation: Anti-Reformist Elites and Resilient Civil Society". *Democratization*, vol. 19, no. 2 (2012*a*): 209–29.

———. "Indonesia: Yudhoyono's Legacy between Stability and Stagnation". In *Southeast Asian Affairs 2012*, edited by Daljit Singh, and Pushpa Thambipillai. Singapore: Institute of Southeast Asian Studies, 2012*b*.

Mietzner, Marcus and Edward Aspinall. "Problems of Democratization in Indonesia: An Overview". In *Problems of Democratization in Indonesia: Elections, Institutions and Society*, edited by Marcus Mietzner and Edward Aspinall. Singapore: Institute of Southeast Asian Studies, 2010.

Moreno, Erika, Brian F. Crisp, and Matthew Soberg Shugart. "The Accountability Deficit in Latin America". In *Democratic Accountability in Latin America*, edited by Scott Mainwaring and Christopher Welna. New York: Oxford University Press, 2003.

Morishita, Akiko. "Contesting Power in Indonesia's Resource-Rich Regions in the Era of Decentralization: New Strategy for Central Control over the Regions". *Indonesia*, vol. 86 (October 2008): 81–108.

Morlino, Leonardo. "What is a 'Good' Democracy?". *Democratization*, vol. 11, no. 5 (2004): 10–32.

Morrell, Elizabeth. "Local Agency and Region Building in Indonesia's Periphery: Shifting the Goalposts for Development". *Asian Journal of Political Science*, vol. 18, no. 1 (2010): 48–68.

Mulgan, Richard. "'Accountability': An Ever-Expanding Concept?". *Public Administration*, vol. 78, no. 3 (2000): 555–73.

———. "One Cheer for Hierarchy: Accountability in Disjointed Governance". *Political Science*, vol. 55, no. 2 (2003): 6–18.

Müller, Wolfgang C. and Thomas M. Meyer. "Meeting the Challenges of Representation and Accountability in Multi-Party Governments". *West European Politics*, vol. 33, no. 5 (2010): 1065–92.

Mutebi, Alex M. "Recentralising while Decentralising: Centre-Local Relations and 'CEO' Governors in Thailand". *The Asia Pacific Journal of Public Administration*, vol. 26, no. 1 (June 2004): 33–53.

———. "Government and Citizen Engagement at the Local Level in Thailand: Nan Municipality's 'Roundtables' and 'Expert Panels'". *Asia Pacific Perspectives*, vol. 5, no. 2 (2005): 16–28.

———. "Explaining the Failure of Thailand's Anti-Corruption Regime". *Development and Change*, vol. 39, no. 1 (2008): 147–71.

Nagai, Fumio, Nakharin Mektrairat, and Funatsu Tsuruyo. *Local Government in Thailand: Analysis of the Local Administrative Organization Survey*. Joint Research Program Series No. 147. Chiba: Institute of Developing Economies, 2008.

Nardi, Dominic J. "Thai institutions: Constitutional Court". *New Mandala*, 10 August 2010. Available at <http://asiapacific.anu.edu.au/newmandala/2010/08/10/thai-institutions-constitutional-court> (accessed 1 April 2013).

Narykhiew, Nerisa and Kornchanok Raksaseri. "General Teeradej Voted in as Speaker". *The Nation Online*, 23 April 2011. Available at <http://www.nationmultimedia.com/2011/04/23/national/Teeradej-takes-Senate-speaker-post-30153756.html> (accessed 27 July 2011).

Nelson, Michael H. "Analyzing Provincial Political Structures in Thailand: Phuak, Trakun and Hua Khanaen". Working Paper Series no. 79. Hong Kong: City University of Hong Kong, 2005.

————. "A Proportional Election System for Thailand?". *KPI Thai Politics Up-date*, no. 2 (2007). Available at <http://www.academia.edu/ 2085391/A_Proportional_ Election_System_for_Thailand> (accessed 1 April 2013).

————. "Looking Back Before the Election of 2011: Thailand's Constitutional Referendum and the Election of 2007". *European-Asian Journal of Law and Governance*, vol. 1, no. 1 (2011): 49–74.

New Straits Times. "Yingluck Survives No-Confidence Vote". *New Straits Times Online*, 28 November 2012. Available at <http://www.nst.com.my/latest/ yingluck-survives-no-confidence-vote-1.177948> (accessed 5 April 2013).

Nogsuan, Siripan. "The 2005 General Elections in Thailand: Toward a One-Party Government". *Kasarinlan: Philippine Journal of Third World Studies*, vol. 20, no. 1 (2005): 48–71.

Nohlen, Dieter. "Electoral Systems and Electoral Reforms in Latin America". In *Institutional Design in New Democracies: Eastern Europe and Latin America*, edited by Arend Lijphart and Carlos H. Waisman. Boulder/Oxford: Westview Press, 1996.

Norris, Pippa. *Driving Democracy: Do Power-Sharing Institutions Work?* Cambridge/ New York: Cambridge University Press, 2008.

Norton, Elliot. "Illiberal Democrats versus Undemocratic Liberals: The Struggle Over the Future of Thailand's Fragile Democracy". *Asian Journal of Political Science*, vol. 20, no. 1 (2012): 46–69.

Ockey, James. "Thailand in 2006: Retreat from Democracy to Military Rule". *Asian Survey*, vol. 47, no. 1 (2007): 133–40.

O'Donnell, Guillermo. "Delegative Democracy". *Journal of Democracy*, vol. 5, no. 1 (1994): 55–69.

————. "Illusions about Consolidation". *Journal of Democracy*, vol. 7, no. 2 (1996): 34–51.

————. "Horizontal Accountability in New Democracies". *Journal of Democracy*, vol. 9, no. 3 (1998): 112–26.

————. "Horizontal Accountability in New Democracies". In *The Self-Restraining State: Power and Accountability in New Democracies*, edited by Andreas Schedler, Larry Diamond, and Marc F. Plattner. Boulder/London: Lynne Rienner Publishers, 1999.

————. "Horizontal Accountability: The Legal Institutionalization of Mistrust". In *Democratic Accountability in Latin America*, edited by Scott Mainwaring and Christopher Welna. New York: Oxford University Press, 2003.

O'Donnell, Guillermo and Philippe Schmitter. *Transitions from Authoritarian Rule, Part 4: Tentative Conclusions about Uncertain Democracies*. Baltimore: Johns Hopkins University Press, 1986.

Osman, Salim. "Political Fallout from Bid to Impeach Boediono". *The Jakarta Globe*, 17 December 2012. Available at <http://thejakartaglobe.beritasatu.

com/archive/political-fallout-from-bid-to-impeach-boediono/> (accessed 28 February 2013).

Painter, Martin. "Thaksinocracy or Managerialization? Reforming the Thai Bureaucracy". Working Paper Series, no. 76. City University of Hong Kong, May 2005. Available at <http://www6.cityu.edu.hk/searc/Data/FileUpload/269/WP76_05_Martin.pdf> (accessed 13 May 2013).

Palatino, Mong. "Nuisance Candidates". *The Diplomat Online*, 20 April 2010. Available at <http://the-diplomat.com/philippines-election-2010/insiders-diary/nuisance-candidates.html> (accessed 2 August 2011).

Pangadaran, Satrya and Dian Parluhutan. "Judicial Impeachment Mechanism in the Republic of Indonesia and the United States of America: A Constitutional Law Comparison". *Law Review*, vol. 11, no. 1 (2011): 123–37.

Pangalangan, Raul. "The Philippines' Sandiganbayan: Anti-Graft Courts and the Illusion of Self-Contained Anti-Corruption Regimes". In *New Courts in Asia*, edited by Andrew Harding and Penelope Nicholson. New York: Routledge, 2010.

Parreño, Earl. "Pork". In *Pork and Other Perks: Corruption and Governance in the Philippines*, edited by Sheila Coronel. Quezon City: Philippine Center for Investigative Journalism, 1998.

Pepinsky, Thomas B. and Maria M. Wihardja. "Decentralization and Economic Performance in Indonesia". *Journal of East Asian Studies*, vol. 11, no. 3 (2011): 337–71.

Perron, Louis. "Election campaigns in the Philippines". In *The Routledge Handbook of Political Management*, edited by Dennis W. Johnson. London/New York, 2008.

———. "Election Campaigns and the Political Consulting Industry in the Philippines". *Zeitschrift für Politikberatung*, vol. 2, no. 4 (2009): 625–40.

Philippine Daily Inquirer. "Saying He Can't Lie, Fr. Ed Admits Taking P500,000". *Philippine Daily Inquirer*, 13 October 2007. Available at <http://newsinfo.inquirer.net/inquirerheadlines/nation/view/20071013-94297/Saying_he_can> (accessed 5 March 2013).

Philp, Mark. "Delimiting Democratic Accountability". *Political Studies*, vol. 57 (2009): 28–53.

Phongpaichit, Pasuk. "Thai Politics Beyond the 2006 Coup, Excerpt of Supha Sirimanond Memorial Lecture", 2006. Available at <http://pioneer.netserv.chula.ac.th/~ppasuk/thaipoliticsbeyondthecoup.pdf> (accessed 13 May 2013).

Phongpaichit, Pasuk and Chris Baker. "Business Populism in Thailand". *Journal of Democracy*, vol. 16, no. 2 (2005): 58–72.

———. *Thaksin*, 2nd ed. Bangkok: Silkworm Books, 2009.

———. "The Mask-Play Election: Generals, Politicians and Voters at Thailand's 2007 Poll". Working Paper Series no. 144. Asia Research Institute, September 2010. Available at <http://www.ari.nus.edu.sg/docs/wps/wps10_144.pdf> (accessed 27 July 2011).

Pitkin, Hanna F. *The Concept of Representation*. Berkeley: University of California Press, 1967.

Pongsawat, Pitch. "Middle-Class Ironic Electoral Cultural Practices in Thailand: Observing the 2005 National Assembly Election and Its Aftermath". In *Elections as Popular Culture in Asia*, edited by Chua Beng Huat. New York: Routledge, 2007.

Pongsudhirak, Thitinan. "Thailand's Transformation". Paper presented at ISEAS Regional Outlook, Singapore, 8 January 2008. Available at <http://humansecuritygateway.com/documents/ISEAS_ThailandsTransformation.pdf> (accessed 13 May 2013).

Porcalla, Delon. "Noynoy: Congressional Pork Barrel stays". *The Philippine Star*, 8 July 2010. Available at <http://www.philstar.com/Article.aspx? articleid= 591347> (accessed 30 August 2011).

Powell, G. Bingham. "Constitutional Design and Citizen Electoral Control". *Journal of Theoretical Politics*, vol. 1, no. 2 (1989): 107–30.

———. "Political Representation in Comparative Politics". *Annual Review of Political Science*, vol. 7 (2004): 273–76.

Powell, Walter W. "Expanding the Scope of Institutional Analysis". In *The New Institutionalism in Organizational Analysis*, edited by Walter W. Powell and Paul J. DiMaggio. Chicago: University of Chicago Press, 1991.

Pridham, Geoffrey. "Southern European Democracies on the Road to Consolidation: A Comparative Assessment of the Role of Political Parties". In *Securing Democracy: Political Parties and Democratic Consolidation in Southern Europe*, edited by Geoffrey Pridham. New York: Routledge, 1990.

———. *The Dynamics of Democratization: A Comparative Approach*. London/ New York: Continuum, 2000.

Priwitzer, Kerstin and Patrick Ziegenhain. "Representatives from Muslim Mindanao in the Congress of the Philippines: Intermediaries for the People or Self-Interested Local Bosses?". In *Conflict in Moro Land: Prospects for Peace?*, edited by Arndt Graf, Peter Kreuzer, and Rainer Werning. Pulau Pinang: Universiti Sains Malaysia, 2009.

Punyaratabandhu, Suchitra. "Thailand in 1997: Financial Crisis and Constitutional Reform". *Asian Survey*, vol. 38, no. 1 (1998): 161–67.

Quimpo, Nathan Gilbert. "The Philippines: Predatory Regime, Growing Authoritarian Features". *The Pacific Review*, vol. 22, no. 3 (2009): 335–53.

———. "Countries at the Crossroads: Philippines". Washington, D.C.: Freedom House, 2011. Available at <http://www.freedomhouse.org/sites/default/files/inline_images/PHILIPPINESfinal.pdf> (accessed 28 February 2013).

Quiros, Conrado de. "There's the Rub, 'Dagdag-bawas'". *Philippine Daily Inquirer*, 2 October 2012. Available at <http://opinion.inquirer.net/37944/dagdag-bawas> (accessed 28 February 2013).

Ramos, Charmaine. "Decentralization and Democratic Deepening in the Philippines". In *Decentralization Interrupted: Studies from Cambodia, Indonesia, Philippines and Thailand*, edited by Denden Alicias et al. Quezon City: Institute for Popular Democracy, 2007.

Randall, Vicky and Lars Svasand. "Party Institutionalization and the New Democracies". In *Democracy and Political Change in the 'Third World'*, edited by Jeff Haynes. London/New York: Routledge, 2001.

Rastika, Icha and Tri Wahono. "KPK Didesak Usut Calo Anggaran di DPR". *Kompas-Online*, 29 June 2011. Available at <http://nasional.kompas.com/read/2011/06/29/11284141/KPK.Didesak.Usut.Calo.Anggaran.di.DPR> (accessed 4 August 2011).

Rasyid, Ryaas. "Regional Autonomy and Local Politics in Indonesia". In *Local Power and Politics in Indonesia: Decentralisation and Democratisation*, edited by Edward Aspinall and Greg Fealy. Singapore: Institute of Southeast Asian Studies, 2003.

Reformina, Ina and R.G. Cruz. "Mikey Seeks to be Voice of Security Guards in Congress". *ABS-CBN News Online*, 23 March 2010. Available at <http://www.abs-cbnnews.com/nation/03/23/10/mikey-seeks-be-voice-security-guards-congress> (accessed 19 July 2011).

Reilly, Benjamin. *Democracy and Diversity: Political Engineering in the Asia-Pacific*. Oxford: Oxford University Press, 2006.

Revianur, Aditya. "MK: Ambang Batas Parlemen Tak Berlaku Nasional". *Kompas Online*, 29 August 2012.

Rivera, Temario C. "In Search of Credible Elections and Parties: The Philippine Paradox". In *Chasing the Wind: Assessing Philippine Democracy*, edited by Felipe B. Miranda, Malaya C. Ronas, Ronald D. Holmes, and Temario C. Rivera. Quezon City: Commission on Human Rights of the Philippines, 2011.

Rocamora, Joel. "Dissidence and Development: Perspective for a Tri-People Approach". In *Rebels, Warlords and Ulama: A Reader on Muslim Separatism and the War in the Southern Philippines*, edited by Eric Gutierrez et al. Quezon City: Institute for Popular Democracy, 2004.

———. "Decentralization Interrupted: Notes for Comparison". In *Decentralization Interrupted: Studies from Cambodia, Indonesia, Philippines and Thailand*, edited by Denden Alicias et al. Quezon City: Institute for Popular Democracy, 2007.

Rohdewohld, Rainer. "Decentralization and the Indonesian Bureaucracy: Major Changes, Minor Impact?". In *Local Power and Politics*, edited by Edward Aspinall and Greg Fealy. Singapore: Institute of Southeast Asian Studies, 2003.

Romero, Paolo and Marvin Sy. "GMA: Get Out of My Way". *The Philippine Star*, 24 July 2007. Available at <http://www.live.philstar.com/headlines/7991/gma-get-out-my-way> (accessed 28 February 2013).

Rood, Steven. "Forging Sustainable Peace in Mindanao: The Role of Civil Society". *Policy Studies* 17. Washington, D.C.: East-West Center Washington, 2005. Available at <http://www.eastwestcenter.org/fileadmin/stored/pdfs/PS017.pdf> (accessed 23 August 2011).

————. "Citizens and Poll Workers Declare First Automated Elections in the Philippines a Success, but Flaws Remain". *The Asia Foundation: In Asia. Weekly Insight and Features in Asia*, 4 August 2010. Available at <http://asiafoundation.org/in-asia/2010/08/04/citizens-and-poll-workers-declare-first-automated-elections-in-philippines-a-success-but-flaws-remain> (accessed 28 February 2013).

Rose-Ackerman, Susan. *From Elections to Democracy: Building Accountable Government in Hungary and Poland*. Cambridge/New York: Cambridge University Press, 2005.

Rufo, Aries. "Arroyo Issues Midnight Madness of Appointments". abs-cbnNEWS.com/Newsbreak, 3 June 2010. Available at <http://www.abs-cbnnews.com/nation/06/03/10/arroyo-issues-midnight-madness-appointments> (accessed 5 September 2011).

Rüland, Jürgen. "Politisch-institutionelle Reformen und Dezentralisierung: Thesen zum Forschungsstand". In *Subsidiarität in der Entwicklungszusammenarbeit. Dezentralisierung und Verwaltungsreformen zwischen Strukturanpassung und Selbsthilfe*, edited by Klaus Simon, Albrecht Stockmeyer, and Harald Fuhr. Baden Baden: Nomos, 1993.

————. "Constitutional Debates in the Philippines: From Presidentialism to Parliamentarism?". *Asian Survey*, vol. 43, no. 3 (2003): 461–84.

Rüland, Jürgen, Michael Nelson, Clemens Jürgenmeyer, and Patrick Ziegenhain. *Parliaments and Political Change*. Singapore: Institute of Southeast Asian Studies, 2005.

Saelee, Sarun. "Provincial governor reshuffle confirmed transparent". *National News Bureau of Thailand*, 29 September 2010. Available at <http://thainews.prd.go.th/en/news.php?id=255309290013> (accessed 24 August 2011).

Salaverria, Leila, Gil C. Cabacungan Jr., and Norman Bordadora. "DoJ Blames High Court for Honasan Release". *The Inquirer Online*, 24 April 2007. Available at <http://newsinfo.inquirer.net/inquirerheadlines/nation/view/20070424-62085/DoJ_blames_high_court_for_Honasan_release> (accessed 30 March 2009).

Sandschneider, Eberhard. *Stabilität und Transformation politischer Systeme*. Opladen: Leske+Budrich, 1995.

Sartori, Giovanni. *Comparative Constitutional Engineering: An Inquiry into Structures, Incentives, and Outcomes*. New York: New York University Press, 1994.

Scharpf, Fritz W. *Games Real Actors Play: Actor-Centered Institutionalism in Policy Research*. Boulder/Oxford: Westview Press, 1997.

Schedler, Andreas. "Conceptualizing Accountability. In *The Self-Restraining State: Power and Accountability in New Democracies*, edited by Andreas Schedler,

Larry Diamond, and Marc F. Plattner. Boulder/London: Lynne Rienner Publishers, 1999*a*.

――――. "Restraining the State: Conflicts and Agents of Accountability". In *The Self-Restraining State: Power and Accountability in New Democracies*, edited by Andreas Schedler, Larry Diamond, and Marc F. Plattner. Boulder/London: Lynne Rienner Publishers, 1999*b*.

――――, ed. *Electoral Authoritarianism: The Dynamics of Unfree Competition*. Boulder: Lynne Rienner, 2006.

Schmidt, Adam. "Indonesia's 2009 Elections: Performance Challenges and Negative Precedents". In *Problems of Democratization in Indonesia: Elections, Institutions and Society*, edited by Marcus Mietzner and Edward Aspinall. Singapore: Institute of Southeast Asian Studies, 2010.

Schmitter, Philippe C. "The Limits of Horizontal Accountability". In *The Self-Restraining State: Power and Accountability in New Democracies*, edited by Andreas Schedler, Larry Diamond, and Marc F. Plattner. Boulder: Lynne Rienner Publishers, 1999.

Schütte, Sofie Arjon. "Government Policies and Civil Society Initiatives Against Corruption". In *Democratization in Post-Suharto Indonesia*, edited by Marco Bünte and Andreas Ufen. London/New York: Routledge, 2009.

Seabright, Paul. "Accountability and Decentralization in Government: An Incomplete Contracts Model". *European Economic Review*, vol. 40, no. 1 (1996): 61–89.

Selee, Andrew. "Exploring the Link Between Decentralization and Democratic Governance". In *Decentralization and Democratic Governance in Latin America*, edited by Joseph S. Tulchin and Andrew Selee. Washington, D.C.: Woodrow Wilson International Center for Scholars, 2004.

Senate of the Philippines. "Senate Resolution No. 10", 2008. Available at <http://www.senate.gov.ph/14th_congress/resolutions/sjr-10.pdf> (accessed 5 March 2013).

――――. "Composition of the Senate", 2013. Available at <http://www.senate.gov.ph/senators/composition.asp> (accessed 5 March 2013).

Seymour, Richard and Sarah Turner. "Otonomi Daerah: Indonesia's Decentralisation Experiment". *New Zealand Journal of Asian Studies*, vol. 4, no. 2 (2002): 33–51.

Sherlock, Stephen. "Indonesia's Regional Representative Assembly: Democracy, Representation and the Regions". A report on the Dewan Perwakilan Daerah (DPD). CDI Policy Papers on Political Governance. Canberra: Centre for Democratic Institutions, 2006.

――――. "The Indonesian Parliament after Two Elections: What has Really Changed?". CDI Policy Papers on Political Governance. Canberra: Centre for Democratic Institutions, 2007.

――――. "Indonesia's 2009 Elections: The New Electoral System and the Competing Parties". CDI Policy Papers on Political Governance. Canberra: Centre for Democratic Institutions, 2009.

―――. "The Parliament in Indonesia's Decade of Democracy: People's Forum or Chamber of Cronies?". In *Problems of Democratization in Indonesia: Elections, Institutions and Society*, edited by Marcus Mietzner and Edward Aspinall. Singapore: Institute of Southeast Asian Studies, 2010.

Shin, Jae Hyeok. "Electoral System Choice and Parties in New Democracies: Lessons from the Philippines and Indonesia". In *Party Politics in Southeast Asia: Clientelism and Electoral Competition in Indonesia, Thailand, and the Philippines*, edited by Dirk Tomsa and Andreas Ufen. London/New York: Routledge, 2013.

Shugart, Mathew Soberg and John Carey. *Presidents and Assemblies: Constitutional Design and Electoral Dynamics*. Cambridge/New York: Cambridge University Press, 1992.

Sihaloho, Markus Junianto, Bre Nanginna, and Anita Rachman. "Will the Yogyakarta Sultan Be Leader in Name Only with New Law?". *Jakarta Globe*, 4 December 2010. Available at <http://www.thejakartaglobe.com/news/will-the-yogyakarta-sultan-be-leader-in-name-only-with-new-law/410023> (accessed 25 August 2011).

Sihite, Ezra. "Yogyakarta Sultan Keeps His Hold on Governorship". *Jakarta Globe*, 31 August 2012. Available at <http://www.thejakartaglobe.com/politics/yogyakarta-sultan-keeps-his-hold-on-governorship/541364> (accessed 26 March 2013).

Sijabat, Ridwan Max. "Golkar, PDI-P Insist on 5% Threshold as Debate Heats up". *The Jakarta Post Online*, 28 May 2011*a*. Available at <http://www.thejakartapost.com/news/2011/05/28/golkar-pdi-p-insist-5-threshold-debate-heats.html> (accessed 25 August 2011).

―――. "Sultan calls on government not to betray Constitution". *The Jakarta Post Online*, 2 March 2011*b*. Available at <http://www.thejakartapost.com/news/2011/03/02/sultan-calls-government-not-betray-constitution.html> (accessed 25 August 2011).

―――. "Parties still at odds over election system". *The Jakarta Post Online*, 29 March 2012*a*.

―――. "DPD seeks more authority in lawmaking". *The Jakarta Post Online*, 7 November 2012*b*.

Sinpeng, Aim. "Thailand's electoral rules". *New Mandala*, 30 May 2011. Available at <http://asiapacific.anu.edu.au/newmandala/2011/05/30/thailands-electoral-rules> (accessed 2 April 2013).

Sirivunnabood, Punchada. "Building Local Party Organizations in Thailand: Strenghtening Party Rootedness or Serving Elite Interests?". In *Party Politics in Southeast Asia: Clientelism and Electoral Competition in Indonesia, Thailand, and the Philippines*, edited by Dirk Tomsa and Andreas Ufen. London/New York: Routledge, 2013.

Sisante, Jam. "Aquino abolishes Presidential Anti-Graft Commission". GMANews. TV, 24 November 2010. Available at <http://www.gmanetwork.com/news/

story/206758/news/nation/aquino-abolishes-presidential-anti-graft-commission> (accessed 13 March 2013).

Slater, Dan. "Indonesia's Accountability Trap: Party Cartels and Presidential Power after Democratic Transition". *Indonesia*, vol. 78 (2004): 61–92.

————. "Democracy yes, Accountability no? Voters have done everything they can do for democracy: The same cannot be said for the elites". *Inside Indonesia*, vol. 95, no. 1 (2009): 1–5.

Sobari, Wawan. "Legalizing transactional politics". *The Jakarta Post Online*, 17 June 2010. Available at <http://www.thejakartapost.com/news/2010/06/17/legalizing-transactional-politics.html> (accessed 28 July 2011).

Social Weather Stations. "The 2011 Survey on Good Local Governance", 2011. Available at <http://asiafoundation.org/resources/pdfs/The2011SurveyonGoodLocal Governance.pdf> (accessed 18 February 2013).

Stapenhurst, Rick and Mitchell O'Brien. "Accountability in Governance". World Bank PREM (Poverty Reduction and Economic Management) Note No. 4. Washington, D.C.: The World Bank, 2008.

Steffani, Winfried. "Zur Unterscheidung parlamentarischer und präsidentieller Regierungssysteme". *Zeitschrift für Parlamentsfragen*, vol. 14, no. 3 (1983): 390–401.

Streeck, Wolfgang and Kathleen Thelen. "Institutional Change in Advanced Political Economies". In *Beyond Continuity: Institutional Change in Advanced Political Economies*, edited by Wolfgang Streeck and Kathleen Thelen. Oxford/New York: Oxford University Press, 2005.

Sukma, Rizal. "Indonesian Politics in 2009: Defective Elections, Resilient Democracy". *Bulletin of Indonesian Economic Studies*, vol. 45, no. 3 (2009): 317–36.

————. "Indonesia's 2009 Elections: Defective System, Resilient Democracy". In *Problems of Democratization in Indonesia: Elections, Institutions and Society*, edited by Marcus Mietzner and Edward Aspinall. Singapore: Institute of Southeast Asian Studies, 2010.

Sulistiyanto, Priyambudi and Maribeth Erb. "Indonesia and the Quest for 'Democracy'". In *Deepening Democracy in Indonesia: Direct Elections for Local Leaders (Pilkada)*, edited by Priyambudi Sulistiyanto and Maribeth Erb. Singapore: Institute of Southeast Asian Studies, 2009.

Suwanmala, Charas and Dana Weist. "Thailand's Decentralization: Progress and Prospects". In *Decentralization Policies in Asian Development*, edited by Shinuchi Ichimura and Roy Bahl. Singapore: World Scientific Publishing, 2009.

Sy, Marvin. "Palace Defends Entry of GMA's Sister-in-law as Party-List Lawmaker". *The Philippine Star*, 26 April 2009. Available at <http://www.philstar.com/headlines/461005/palace-defends-entry-gmas-sister-law-party-list-lawmaker> (accessed 5 March 2013).

———. "Miriam hits Binay for opposing anti-dynasty bill". *The Philippine Star*, 27 November 2012. Available at <http://www.philstar.com/headlines/2012/11/27/874513/miriam-hits-binay-opposing-anti-dynasty-bill> (accessed 28 February 2013).

Szep, Jason. "Analysis: A Debate over Autonomy in Thailand's Restive South". *Reuters US Edition*, 23 June 2011. Available at <http://www.reuters.com/article/2011/06/23/us-thailand-election-muslims-idUSTRE75M0Q220110623> (accessed 24 August 2011).

Tan, Paige Johnson. "Anti-Party Attitudes in Southeast Asia". In *Party Politics in Southeast Asia: Clientelism and Electoral Competition in Indonesia, Thailand, and the Philippines*, edited by Dirk Tomsa and Andreas Ufen. London/New York: Routledge, 2013.

Tanchai, Woothisarn. "Decentralization and Local Governance: Revisition and Revitalization for Local Governments in Thailand". Presentation at DELGOSEA Capacity Development Workshop for Local Coaches, Pattaya, 18 November 2010. Available at <http://www.delgosea.eu/cms/layout/set/print/content/download/403/3471/file/Decentralization%20and%20Local%20Governance%20in%20Thailand.pdf> (accessed 10 August 2011).

Teehankee, Julio. "Consolidation or Crisis of Clientelistic Democracy? The 2004 Synchronized Elections in the Philippines". In *Between Consolidation and Crisis: Elections and Democracy in Five Nations in Southeast Asia*, edited by Aurel Croissant and Beate Martin. Münster: LIT, 2006.

———. "Clientelism and Party Politics in the Philippines". In *Party Politics in Southeast Asia: Clientelism and Electoral Competition in Indonesia, Thailand, and the Philippines*, edited by Dirk Tomsa and Andreas Ufen. London/New York: Routledge, 2013.

The Nation Online. "No Dictation on the Charter: CNS Chief". *The Nation Online*, 20 December 2006. Available at <http://www.nationmultimedia.com/2006/12/20/headlines/headlines_30022102.php> (accessed 16 December 2009).

———. "Chaovarat Rules Out Politics in Reshuffle". *The Nation Online*, 11 March 2009. Available at <http://www.nationmultimedia.com/home/Chaovarat-rules-out-politics-in-reshuffle-30097609.html> (accessed 24 August 2011).

———. "Royalist to Become Governor in Chiang Mai". *The Nation Online*, 29 September 2010. Available at <http://www.nationmultimedia.com/home/2010/09/29/politics/Royalist-to-become-governor-in-Chiang-Mai-30138944.html> (accessed 24 August 2011).

Tilly, Charles. "Means and Ends of Comparison in Macrosociology". *Comparative Social Research*, vol. 16 (1997): 43–53.

Timbermann, David G. *A Changeless Land: Continuity and Change in Philippine Politics*. Singapore: Institute of Southeast Asian Studies, 1991.

Times Online. "Thaksin Shinawatra: The Full Transcript of His Interview with The Times". *Times Online*, 9 November 2009. Available at <http://de.scribd.

com/doc/34822200/Thaksin-Shinawatra-the-full-transcript-of-his-interview-with-The-Times> (accessed 24 August 2011).

Tiongson-Mayrina, Karen. "Ampatuan Clan the Biggest Winner in May 2010 Polls". *GMA News Research*, 18 July 2010. Available at <http://www.gmanetwork.com/news/story/196376/news/specialreports/ampatuan-clan-the-biggest-winner-in-may-2010-polls> (accessed 28 February 2013).

Tomsa, Dirk. "The Indonesian Party System after the 2009 Elections: Towards Stability?". In *Problems of Democratization in Indonesia: Elections, Institutions and Society*, edited by Marcus Mietzner and Edward Aspinall. Singapore: Institute of Southeast Asian Studies, 2010.

———. "What Type of Party? Southeast Asian Parties between Clientelism and Electoralism". In *Party Politics in Southeast Asia: Clientelism and Electoral Competition in Indonesia, Thailand, and the Philippines*, edited by Dirk Tomsa and Andreas Ufen. London/New York: Routledge, 2013.

Tsebelis, George. "Decision-Making in Political Systems: Veto Players in Presidentialism, Parliamentarism, Multicameralism and Multipartyism". *British Journal of Political Science*, vol. 25 (1995): 289–325.

Uchimura, Hiroko and Yurika Suzuki. "Fiscal Decentralization in the Philippines after the 1991 Code: Intergovernmental Fiscal Relationships and the Roles of Fiscal Transfers". In *Fiscal Decentralization and Development: Experiences of Three Developing Countries in Southeast Asia*, edited by Hiroko Uchimura. New York: Palgrave Macmillan, 2012.

Ufen, Andreas. "Political Party and Party System Institutionalization in Southeast Asia: Lessons for Democratic Consolidation in Indonesia, the Philippines and Thailand". *The Pacific Review*, vol. 21, no. 3 (2008): 327–50.

———. "Political Parties and Democratization in Indonesia". In *Democratization in Post-Suharto Indonesia*, edited by Marco Bünte and Andreas Ufen. London/New York, 2009.

Uwanno, Borwornsak and Wayne D. Burns. "The Thai Constitution of 1997: Sources and Process". *University of British Columbia Law Review*, vol. 32, no. 1 (1998): 227–47. Available at <http://www.thailawforum.com/articles/constburns1.html> (accessed 10 September 2012).

Uy, Jocelyn R. "Comelec OKs Disabled Party But Disqualifies Anti-Rebel Group". *Philippine Daily Inquirer Online*, 8 November 2012. Available at <http://newsinfo.inquirer.net/303732/comelec-oks-disabled-party-but-disqualifies-anti-rebel-group> (accessed 18 February 2013).

Valenzuela, J. Samuel. "Democratic Consolidation in Post-Transitional Settings: Notion, Process, and Facilitating Conditions". In *Issues in Democratic Consolidation: The New South American Democracies in Comparative Perspective*, edited by Scott Mainwaring, Guillermo O'Donnell, and J. Samuel Valenzuela. Notre Dame: University of Notre Dame Press, 1992.

Van de Sand, Klemens. "IFAD's Perspective on Decentralization Issues". In *Technical Consultation on Decentralization for Rural Development*, edited by Food and Agriculture Organization. Rome: FAO, 1999.

Vatikiotis, Michael. "Thailand on the Mend?". *New York Times Online*, 21 September 2006. Available at <http://www.nytimes.com/2006/09/21/opinion/21iht-edvatik.2890032.html> (accessed 18 July 2011).

Villanueva, Marichu. "Palace assures automatic release of LGUs' IRA". *The Philippine Star Online*, 5 October 2000. Available at <http://www.philstar.com/nation/105509/palace-assures-automatic-release-lgus%C2%92-ira> (accessed 6 March 2013).

————. "GMA orders release of IRA to LGUs". *The Philippine Star Online*, 31 January 2001. Available at <http://www.philstar.com/headlines/89615/gma-orders-release-ira-lgus> (accessed 6 March 2013).

von Luebke, Christian. "The Politics of Reform: Political Scandals, Elite Resistance, and Presidential Leadership in Indonesia". *Journal of Current Southeast Asian Affairs*, vol. 29, no. 1 (2010): 79–94.

Weisband, Edward and Alnoor Ebrahim. "Introduction: Forging Global Accountabilities". In *Global Accountabilities: Participation, Pluralism, and Public Ethics*, edited by Alnoor Ebrahim and Edward Weisband. Cambridge/New York: Cambridge University Press, 2007.

Welzel, Christian. "Systemwechsel in der globalen Systemkonkurrenz: Ein evolutionstheoretischer Erklärungsversuch". In *Systemwechsel 1*, edited by Wolfgang Merkel. Opladen: Leske + Budrich, 1996.

Wilson, Ian. "The Rise and Fall of Political Gangsters in Indonesian Democracy". In *Problems of Democratization in Indonesia: Elections, Institutions and Society*, edited by Marcus Mietzner and Edward Aspinall. Singapore: Institute of Southeast Asian Studies, 2010.

Wong, Jeffrey. "D in: De". In *Decentralization Interrupted: Studies from Cambodia, Indonesia, Philippines and Thailand*, edited by Alicias, Denden et al. Quezon City: Institute for Popular Democracy, 2007.

Wongpreedee, Achakorn. "Decentralization and Its Effect on Provincial Political Power in Thailand". *Asian and African Area Studies*, vol. 6, no. 2 (2007): 454–70.

————. "The Effect of Decentralization on Phitsanulok City of Thailand: Transitional Period from Mechanical Politics to Good Governance". Presentation at the 7th Seminar of the Institute Forte for Comparative Studies in Local Governance (COSLOG), Graduate Institute of Policy Studies (GRIPS), Tokyo, 17 March 2009. Available at <http://www3.grips.ac.jp/~coslog/activity/02/seminar_h20/file/No7seminar_ppt.pdf> (accessed 10 August 2011).

Wongpreedee, Achakorn and Chandra Mahakanjana. "Decentralization and Local Governance in Thailand". In *Public Administration in Southeast Asia: Thailand, Philippines, Malaysia, Hong Kong, and Macao*, edited by Evan M. Berman. Boca Raton/London/New York: CRC Press, 2006.

World Bank. "The Philippines: Towards a Better Investment Climate for Growth and Productivity", 2005. Available at <http://s3.amazonaws.com/zanran_

storage/www.enterprisesurveys.org/ContentPages/53301065.pdf> (accessed 5 March 2013).

——— (no data). "Discussion Draft: Civil Service Reform". Available at <http:// siteresources.worldbank.org/INTPHILIPPINES/Resources/DB06-CivilService Reform.pdf> (accessed 28 February 2013).

Yilmaz, Serdar, Yakup Beris, and Rodrigo Serrano-Berthet. "Linking Local Government Discretion and Accountability in Decentralization". *Development Policy Review*, vol. 28, no. 3 (2010): 259–93.

Yuda, Hanta. "The Conflict within SBY's coalition". *The Jakarta Post Online*, 13 January 2011. Available at <http://www.thejakartapost.com/news/ 2011/01/13/the-conflict-within-sby%E2%80%99s-coalition.html> (accessed 10 February 2013).

Yudhoyono, Susilo Bambang. "Gunakan Kekuasaan Secara Proporsional". Speech delivered in Kupang, 9 February 2011. Quoted in *Portal Nasional Republik Indonesia*. Available at <http://www.indonesia.go.id/id/index.php?option=com_ content&task=view&id=14217&Itemid=701> (accessed 10 February 2011).

Zabriskie, Phil. "The Punisher". *TIME Magazine Online*, 19 July 2002. Available at <http://www.time.com/time/magazine/article/0,9171,265480,00.html> (accessed 11 March 2013).

Ziegenhain, Patrick. *The Indonesian Parliament and Democratization*. Singapore: Institute of Southeast Asian Studies, 2008.

Zimmermann, Ronja. "Rechtsstaatlichkeit und Demokratie in den Philippinen". Master Thesis, Department of Political Science, University of Trier, 2012a. Available at <http://www.uni-trier.de/fileadmin/fb3/POL/pubs/MA_ Zimmermann.pdf> (accessed 14 March 2013).

———. "Alte Bande reißen nicht? Richterliche (Un-) Abhängigkeit am philippinischen Supreme Court". *Internationales Asienforum*, vol. 43, nos. 3–4 (2012b): 325–50.

LIST OF INTERVIEWS

In the Philippines

Alex Brillantes, Professor at the National College of Public Administration and Governance, University of the Philippines, Quezon City, 18 September 2007.

Aquilino 'Nene' Pimentel, Member of the Senate of the Philippines (2001–10), Manila, 4 September 2007.

Benjamin "Ben" Diokno, Professor of Economics at the University of the Philippines, Former Secretary of the Department of Budget and Management (DBM) between 1998 and 2001, Quezon City, 14 September 2007.

Bernadino "Bernie" Sayo, Undersecretary, Presidential Legislative Liaison Office (PLLO), Quezon City, 13 September 2007.

Carolina Hernandez, Emeritus Professor of Political Science, University of the *Philippines*, Quezon City, 24 August 2007.

Dina Abad, Former Member of the House of Representatives, Manila, 5 September 2007.

Djorina Velasco, Democracy Watch Department, Institute of Popular Democracy, Quezon City, 22 August 2007.

Earl Parreño, Journalist and Book Author, Manila, 28 August 2007.

Florencio "Butch" Abad, Former Secretary of Education, Manila, 12 September 2007 (since 2010, Secretary of the Department of Budget and Management).

Francisco Magno, Executive Director, La Salle Institute of Governance, Manila, 1 September 2009.

Glenda Gloria, Journalist, Chief Operating Officer of ABS-CBN News Channel, Quezon City, 20 August 2007 and 26 August 2009.

Herwig Mayer, Program Manager, Decentralization Program of GTZ, Makati City, 14 September 2007 and 2 September 2009.

Joel Rocamora, Director, Secretary of the National Anti-Poverty Commission, Quezon City, 5 October 2010.

Jose Luis 'Chito' Gascon, Former Undersecretary of Education, Quezon City, 10 September 2007.

Julio Teehankee, Associate Professor of Political Science, De La Salle University, Manila, 28 August 2007.

Loretta "Etta" Ann Rosales, Akbayan, Former Member of the House of Representatives, Manila, 8 September 2007 (since September 2010, Chairperson of the Commission on Human Rights of the Philippines).

Millet Apostol, Committee Secretary on Foreign Affairs, House of Representatives, Quezon City, 12 September 2007.

Mujiv S. Hataman, Member of the House of Representatives, Party List A-MIN, Quezon City, 13 September 2007 (since 2011, Regional Governor of the Autonomous Region in Muslim Mindanao).

Nereus 'Neric' Acosta, Former Member of the House of Representatives, Manila, 6 September 2007.

Nieves 'Bing' Osorio, Former Undersecretary of Finance, Quezon City, 18 September 2007.

Prospero 'Popoy' de Vera, Professor at the National College of Public Administration and Governance, University of the Philippines, Quezon City, 13 September 2007.

Risa Hontiveros-Baraquel, Member of the House of Representatives, Quezon City, 29 August 2007,

Rodolfo 'Pong' Biazon, Member of the Senate of the Philippines (1992–95, 1998–2010), Manila, 5 September 2007.

Rodolfo Vicerra, Director-General, Congressional Planning and Budget Department, House of Representatives, 3 September 2007.

Romulo Miral, Executive Director, Congressional Planning and Budget Department, House of Representatives, 3 September 2007.

Ronald 'Ronnie' Holmes, Department of Political Science, De La Salle University, Manila, 30 August 2007 and 24 August 2009.

Teresita "Ging" Quintos-Deles, Former Special Advisor to the President on the Peace Process in Mindanao (2003–05), Manila, 14 September 2007 (since July 2010 again Presidential Adviser on the Peace Process in Mindanao).

In Thailand

Boonyad Sukthinthai, Member of the House of Representatives, Democrat Party, Bangkok, 14 October 2010.

Chaturon Chaisang, Former Member of the House of Representatives and Deputy Prime Minister, Thai Rak Thai, Bangkok, 17 August 2009.

Kittisak Prokati, Professor at the Faculty of Law, Thammasat University, Bangkok, 13 August 2009.

Kraisak Choonhavan, Member of the House of Representatives, Democrat Party, Bangkok, 17 August 2009.

Michael H. Nelson, Faculty of Political Science, Chulalongkorn University, 18 August 2009 in Bangkok and 15 October 2010 in Nonthaburi.

Naruemon Thabchumpon, Professor at the Faculty of Political Science, Chulangalongkorn University, Bangkok, 14 August 2009.

Nataphol Teepsuwan, Director General of Democrat Party, Member of the House of Representatives, Bangkok, 11 October 2010.

Nick Nostitz, Freelance Journalist, Bangkok, 15 August 2009.

Ong-art Klampaiboon, Minister to the Prime Minister's Office, Democrat Party, Bangkok, 14 October 2010.

Prinya Thaewanarumitkul, Vice Rector for Student Affairs, Thammasat University, Bangkok, 18 August 2009.

Suthipon Thaveechaiyagarn, Secretary General of the Election Commission of Thailand, Bangkok, 17 August 2009.

Thanet Charoenmuang, Professor of Political Science and Public Administration, Chiang Mai University, Chiang Mai, 24 September 2010.

In Indonesia

A. Rasyid Saleh, Ministry of Home Affairs, Jakarta, 17 March 2008.

Afriadi Hasibuan, Ministry of Home Affairs, Jakarta, 27 March 2008.

Agung Nugroho, Dean of the Faculty of Business Administration, Universitas Atma Jaya Jakarta, Jakarta, 15 March 2008.

Ahmad Yani, Ministry of Finance, Jakarta, 27 March 2008.

Alit Merthayasa, Foundation for Innovation in Local Government (Yayasan Inovasi Pemerintahan Daerah), Jakarta, 12 March 2008.

Andi Syamsu Alam, Supreme Court of Indonesia, Head of Religious Courts Affairs, Jakarta, 25 March 2008.

Anung Sugihantono, Head of the Regional Planning Board of the Province of Central Java, Semarang, 19 March 2008.

Aruna Bagchee, Governance Advisor, Decentralization Support Facility, Jakarta, 13 March 2008.

Asmawi Rewansyah, Ministry of Administrative Reform, Jakarta, 26 March 2008.

Bambang Prihandono, Senior Lecturer, Department of Political Science, Atma Jaya University Yogyakarta, Yogyakarta, 22 March 2008.

Barbara Garbe-Hanssen, Counsellor for Development Cooperation, German Embassy at the Republic of Indonesia, Jakarta, 17 March 2008.

Eko Subowo, Directorate of Regional Autonomy, Ministry of Home Affairs, Jakarta, 14 March 2008.

Elke Rapp, Democratic Reform Support Program, USAID, Jakarta, 10 March 2008.

Fx. Hadi Rudyatmo, Vice Mayor of the City of Surakarta, Surakarta, 24 March 2008.

Heru Subiyantoro, Directorate General of Fiscal Balance, Ministry of Finance, Jakarta, 12 March 2008.

Hetifah Sj. Siswanda, Director of the NGO Consortium B-Trust, Jakarta, 14 March 2008 (since 2009, Member of Parliament, Golkar).

Himawan Hariyoga, State Ministry of National Development Planning (Bappenas), Jakarta, 27 March 2008.

I Made Suwandi, Director of Regional Affairs, Ministry of Home Affairs, Jakarta, 17 March 2008.

Joel Friedmann, Director of the Governance Reform Support Project, Canadian International Development Agency, Jakarta, 14 March 2008.

Joko Widodo (Mayor of Surakarta), Surakarta, 23 March 2008 (since 2012, Governor of Jakarta).

Lenny N. Rosalin, Head at the Division for Women Empowerment, Ministry for Women's Affairs, Jakarta, 25 March 2008.

M. Ainul Asikin, Head of the Local Planning Board in the city of Mataram, Mataram, 11 March 2008.

M. Farchan, Head of the Local Planning Board in the city of Semarang, Semarang, 19 March 2008.

Roni Ihram Maulana, Director of Monitoring, Anti Corruption Clearing House (KPK), Jakarta, 25 March 2008.

Roy Valiant Salomo, Head of Department, Faculty of Social and Political Science, University of Indonesia, Jakarta, 17 March 2008.

Siti Musdah Mulia, Research Professor, Indonesian Institute of Sciences, Jakarta, 18 March 2008.

Son Diamar, State Ministry of National Development Planning (Bappenas), Jakarta, 17 March 2008.

Suprayoga Hadi, State Ministry of National Development Planning (Bappenas), Jakarta, 13 March 2008.

Syamsul Arief Rivai, Directorate of Regional Development, Ministry of Home Affairs, Jakarta, 13 March 2008.

INDEX

About the Author

During the time of the writing of this book, **Patrick Ziegenhain** was Assistant Professor (Akademischer Rat) at the Department of Political Science, University of Trier, Germany. After a term as Visiting Professor at De la Salle University, Manila, Philippines in 2014, he is now working at the Department of Southeast Asian Studies, Frankfurt, Germany.

Since 2005, Patrick Ziegenhain holds a PhD in Political Science from Albert-Ludwigs-University in Freiburg, Germany. He is author of the book *The Indonesian Parliament and Democratization*, published by ISEAS in 2008, and co-author of the book *Parliaments and Political Change in Asia*, published by ISEAS in 2005.

www.ingramcontent.com/pod-product-compliance
Lightning Source LLC
Chambersburg PA
CBHW060148280326
41932CB00012B/1677